The Complete Guide to
Building Your Home for Less

The ultimate money-saving reference for constructing or remodeling your home

MICHAEL CONROY

BETTERWAY BOOKS
CINCINNATI, OHIO

The Complete Guide to Building Your Home for Less. Copyright © 2005 by Michael Conroy. Printed and bound in the United States. All rights reserved. No part of this book may be reproduced in any form or by any electronic or mechanical means including information storage and retrieval systems without permission in writing from the publisher, except by a reviewer, who may quote brief passages in a review. Published by Betterway Books, an imprint of F+W Publications, Inc., 4700 East Galbraith Road, Cincinnati, Ohio, 45236. First edition.

Distributed in Canada by Fraser Direct
100 Armstrong Avenue
Georgetown, Ontario L7G 5S4
Canada

Distributed in the U.K. and Europe by
David & Charles
Brunel House
Newton Abbot
Devon TQ12 4PU
England
Tel: (+44) 1626 323200
Fax: (+44) 1626 323319
E-mail: mail@davidandcharles.co.uk

Distributed in Australia by Capricorn Link
P.O. Box 704
Windsor, NSW 2756
Australia

Other fine Betterway Books are available from your local bookstore or direct from the publisher.

09 08 07 06 05   5 4 3 2 1

Library of Congress Cataloging-in-Publication Data

Conroy, Michael, 1966-
    The complete guide to building your home for less / Michael Conroy. -- 1st ed.
        p.   cm.
    Includes index.
    ISBN 1-55870-769-7 (pbk: alk. paper)
    1. House construction--Amateurs' manuals. 2. House construction--Cost control. 3. Contractors--Selection and appointment.
I. Title.
TH4815.C665   2005
690'.837--dc22
2005011022

Acquisitions editor: Jim Stack
Editor: Amy Hattersley
Designer: Brian Roeth
Production coordinator: Jennifer Wagner
Technical Illustrator: Len Churchill

F+W PUBLICATIONS, INC.

READ THIS IMPORTANT SAFETY NOTICE

To prevent accidents, keep safety in mind while you work. Use the safety guards installed on power equipment; they are for your protection. When working on power equipment, keep fingers away from saw blades, wear safety goggles to prevent injuries from flying wood chips and sawdust, wear hearing protection and consider installing a dust vacuum to reduce the amount of airborne sawdust in your woodshop. Don't wear loose clothing, such as neckties or shirts with loose sleeves, or jewelry, such as rings, necklaces or bracelets, when working on power equipment. Tie back long hair to prevent it from getting caught in your equipment. People who are sensitive to certain chemicals should check the chemical content of any product before using it. The authors and editors who compiled this book have tried to make the contents as accurate and correct as possible. Plans, illustrations, photographs and text have been carefully checked. All instructions, plans and projects should be carefully read, studied and understood before beginning construction. In some photos, power tool guards have been removed to more clearly show the operation being demonstrated. Always use all safety guards and attachments that come with your power tools. Due to the variability of local conditions, construction materials, skill levels, etc., neither the author nor Popular Woodworking Books assumes any responsibility for any accidents, injuries, damages or other losses resulting from the material presented in this book. Prices listed for supplies and equipment were current at the time of publication and are subject to change. Glass shelving should have all edges polished and must be tempered. Untempered glass shelves may shatter and can cause serious bodily injury. Tempered shelves are very strong and if they break will just crumble, minimizing personal injury.

ABOUT THE AUTHOR

Mike Conroy resides in Decatur, Illinois. Mike built his first house, on his own, when he was 23 years old. He has been in and around the construction industry ever since. Mike started working for the City of Decatur in 1996 as a neighborhood services officer. While holding this position he obtained American Association of Code Enforcement (A.A.C.E.) certification as a housing code enforcement officer. In 1999 he transferred within the city to the position of rehabilitation construction specialist, which he still holds. He is also a licensed lead-based paint supervisor, and has been certified in rehab management, program management and cost estimation for rehab. Even though he doesn't physically work construction full time any more, he has never laid down his hammer for very long. Since leaving full-time construction in 1991, Mike has built seven houses and tackled many remodeling projects, working evenings and weekends. He has lived, eaten and breathed construction, both on and off the clock, for 15 years.

PHOTO CREDIT: PATRICK CRAGIN

ACKNOWLEDGEMENTS

I wish to express my thanks to the following: Early to Rise, for direction; Roger Woodson, for believing in me; Cynthia Wadell, for seeing the worth of this work; and God, for everything. This list is not all encompassing, so if you've helped and you're not listed, know that I am grateful. But without these four, this book never would have existed.

TABLE OF CONTENTS

INTRODUCTION . . . 6

CHAPTER ONE

FINDING THE BEST PLACE TO BUILD . . . 9

CHAPTER TWO

DESIGNING FOR VALUE AND LIVING . . . 22

CHAPTER THREE

QUALITY AND COMPROMISE . . . 58

CHAPTER FOUR

BUILDING CODES . . . 69

CHAPTER FIVE

FINDING AND WORKING WITH GENERAL CONTRACTORS AND SUBCONTRACTORS . . . 79

CHAPTER SIX

REDUCING LABOR COSTS . . . 92

CHAPTER SEVEN

DO IT YOURSELF . . . 105

CHAPTER EIGHT

HOW TO BUY MATERIALS . . . 119

CHAPTER NINE

BUDGETING . . . 127

CHAPTER TEN

THE SIX-YEAR MORTGAGE-FREE PLAN . . . 146

CHAPTER ELEVEN

THE SUCCESSFUL MIND-SET APPLIED
TO CONSTRUCTION . . . 148

CHAPTER TWELVE

WHY REMODEL? . . . 162

CHAPTER THIRTEEN

STRUCTURAL VERSUS COSMETIC
REMODELING . . . 196

APPENDIX A: RECOMMENDED
WEBSITES, PERIODICALS AND
OTHER SOURCES. . . 206

APPENDIX B: MORE SAMPLE
FLOOR PLANS. . . 210

APPENDIX C: CONVERSION CHARTS
AND FORMULAS. . . 244

APPENDIX D: TERMS, SAFETY TIPS
AND MISCELLANEOUS FORMS. . . 248

APPENDIX E: ABOUT LEAD-BASED
PAINT. . . 262

INDEX . . . 273

Knowledge is power. When considering a new home project, this can be the power to do, the power to save or a combination of both.

Money, money, money! This book is full of money. Not literally. You can't turn it over, shake it, and start watching crisp new $20 bills fall at your feet. But if you absorb the knowledge in the following pages and put it into practice, you can save a heap of money while building a new home or remodeling your existing one. Think about it — what would you do with a large amount of equity from your home? What would you do if your mortgage were cut in half? What if you had no mortgage? By reading and applying the information contained in this book, any of these scenarios is possible. I will show you how, even if you start with no equity, you can own your home outright in as little as six years.

Knowledge is power. When considering a new home project, this can be the power to do, the power to save, or a combination of both. The stores are full of great books that will give you the power to do. *The Complete Guide to Building Your Home for Less* does something more than these other books: it gives you the power to save money. I have transformed the "how to build a new house" book into a "how to save while building a new house" book.

I'm not some guy who built one house and is now writing a book about it. I've proven myself time and time again. I've been putting my practices to good use since 1989. Using these techniques, I've kept costs to an average of $43 a square foot on numerous houses. (That's less than half the national average!) Most people are amazed at what I've been able to accomplish. I've even been the focus of a newspaper article lauding my ability to build homes for unbelievably low amounts of money (*Decatur Herald and Review*, Home Section, December 31, 1989). I consistently do what others cannot, and now I want to share my money-saving techniques with you.

Arming yourself with the information contained in this book should be priority number one for every homeowner who wishes to pay less for a home. You don't have to be super smart or super crafty to construct a home for less; you just have to be willing to learn what this book teaches you and apply that knowledge. If you are considering building a new home or remodeling your present one, do yourself a favor and read this book. You'll be glad you did!

Note: If you're remodeling, I suggest you read chapters twelve and thirteen first. Then go back to chapter three and proceed from there. Chapters one and two are directed at new construction, whereas the information in chapters twelve and thirteen deals with remodeling and should be digested before you read the rest of the book.

CHAPTER ONE

FINDING THE BEST PLACE TO BUILD

Finding a great place to build your new home is like finding a great car. You can test-drive it. You can imagine what it'll be like to own it. But until you use it every day, it's all speculation. In order to be as sure as possible, do all the research you can. I start the process with two or three areas as options and work from there. Maybe you've seen a subdivision you want to check out, or you're set on a school district, or you have a friend who just loves her neighborhood. By now, you should have an area or three in mind. I'll show you how to find the perfect location for you.

USE THE GRAPEVINE

Let your family and friends help by being your eyes and ears. Get out and take a drive in your possible areas. Look for sale signs.

Make the effort to talk to some of the current residents. They'll be invaluable in telling you about possible pitfalls or problems in your prospective area or maybe even your potential lot. They'll also provide insight as to the price properties have been selling for, and they'll know what bargains are left for the taking. Check these aspects when looking for lots:

- **School districts:** Even if you don't have children, pay very close attention to which school district your lot lies in. Find out which schools are considered desirable. Will your children be walking to

A faded "For Sale" sign nailed to a tree may mark a bargain.

Many people consider school districts first when choosing a lot.

GLOSSARY

Covenants and Restrictions

Rules and requirements determined by subdivisions for building and living within the community. Be sure to ask for these when considering any land purchase.

BOTTOM LINE

I've had a half-acre pond dug for free. The excavator needed the dirt, and I wanted the pond. We helped each other, and I added beauty and function to my land without increasing the of cost.

BOTTOM LINE

By turning one lot into three lots through subdividing, I was able to gain $25,500 in equity.

school or riding the bus? If they're riding the bus, where's the nearest bus stop?

- **Taxes:** Taxes vary greatly from one area to another. Find out what the tax rate is for each lot you are considering. You don't want to save a ton of money while building your new house just to turn around and pay it all back in taxes.

- **Surrounding areas:** Will the surrounding areas support new construction? Will they appreciate or depreciate in value over the next ten years? How will the area change in the near future? Are there commercial developments or dilapidated properties that will soon affect your lot? Make sure that you would be willing to stay in the area for the long haul even if that's not your plan.

- **Style of homes:** Are the homes around your lot similar to the type of home you're planning to build? Will your house fit in architecturally as well as in value? Building a new two-story Victorian in a post-WWII tract-house subdivision isn't the thing to do.

- **Covenants and restrictions:** Subdivisions have covenants and restrictions that say what you can and cannot build in them. Be sure to get a copy. They typically call out square footages and other restrictions but may also dictate what type of fencing and outbuildings you may have. They may even tell you what you can and can't park in your driveway! Read them carefully and be sure to get written approval from the architectural commission before starting your project. See Figures 1-5A through 1-5E for an example of Covenants and Restrictions.

- **Historical districts:** Check with your local historical society to see if your lot or any of its features is considered historic. If it is, investigate thoroughly what this will mean to you before agreeing to buy.

- **Existing Features:** Are there any natural features you can add or

FIGURE 1-1 When looking for lots in established areas, watch out for historic districts.

Residential   MLS: **166811**   Status: **Active**   Address: **1060 Country Manor** | Price: **$188,900** |

City:	**Mt. Zion**	Parcel No:	**12-17-05-229-009**
County:	**Macon**	Agent Owned:	**Related**
State:	**IL**		
Zip:	**62549**	Tax Year:	**2002**
School:	**Other**	➡ Taxes Apx:	**555**
Elem School:	**Mt. Zion**	Tax Exemption:	**None**
Middle School:	**Mt. Zion**	Contingency:	
High School:	**Mt. Zion**	Protect Period:	**60**
Grid:	**80**	Lake Front:	**No**
Possession:	**At Close**		
Owner Phone:	**454-8013**		
Owner:	**McMillen Builders Inc**		

Rooms:	**8**	Yr Built Apx:	**2004**	
Bedrooms:	**4**	Main SF Apx:	**1,010**	
Bath Master:	**Yes**	Upper SF Apx:	**990**	
Baths Full:	**2**	Lwr SF Apx:		
Baths Partial:	**1**	Total Fin SF	**2,000**	
Baths Total:	**2.50**	BsmtF SF Apx:		
		BsmtUF SF Apx:	**1,010**	

Style: **2 Story**
Exterior: **Vinyl**
Roof: **Shingle**
Drive Construc: **Concrete**
Basement: **Full**
Garage: **2.5 Car, Attached**
Heat: **Forced Air**
Water Heater: **Gas**
Cooling: **Central**

Acres-Apx:

Room	Level	Dim Apx	Flooring
Living Room			
Family Room			
Great Room	1	26x14	Carpet
Dining Room	1	13'6x12	Other
Kitchen	1	13'6x12	Vinyl
Master Bedroom	2	14x13	Carpet
Bedroom	2	14x12	Carpet
Bedroom	2	14x12	Carpet
Bedroom	2	12x10'6	Carpet
Rec Room			
Utility	1	13'6x8	Vinyl

Water: **City**
Sewer: **City**
Gas/Elec Avg $:
Fireplace: **None**
Lot Size Apx: **See remark**

Lead Paint Disc: **No**
Seller Discl: **No**
Appliances: **Dishwasher, Disposal, Range**
Features Exter: **Brick Trim, Concrete Parking, Deck, Landscaped, Workshop Area**
Features Inter: **Cable TV, Cathedral Ceiling, Ceiling Fan, Vinyl Floor, Walk-in Closet, Workshop Area**
Showing Instruc: **Vacant, key box please leave card**

Remarks: **Mt Zion Schools, wonderful family or great room w/cathedral ceilings and sliders to deck. Main floor open, spacious kitchen w/loads of cabinets includes planning desk, main floor laundry. Super master bedroom w/walk-in closet and Mbath w/whirlpool. full basement. Call Becky Ray for more info. Visual tour www.decaturillinoishomes.com. Lot size 47x120x222x218**

Legal: **Lot 16 Country Side 2nd Addn.**

Directions: **South on Baltimore to Florian turn left to Country Manor turn left end of cul de sac.**

C/C: **300**

Listing Agent:	**Becky Ray**	Agent Phone:	**(217) 428-9500**		
Listing Office:	**RE/MAX Executives, Inc**	Office Phone:	**(217) 428-9500**	Lock Box:	**Yes**

Information hereon is believed accurate but is not warranted.
Buyer should verify school districts and all information. Decatur Association of REALTORS   04/30/2004

FIGURE 1-2   This sample real estate listing shows the current taxes (see arrow above) being paid on a property.

FIGURE 1-3 Building a two-story home in a subdivision full of small ranches is not a good idea.

use to your advantage? For example, are there trees, creeks or boulders that will add to the beauty or functionality of the lot? Can you add a pond, a row of shrubs or plantings that will heighten the beauty of the lot? Is there an eyesore nearby that you can cover up with plantings or a fence?

• **Possible subdividing:** Is it possible to subdivide the lot you are looking at purchasing? By turning one lot into two or more, the potential for profit can be large.

• **Utility lines:** Check for buried or overhead utility lines that will affect home placement, outbuilding placement, access, lateral field placement, landscaping or plantings. The plat of your lot will show buried lines and the easements around them.

• **Utility hookups:** Check on the availability and the cost of utility hookups. Check for access to electric, gas, water, sewer, cable, garbage hauling, fire protection, ambulance and phone service. If any of these utilities is not avail-

FIGURE 1-4 When looking at lots, watch out for signs indicating buried utility lines.

Declaration of Protective Covenants and Restrictions for Harrison Park Plats I and II

Filed at the Sangamon County Recorder, January 14, 1987 Document Number S2282

WHEREAS, Harrison Park Development, Inc. an Illinois corporation, hereinafter referred to as "Developer" is the owner of all the lots in Harrison Park Subdivision, Plats I and II situated in:

> the east half of the northwest quarter of the northwest quarter of section 36; and the east half of the northwest quarter of said section 36, all in the township 16 north, range 6 west of the third principal meridian, except the right of way of the Chicago and Northwestern Railway Company. And except that part of the southeast quarter of the northwest quarter of said section lying southeasterly of the right of way of the Chicago and Northwestern Railway Company. Also, except the east 600 feet of that part of the northwest quarter of said section lying north of the Chicago and Northwestern Railroad right of way.

> Sangamon County, Illinois; and

WHEREAS, it is desirable to secure the best use and improvements of the lots therein, and to protect the owners of such lots against such use of other lots therein as would depreciate the value of such property, and to prevent the erection of poorly designed or constructed buildings, and to make the best use of and preserve the natural beauty of said property and to locate the buildings thereon with regards to topographic features; and

WHEREAS, the Developer desires to create a finer quality residential subdivision having a standard of architectural harmony, achieved through consistency of features such as color, texture, material, type or exterior style, placement of landscape flora and the preservation of certain existing wooded areas in their natural state, and through relative consistency of design, and

WHEREAS, to secure such objectives, said Developer desires to subject the lots in said subdivision to the following restrictions and covenants, including but not limited to methods of construction and maintenance as will secure a continuous standard for the proper development of said subdivision.

NOW THEREFORE, KNOW ALL MEN BY THESE PRESENTS, that the aforesaid Developer and owner of said property, hereby declares that all lots in said Harrison Park Subdivision Plats I and II, shall be sold, transferred and conveyed subject to the following covenants and restrictions:

1. USE RESTRICTION.

Developer hereby creates an ARCHITECTURAL CONTROL COMMITTEE (ACC) composed of Kenneth G. Cole, Patrick J. Forkin and Kenneth G. Cole Jr. In the event of the death or resignation of any member of said COMMITTEE, the remaining members shall appoint a member to fill the vacancy. The ACC shall have the right to prevent the clearing of a lot and subsequent excavation and grading prior to construction of the main residence upon such a lot according to the following:

A. Prior to the construction of the main residence, a lot owner is required to seek approval of the building plans through the ACC.

B. The ACC shall consider quality of workmanship and materials, external design, location with respect to topography and finished grades, elevations and building lines, location of

FIGURE 1-5A   Sample of covenants and restrictions, page 1 of 5.

driveways and walk ways and the preservation of certain existing trees and wooded areas.

C. To comply with this requirement, each lot owner, prior to any construction on the lot, shall first submit a preliminary plan to the ACC stating in general the type, style, size and general design of the residence to be constructed, along with its location on the building site and the name of the lot owner's general contractor.

D. After approval in writing of the preliminary plan by the ACC, the lot owner shall then submit two (2) sets of the actual plans and specifications of the improvement to be constructed.

E. Such plans and specifications shall include the floor plan, exterior color schemes, and materials, elevations and actual plat plan showing distances from easements and lot lines and the location of the finished grade height of the first floor.

F. The lot owner agrees that he/she will not obtain a building permit until the ACC has approved the final plans. If no objections to the plans are raised by the ACC within seven (7) days of submission of the final plans to said COMMITTEE, the plans shall be deemed to have been approved by said ACC.

After the first sale of forty (40) of the lots in Harrison Park Plats I and II, the ACC, at its option, may delegate the duties specified herein to the Harrison Park Homeowner's Association.

<u>Rights of Way and Easements</u>

Rights of way and easements for installation and maintenance of utilities and drainage facilities are reserved as shown on the recorded plat. Within these easements, no structure, fence, planting or other material, shall be placed or permitted to remain which may damage or impair the function or interfere with the installation and maintenance of utilities, or easements. Any improvements so located shall be removed upon the request of the Developer, its successors or assigns, or any public utility using said area, at the expense of the owner of said lot or tract. The easement area of each lot and all improvements in it shall be maintained continuously by the owner of the lost, except those improvements for which a public utility or authority is obligated to maintain.

Each owner of the building site is a member of HARRISON PARK HOMEOWNERS ASSOCIATION, which ASSOCIATION will be incorporated by DEVELOPER, as an Illinois Not-For-Profit Corporation. Each owner of a building site shall be liable for his proportionate share of the cost (based upon the percentage of the Lot(s) owned by an owner as to the total number of lots in the plat of record as amended from time to time to include additional Harrison Park plats) for the proper maintenance of certain easement areas within the subdivision, which easement areas are described below and which may be amended from time to time to include additional easement areas upon completion and inclusion of addition plats in the subdivision. Any maintenance fee assessed by DEVELOPER or by the HOMEOWNERS ASSOCIATION and not paid within thirty (30) days of its assessment shall constitute a lien upon the property of the delinquent owner. DEVELOPER agrees that for two (2) years from the date of the recording of this instrument it will maintain the easement areas and collect and assess the maintenance fees. After two years, the maintenance of the easement areas and collection of the maintenance fees shall be performed by the HOMEOWNERS ASSOCIATION.

The easement areas to be maintained by the Developer and the Homeowners Association referred to above are the following:

The entrance areas of Harrison Park including the center isle ad the planting areas on each side, east and west of the entrance lying immediately south of Washington Street.

3.   <u>EROSION CONTROL AND LANDSCAPE WASTE</u>

During the clearing and construction, until all exposed dirt from excavation has been removed from the lot or brought to an approved final grade surrounding the dwelling until, and until the lot is

FIGURE I-5B   Sample of covenants and restrictions, page 2 of 5.

permanently landscaped with vegetation or landscaping material, the lot owner shall prevent the erosion and washing of soil from the lot of employing the following measures:

A.   Disposing of all landscape waste, such as brush, weeds, removed trees, and excess dirt, in a lawful fashion by burial, incineration or removal, without casing damage to an adjacent lot or other property within Harrison Park Subdivision

B.   In the cause of making improvements to a lot, the owner shall place, or require a General or Sub Contractor to place, all excavated soils deposited within the lot at least five (5) feet from any lot line, and the owner or General or Sub Contractor shall not place any soil piles on an easement or right-of-way of record. During and prior to completion of construction efforts the lot owner or contractor of the lot owner's designation shall erect and maintain a water permeable cloth dike of suitable strength and durability across the front of a lot and around the perimeter of excavated soil piles or shall employ other effective means to prevent such soils from eroding or washing in easements or rights of way or other lots. Such dikes or other systems shall be maintained until the excess soil has been brought to approved final grade or removed from the lot.

C.   Immediately after the final grade has been established and approved on the lot surrounding the building site, the lot owner shall provide and install vegetation to cover exposed soils by planting approved ground cover, sodding, seeding and strawing, or covering the exposed areas with approved landscape material to prevent erosion. Drainage easements on lots shall be maintained by the lot owner according to the plat of record and the specifications of final grade as approved by the City Engineer.

D.   Soils, mud and landscape waste carried from a lot onto other properties and common areas such as easements, rights of way and roadways, by erosive forces or by vehicles leaving a construction site, shall be cleaned up daily or as necessary at the expense of the lot owner.
The Developer, his successors and assigns, shall have the right to enter a lot at any time for the purpose of preventing and arresting undue erosion at the expense of the lot owner if the lot owner or his designated contractor is unwilling or unable to prevent such erosion.

4.   **CONSTRUCTION MATERIAL WASTE**

At each building site, excess material and waste from construction shall be gathered and disposed of regularly in a lawful fashion. No lot shall be used or maintained at anytime for a dumping ground.

5.   **DRIVEWAYS**

Driveways shall be constructed of concrete, asphalt or other material as approved by the Architectural Control Committee.

6.   **NUISANCES AND TRASH, ETC**

a.   No noxious or offensive trade or activities shall be carried on in said subdivision, nor shall anything be done therein or thereon which may be or become an annoyance or nuisance to the neighborhood.

b.   No structure of a temporary character, trailer, basement, shack, garage, barn or other outbuilding shall be erected or placed on any lot at any time, except during the construction period without approval of the Architectural Control Committee. No derelict vehicles shall be kept or stored on any lot.

c.   No animals, livestock or poultry of any kind shall be raised, bred or kept on any lot in said subdivision except for dogs and cats and other common pet animals, and not for any commercial purposes.

d.   All weeds shall be kept cut on sold vacant lots, and no such vacant lot shall be permitted to fall into an unsightly condition, except that the lot owner shall not be obligated to clear natural wooded areas of brush and undergrowth.
No lot shall be used or maintained as a dumping ground for rubbish, and all trash, garbage or other waste shall be kept in sanitary containers. Any vacant lot which falls into an unsightly condition may be mowed or cleaned up by the subdivider at the

FIGURE 1-5C Sample of covenants and restrictions, page 3 of 5.

expense of the owner.

e.   No permanent fence shall be constructed in front of a residence without the prior approval of the Architectural Control Committee. In case of corner lots, both street sides of the residence shall be considered as front lines.

7.   ROOFLINES AND MATERIAL

The roof pitch of the main roof of a building shall not rise less than five (5) vertical feet in twelve (12) horizontal feet. The color and type of material of the roof covering shall be brown or black shingles, shakes, or tiles. Specific exceptions may be granted by the Architectural Control Committee if such an exception meets the standards of quality and design for the subdivision.

8.   SIDEWALKS

After the construction of the sidewalk in front of a lot and acceptance by the City Engineer or his representative, the lot owner shall be responsible for replacing at his own expense, any broken section.

9.   BUILDING SITE or LOT

As used in this instrument, means all or any part of a single tract of land upon which is constructed, intended to located, or located on single-family dwelling.

10.   DURATION OF RESTRICTIONS

The aforesaid covenants shall run with the land and shall be binding upon all parties and all persons claiming under them for a period of twenty-five (25) years from the date these covenants are recorded, after which time said covenants shall be automatically extended for successive periods of ten (10) years, unless an instrument signed by more than seventy-five (75%) percent of the then record owners of the building sites delineated in Plats I and II and any other plats of said Harrison Park Subdivision, has been recorded in the office of the Recorder of Deeds of Sangamon County, Illinois, each building site having one vote, agreeing to change or rescind said covenants in _____ or in part.

11.   REMEDIES FOR VIOLATION

In the event of a violation or breach of any of these covenants and restrictions by any person or entity subject such covenants and restrictions, a person or entity enjoying the benefit of these restrictions, shall have the right to proceed in a judicial action at law or in equity to compel compliance _____ the terms of these covenants and restrictions, or to prevent the breach or violation of them. Developer shall, in addition, have the right to such compensation for actual expenses incurred as a result of any such breach or violation.

12.   SEVERABILITY

Invalidation of one of these covenants or restrictions by judgment or other order shall not in any manner affect any of the other covenants, which shall remain in full force and affect.

IN WITNESS WHEREOF, Harrison Park Development, Inc. has caused this instrument to be executed by its duly authorized officers, pursuant to authority of its Board of Directors, this ___14th___ day of January, 1987.

_____

                                               Harrison Park Development, Inc.
                                             President or Vice-President

Attest: _____
                         Secretary

FIGURE 1-5D   Sample of covenants and restrictions, page 4 of 5.

STATE OF ILLINOIS)
COUNTY OF SANGAMON) SS.

I, the undersigned, a Notary Public in and for the County and State aforesaid, do hereby certify that Kenneth G. Cole and Patrick J Forkin, to me personally known to be, respectively, the President and Secretary of Harrison Park Development, Inc. and also known to me to be the persons whose names are subscribed to the foregoing instrument, appeared before me this day in Person and acknowledged that they signed, seals ad delivered the aforesaid instrument, and the said Kenneth G. Cole as such Presidet, affixed te corporate seal of said Harrison Park Development, Inc. thereto, all as the free and voluntary act of said corporation, for the uses and purposes therein set forth, being duly authorized therunto.

IN WITNESS WHEREOF, I have hereunto set my hand and seal this 14th day of January 1987.

_____
Notary Public

My Commission Expires

4/29/89

FIGURE 1-5E Sample of covenants and restrictions, page 5 of 5.

able, find out what it'll cost you to make it available or to use an alternative. Examples of alternatives include using propane instead of natural gas or a satellite dish instead of cable TV.

- **Unwanted lots:** Don't be afraid to look at the lot no one wants if you can find out why they don't want it. Once you know why it's not desirable, find out what it would cost to fix or remove the undesirable condition. A buddy of mine once bought adjacent lots, one half an acre and one three acres in size, for 22 percent of their value because they had no improved road access. No one was willing to install the road. He was. When you add the cost of the road, his purchase was made for 46 cents on the dollar. By doing what others wouldn't, he gained a fair amount of equity.

- **Flood plain insurance:** Flood plain insurance is expensive, and most lenders will require it as long as you have a mortgage.

RESALE VALUE

If you're not making money on the deal, you're losing it. The main thing I consider when looking at lots is resale value. To determine your house's resale value, you will have to consider several elements. I'll tell you in the next few paragraphs how to find your resale value.

BOTTOM LINE
If a $20,000 building lot may be purchased for $10,000 because it's totally wooded, and you can remove the trees from the building site for $3000, you stand to make $7000 in equity!

GLOSSARY

Resale Value
The price you'd expect to sell your completed house for on the open market.

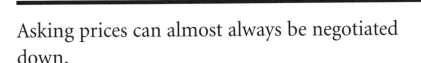

Asking prices can almost always be negotiated down.

If you could pick up a house and move it from one neighborhood to another every day for a week, the value of that house would vary dramatically with each move. The same house with the same amenities will often have a drastically different price from neighborhood to neighborhood and subdivision to subdivision. This is why real-estate agents say that the three most important factors in a house's value are location, location, and location. To maximize your return, maximize your resale value.

The cost of construction on one lot will be almost identical to the cost of construction of the same house on another similar lot. To determine your possible return for different areas, you must determine what houses similar to the one you plan to build are selling for in those areas. You must also determine the cost of the land. An agent can be very useful but not necessary at this stage of the game. If you have an agent with whom you do business, who is willing to help you, it is a good idea to call and ask for help in finding three comparables. If you must (or choose to) do this on your own, visit your local government agency that keeps the records on recent real-estate sales. The sale prices of homes in your area will be on public record and may even be available online from this office. Check the sales records for homes similar to your own and find out what they are selling for. By finding these comparables you can get a good idea of what your new home will be worth. Be sure to find actual sale prices; never calculate what your home will be worth using appraised values or what a broker or banker quotes as the value. Actual sales are the only way to determine what price the market will bear for your home. By researching these values you'll be able to determine which neighborhoods will return the most money on your investment.

Consider such features as garages, lot sizes, exterior finishes, whirlpools, kitchens and baths when determining if a house is comparable or not. Houses must be in similar areas and school districts, have similar amenities and be of similar design to be considered comparable. Once you have found three comparables, fill out the Possible Return Chart (Figure 1-6). List the selling price of the comparables, then add or subtract from that price by indicating whether your home has more value or less in the listed areas. By adding and subtracting the value of the differing amenities for each house, you should be able to get a relatively good idea of what your home will be worth. Your lending institution will require that you hire a licensed appraiser to do this before

Before building the first home in a subdivision, make sure that others will follow.

you get a loan, but I like the appraiser to confirm what I already know, not shock me with what my home will be worth. You should know whether your return is there before you buy a lot, and this chart will help determine whether it will be or not.

NEGOTIATING THE PRICE

Don't just accept the deal without trying to sweeten the pot. There's no guarantee of success. I have paid full price when I had to. But use your imagination and find some reason why you deserve a better price. Here's a list of reasons I've used before:

- **The last lot:** The last lot in a subdivision is usually the last for a reason. If the reason is not enough to deter you from purchasing it, get a better deal.
- **The first lot:** For a subdivision owner to see lot sales, he needs action in his subdivision. To jump-start the action, an owner may cut you a deal if you'll start construction right away. They may even front you

BOTTOM LINE

If you can get a lot fronted, you will pay no interest during construction. On a $20,000 lot, you'll save $800 in interest over six months on an 8 percent loan.

POSSIBLE RETURN CHART

	Your Home	Comparable #1	Comparable #2	Comparable #3
Selling Price				
Square Footage				
# of Bedrooms				
# of Baths				
Lot Size				
Garage(s)				
Outbuilding(s)				
Foundation				
Other Amenity				
Other Amenity				
Other Amenity				
Other Amenity				
Total of Additions				
Total of Subtractions				
Total (= selling price + additions − subtractions)				
Possible Return (= average of three totals)				

FIGURE 1-6 Use this chart to determine what your completed house will be worth.

GLOSSARY

Front
Allowing access and usage while agreeing to accept payment at a predetermined later date.

the lot so you don't pay for it until you're finished with construction.

- **Budget:** Take this actual conversation: "I'm on a budget. I can only afford to pay ____ dollars for your lot, but I would really like to build my home on it," I told the seller as he rolled his eyes and sighed. Exasperated, he leaned over the hood of his truck, stroked his chin, and said, "The rest of the lots sold for $2000 more." I countered with, "I know, I know. But my wife really has her heart set on this lot and I only have ____ dollars." Leaning up from the truck, he scratched his head and said, "OK, but you're getting a heck of a deal." I assured him, "Oh, I know, I know."
- **"Please":** If the budget issue isn't enough to sway the seller, say please! Please can be a powerful word if you mean it.
- **Bring the family:** If "please" fails, sic the kids on them! When I was a young man, my buddies and I all dreamed of building a house on a particular secluded lot. It sat way off the street and had great shade trees on it — private and unique. We all agreed it was the perfect place to live. But there was one little problem: it wasn't for sale. Many, many people tried over the years to buy it. No one had any luck until my buddy tried, and he got it at a great price! When I asked him how he did it, he replied, "The owner was an older lady, so I loaded up the wife and kids, and we visited for over an hour. Done deal." Now that was a smart family outing!
- **Summer frustration:** Some lots need to be maintained (mowed) while they sit vacant, and all lots are subject to property taxes. Most individual owners get tired of maintaining and paying for something they're really not getting a perceived value from. Catching an owner right before or after mowing season or before tax payment time will give you some leverage for negotiating.

INSURING YOUR INVESTMENT

Insurance is a necessary evil. You must protect your investment. However, it's the amount of protection that needs to be decided. At a minimum, liability insurance and a builder's risk policy are musts. I don't overinsure, and I keep my deductibles high. You may have a different view on what you need, and there's nothing wrong with that. I would never adamantly try to talk someone out of extra insurance. All I can do is tell you what I do to keep costs down. To save dollars on premiums, follow these guidelines:

- **High deductibles:** Rates go down as deductibles go up.
- **Skip the outriders:** Your insurance agent will want to cover everything from the materials and tools to your dog's hind legs. Don't pay

for coverage unless you feel you need it. I've never had a tool or material stolen from a job site. Have I been lucky? Of course! Does that guarantee you'll have the same luck? Of course not! Talk to other builders and residents of the area in which you'll be building to see what, if any, problems they are having. Then make an educated decision on which is more prudent, paying the premium or taking the risks involved in not having the extra coverage.

- **Pay in full:** Some companies charge extra fees if you pay monthly. Consider paying for a year in advance to save money.

BOTTOM LINE

If you are paying interest on the money you're using to finance the construction of your new home, always consider whether it's more economical to pay now and thus start accumulating interest immediately, or to pay later and not incur interest charges until that time. Remember, when a loan is involved, time is always a factor. Interest never sleeps and is always accumulating on the balance of your loan.

CHAPTER TWO

DESIGNING FOR VALUE AND LIVING

Now that you've picked the best place to build, it's time to think about a design for your new home. Design your house around the way you really live, not the way you want others to think you live. We'll look at several aspects of your situation to help you determine how to design a house that best suits your needs. By realizing how you utilize your existing home, you can better design your new one. Maybe you've been in a house that seems perfect to you, or maybe you've seen features in a friend's home that you'd like to incorporate into yours. Whether it is an interior space or an exterior accoutrement, I'll not only show you how to do it but how to do it for less.

DESIGNING FOR THE LOT

Look at your lot. Get out onto it. Walk around and look at the views. Check the grade. Walk the perimeter, then the area where you'd like to build. Before even beginning the design process you should be as familiar with your lot's features—both positive and negative—as possible. Ask yourself the following questions:

- **Distinctive features:** Are there distinctive features that will affect your choice of design? For example, is your lot naturally sloping in a way that would facilitate a walk-out basement?
- **Restrictive features:** Are there restrictive features that will affect your choice of design? For example, are there only one or two places on the lot where the house can be sited? Is your lot long and narrow?
- **Natural features:** Are there natural features that you don't want to disturb, such as trees or animal habitat?

GLOSSARY

Grade
The incline, or slope, of your lot.

• **Vistas:** Are there certain vistas you'd like to view from inside the house?

DETERMINING THE BUILDABLE AREA OF YOUR LOT

This section will help you to lay out the lot so the buildable area can be determined. Before beginning, note the following items that should be included in the layout of your lot.

• **Natural features:** All trees, creeks, boulders, fences, etc.

• **Obstructions:** Overhanging branches, wires and other elements that will affect placement and construction.

• **Setbacks:** Zoning setback requirements are available through your local building and zoning department.

Make a drawing of your lot in Box 2-1, similar to Figure 2-2. Show your lot size and shape, natural features, zoning setbacks and the maximum buildable area.

DESIGNING FOR YOUR BUDGET

Decide what you really need, then calculate the cost. We all want beautiful homes packed with great features, but remember that someone has to pay for those features — you. Rather than figuring out how much money

FIGURE 2-1 This sloping lot facilitated installing a walk-out basement.

GLOSSARY

Buildable Area
The area of your lot, after obstructions and setbacks are taken into account, on which a house can be constructed.

GLOSSARY

Zoning Setback
The distance you must set the house back from the lot lines as determined by your local building and zoning department. Check the government listings in your phone book to find your local zoning office.

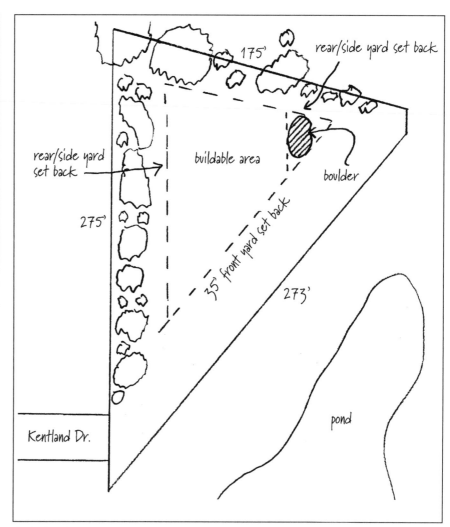

FIGURE 2-2   Triangular-shaped lot with restrictive features, making a small buildable area.

you can afford to spend, start instead by deciding what features you genuinely need and costing them out. With this method you'll get a home that's beautiful and functional without breaking the bank. For example, if you find a plan that you really like but it has an extra bedroom and den that you do not need, cut those spaces from the plan. You will save square footage, and therefore dollars, when you build. Another way to save is to cut out design features that you really don't want or need. By removing unnecessary items from your plan, you will be able to build for less.

The *Journal of Light Construction* had a great article on saving trees while building in the September 2001 issue.

Box 2-1 Draw your lot with setbacks and features here to determine the buildable area.

BOTTOM LINE

Smaller houses don't always mean lower resale values. I sold a house for the same price as a very similar one that was in the same subdivision. My house had the same types of rooms and amenities, but was 250 square feet smaller. Bigger is not always better!

Fill out the Room Use Checklist (Figure 2-3) to determine which areas you'll need in your new home. Fill in a space for every room, including the furnace room, laundry room, closets, unfinished attics and basements and other storage areas. Think carefully about how often you use these spaces. If you have a formal dining room (or any other room) but rarely use it, say so. It may be a very pretty room, but if it's unused it's wasted space. Could this space be more useful if it had another function? Could the space serve multiple functions? Fill out the form, keeping these questions in mind.

Now review the form. Really consider the last column. Do you need this area? Even if you have a room full of furniture, you don't have to build a space for it if you won't use the room.

If you want to add areas that you don't have in your current residence, talk to people with lifestyles and family structures close to your own. Do they have these types of rooms? How often do they use them? Keeping in mind the cost, if they had it to do over again, would they still add that space? Would they trade that space for a more useful one? Once you decide you want the new room, add it to the last column of the Room Use Checklist.

Now that you've determined which rooms you really need, determine how big they need to be. Fill out the Room Size Determination form (Figure 2-4). When you list the size of an existing room, list only the area of the room that's actually put to use. If you have a 15×24-foot living room but your furniture takes up only 12×16 feet of the space, the rest is wasted. Even if you don't utilize a space, it will still cost you dollars. You have to pay to build it, to heat and cool it, and to maintain it. It makes much more sense to cut that space out or put the square footage in another area that you *will* use. One key to great design is eliminating unused and wasted space.

By determining what rooms you want and need and how large they have to be, you have a great start on designing your perfect home.

DESIGNING FEATURES

To keep costs down, use self-control and shop around when considering features. We all have some wants — things we don't necessarily need but would really like to have. Fireplaces, whirlpool tubs, home theaters, intercoms, alarm systems and garbage disposals are all good examples of wanted but not needed features. Many of these features can get very expensive. By shopping around and possibly handling some things yourself, wanted features can be added without blowing the budget. Use common sense when purchasing, and do some research into the possi-

ROOM USE CHECKLIST

Room/Area	How often used? N = never S = seldom O = often A = always	Do I need/want this area? Y = yes N = no	Can I trade or share this area with another? Y = yes N = no	Do I need this area in the new house? Y = yes N = no
Living Room				
Family Room				
Dining Room				
Kitchen				
Bath 1				
2				
3				
Bedroom 1				
2				
3				
4				
Foyer				
Closets				
Laundry Room				
Hallway				
Stairway				
Furnace Room				
Basement				
Garage				
Porch Front				
Rear				
Deck				
Storage building				
Other				
Other				
Other				
Other				
Other				

FIGURE 2-3   Room use checklist.

ROOM SIZE DETERMINATION

Room/Area from last column of Room Use Checklist	Size of existing room or size of wanted room in length x width	Square footage multiply length x width	Total square footage needed
Living Spaces			Add square footage of all rooms together:
Example: Living Room	15 x 24	360	
Garage & Storage			Add square footage of all areas together:
Porches & Decks			Add square footage of all areas together:

FIGURE 2-4 Room size determination.

BOTTOM LINE
Overhead cabinet lighting can be added for as little as $5 in materials.

FIGURE 2-5   Add over-cabinet lighting by installing a switched outlet and a rope light or strand of christmas lights on top of the wall cabinets.

bility of installing some of these features later. Plan for these features now so they can be incorporated into a floor plan. Adding a fireplace, laundry chute or whirlpool can create a problem if it isn't in the design. Some of the items I have added for very few dollars include: separate phone lines, separate Internet lines, laundry chutes, in-the-wall wiring for a home theater, built-in nooks/cubbies/pass-throughs, attic storage areas, pan/tray ceilings, pantries, exposed wood ceilings and cabinet lighting. Use your imagination as well as your self-control. Don't be afraid to ask, "Why can't I?" Do the research and see for yourself if it is possible.

Here are some ways to save on features:

- **Shop around:** Salvage shops that carry scratched and dented items are great places to find bargains. Closeouts and clearance aisles are another.
- **Don't overspend:** If the item for $500 does the same job as a similar item for $1,000, buy the less expensive one. For example, a custom whirlpool tub can cost thousands of dollars, but by designing in the stock white corner unit from my local retailer, which I can buy on sale for $799, I can save a bundle and still have a very impressive tub!

GLOSSARY

Switched Outlet
An electrical outlet whose power is turned on and off by a wall switch or switches.

When done right, extra features don't have to blow your budget.

- **Do it yourself:** Some extras are very simple to install. Do some research on the possibilities before simply dismissing the idea. For example, over-cabinet lighting can be installed simply with a switched outlet and a string of Christmas lights. Total material cost: $5. Other great examples are wiring for phone and cable; materials are inexpensive and installation is easy.

FIVE SAMPLE HOME DESIGNS

Let's look at five types of houses. Each of these styles has its own benefits and drawbacks, which I'll highlight. Keep in mind that if the buildable area of your lot is very large, you can design in whatever style you want and can afford. If, however, the buildable area is small or odd-shaped, you'll have to design within those parameters.

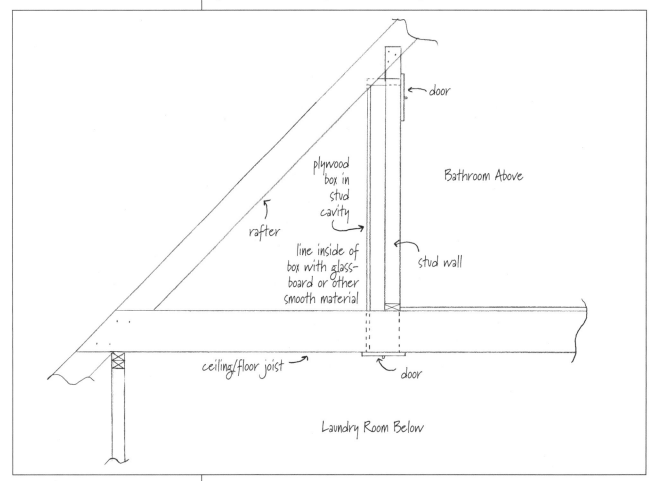

FIGURE 2-6 A laundry chute can be framed with scraps.

FIGURE 2-7   Ranch home.

The Ranch

A ranch home has all living spaces on one level, eliminating the need for stairs. This serves many purposes, including keeping the family close together. It also removes the burden of climbing stairs from occupants who may have trouble with them. Ranches typically cost more to build per square foot than multilevel homes due to foundation and roof costs. Without the ability to stack the floors, you can't get double use out of a roof or a foundation. With the addition of a finished basement, however, a homeowner can effectively double square footage without doubling costs.

This sample plan features three bedrooms, two bathrooms, a two-car attached garage, a laundry room, a large kitchen and a large master suite. The plan is simple but still has great curb appeal. The roof can be easily framed with manufactured trusses. The lack of wasted space provides for "large living" in a small house. The rooms are of adequate size to allow very comfortable living while keeping costs down.

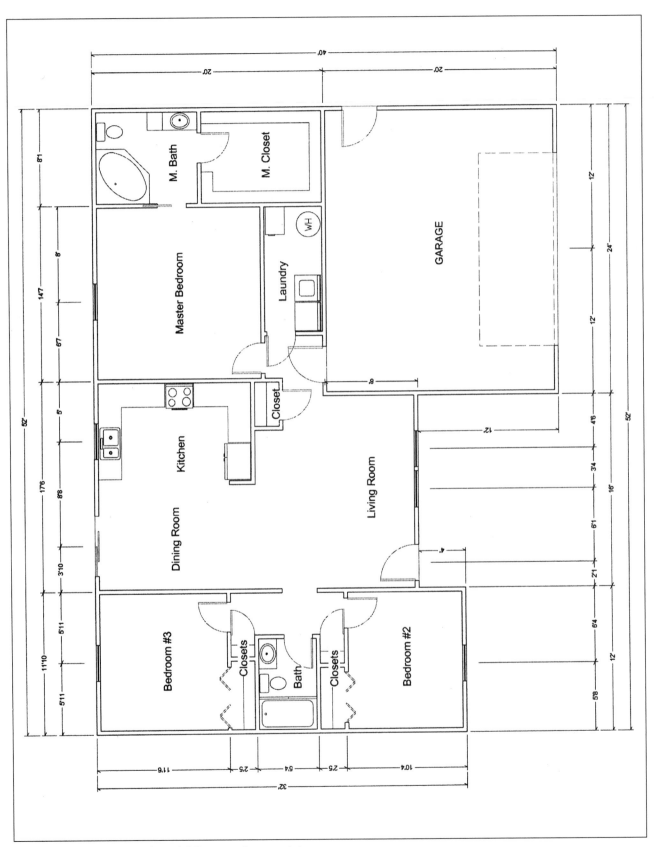

FIGURE 2-8   Floor plan for a 1,313-square-foot ranch home.

You can easily add a covered front porch by extending the roof trusses (cantilevering them) over the front wall of the living room or sloped ceilings in the living room/dining room/kitchen by using cathedral trusses for this area.

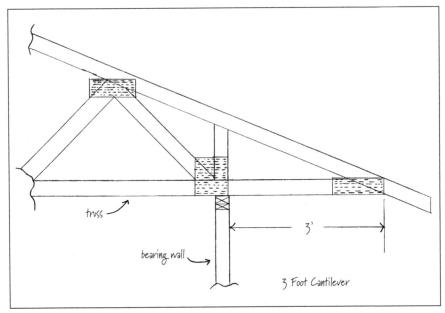

FIGURE 2-9   Cantilevered trusses.

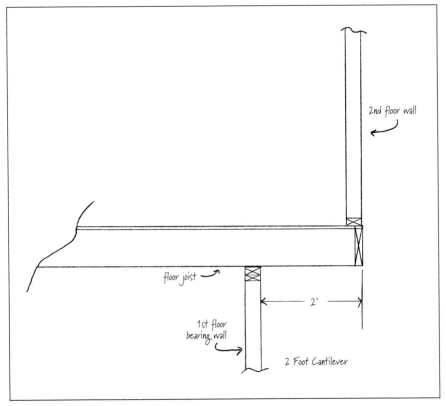

FIGURE 2-10   Cantilevered joists.

GLOSSARY

Footprint

A house's overall width by its overall depth. (See Figure 2-11.)

PROS AND CONS OF RANCH HOUSES

Pros	Cons
■ All living areas on one level.	■ Cost more per square foot to build.
■ Usually resell more quickly and for more per square foot than other styles of homes.	■ Require larger area to build due to larger footprint of house.
■ Ease of construction.	■ Little separation of living spaces.
■ If finished, basement additions can add inexpensive square footage.	

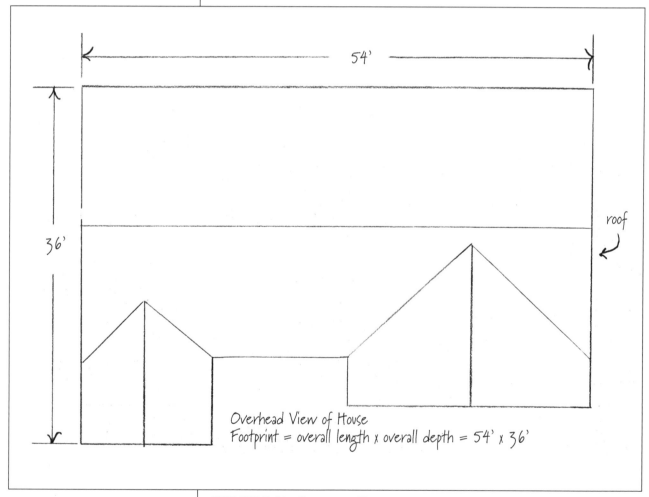

Overhead View of House
Footprint = overall length x overall depth = 54' x 36'

FIGURE 2-11   Footprint of house.

Bedrooms in basements should always have proper egress.

The Two-Story

Multiple-story houses allow for smaller footprints, which means that one can fit on a lot where a ranch may not. It also means lower costs per square foot. Using one foundation to support and one roof to cover two stories at once effectively "shrinks" the size of these sections of the house. This means saved dollars. Having multiple stories also allows for separation of living areas. If a two-story home is built on a basement, the basement and second levels are separated by the main level. This seems to be a nice feature for parents of teenagers, who can put a whole floor between their room and their children's!

The sample plan features three bedrooms, two and a half baths, a den, a two-story foyer, a three-car garage and lots of closet space. This classic

GLOSSARY

Egress
An exit, usually a window, to the exterior of a building. Sections R310 and R311 of the 2003 International Residential Code discuss emergency escape and rescue openings and means of egress in detail.

FIGURE 2-12 Two story home.

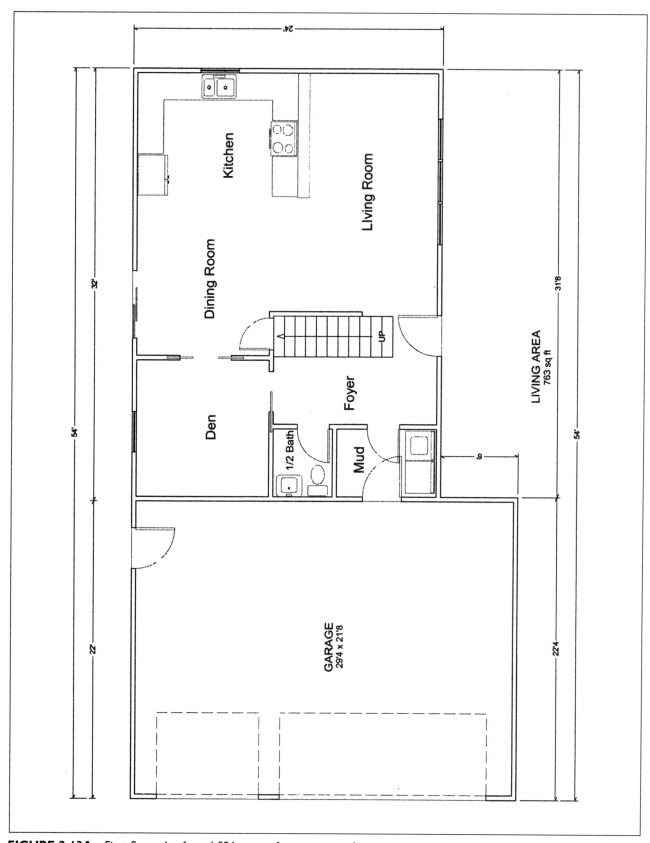

FIGURE 2-13A   First-floor plan for a 1,526-square-foot two-story home.

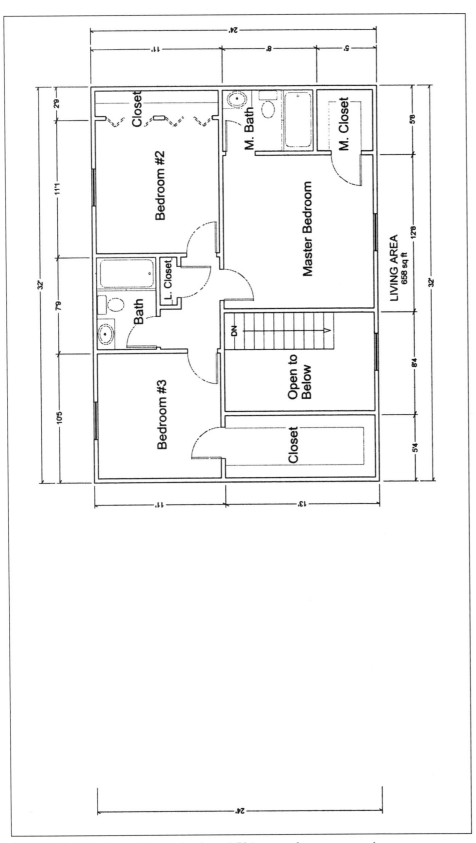

FIGURE 2-13B Second-floor plan for a 1,526-square-foot two-story home.

PROS AND CONS OF TWO STORY HOUSES

Pros	Cons
■ It's cheaper to go up than out.	■ Smaller footprints mean smaller basements.
■ Living spaces can be separated if desired.	■ Upstairs bedrooms may limit your resale clientele.
■ Simple designs still have great curb appeal.	■ Multiple stories usually require an extra half bath compared to ranches.

FIGURE 2-14 Cape Cod home.

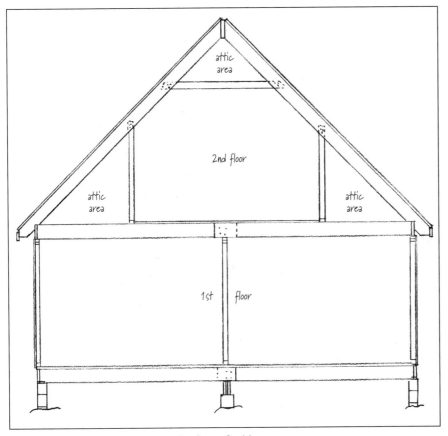

FIGURE 2-15 Cross section of a Cape Cod house.

design has loads of curb appeal while still being a basic rectangle in shape. The open design of the living room, kitchen, and dining room coupled with the two-story foyer makes the first floor of this home seem big. The very simple bathrooms will help to keep costs in check while still providing separate baths for adults and children.

Some possible alterations to this plan would include removing the two-story foyer and adding this square footage to the upstairs, shrinking the garage to two cars, and removing or shrinking the front covered porch.

The Cape Cod

The stacking of floors and the ability to use the attic area for living space make Cape Cods among the most economical houses to build. The dramatic rooflines and dormers make the homes impressive to look at from outside and also allow the easy addition of vaulted ceilings on the inside. Capes can be framed with room-in-attic trusses, but it's much more cost-effective to stick-frame the roof with rafters. While cutting rafters isn't difficult for a pro, a novice may want to get some help cutting a jig or pat-

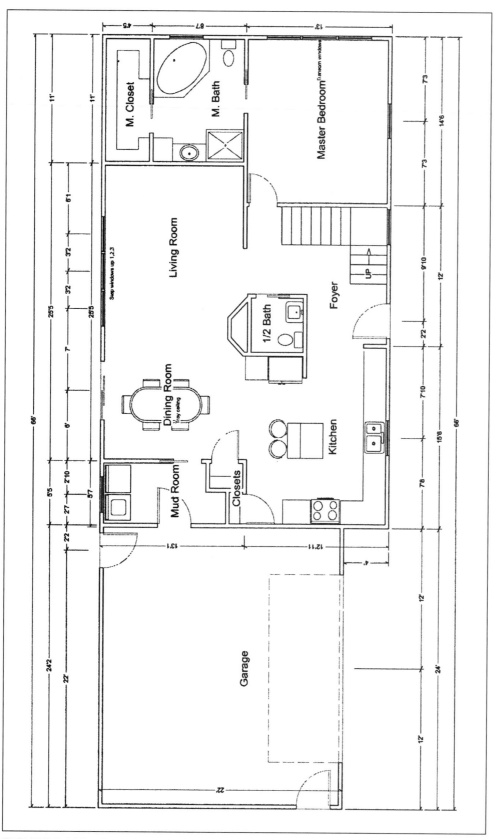

FIGURE 2-16A   First-floor plan of the 1,656-square-foot Cape Cod home.

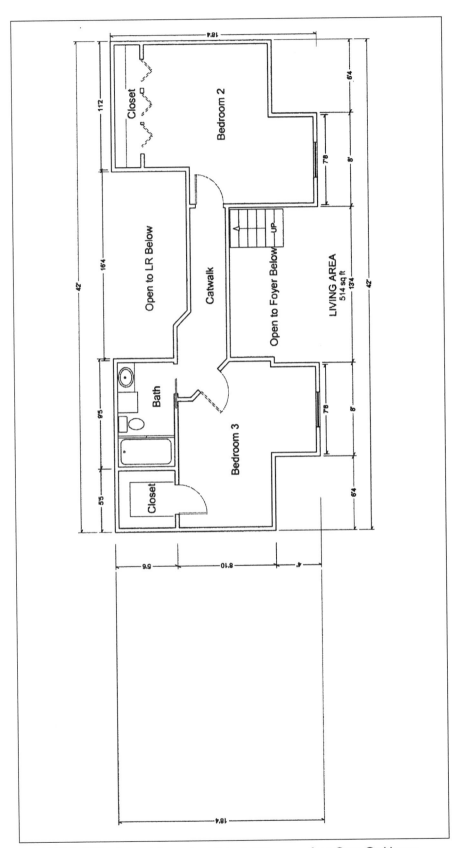

FIGURE 2-16B Second-floor plan of the 1,656-square-foot Cape Cod home.

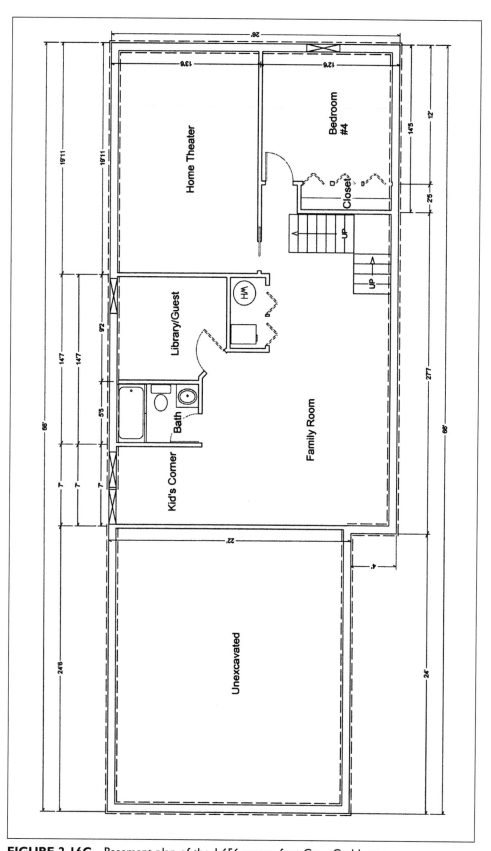

FIGURE 2-16C   Basement plan of the 1,656-square-foot Cape Cod home.

PROS AND CONS
OF CAPE COD HOUSES

Pros	Cons
■ Economical to build.	■ Steep roof pitches may limit the owner's ability to do work.
■ Lots of curb appeal.	■ Second-story walls typically start at 6 feet and angle up to an 8-foot ceiling.
■ Vaulted ceilings can easily be added.	■ Closets on sloped walls have reduced ceiling heights.

tern to lay out the cuts. You'll learn how to find and hire expert help at discount rates in chapter five.

The sample plan features three bedrooms, two and a half baths, vaulted ceilings in living room and foyer, a large master suite on the main level, dormers, a two-car garage and a mud room. This home will have lots of curb appeal and should "live large." By living large, I mean that living in this home will seem like living in a larger house because of the design. I've included a possible basement plan; however, this home may be built on any kind of foundation. The large master bathroom features a corner whirlpool tub with separate stall shower.

Some possible changes would be to add a covered porch, remove the vaulted ceilings and add this square footage to the upstairs, or shrink the master bathroom and closet area.

The Saltbox

The saltbox is really the front half of a Cape Cod house joined with the back half of a two-story house. This combination makes for a pretty good "marriage." By having the curb appeal of a Cape with the extra square footage of a two-story, saltboxes offer the best of both worlds. A salt gives much more flexibility in upstairs design than a Cape. The ability to place windows in the rear wall of the second story for light, ventilation, and egress gives endless choices for design. Salts are one of my favorite kinds of houses. They combine two basic designs and therefore come with the strengths of both styles.

The sample plan features four bedrooms, two and a half baths, both living and family rooms, a two-car attached garage, a vaulted ceiling in the foyer, a two-story ceiling in living room, dormers and a mud room.

GLOSSARY

Room-in-Attic Truss
A manufactured truss that comes with the "attic room" already framed in. It would include the rafters, bottom chords and studs in one ready-to-install piece that was assembled in a factory as shown in figure 2-15.

PROS AND CONS OF SALTBOX HOUSES

Pros	Cons
■ Economical to build. ■ Combine best of two-story and Cape Cod designs. ■ Lots of living room and curb appeal on a small footprint.	■ The cons for salts are the same as the cons for Capes and two-story houses (see pages 38 and 43).

FIGURE 2-17 Saltbox home.

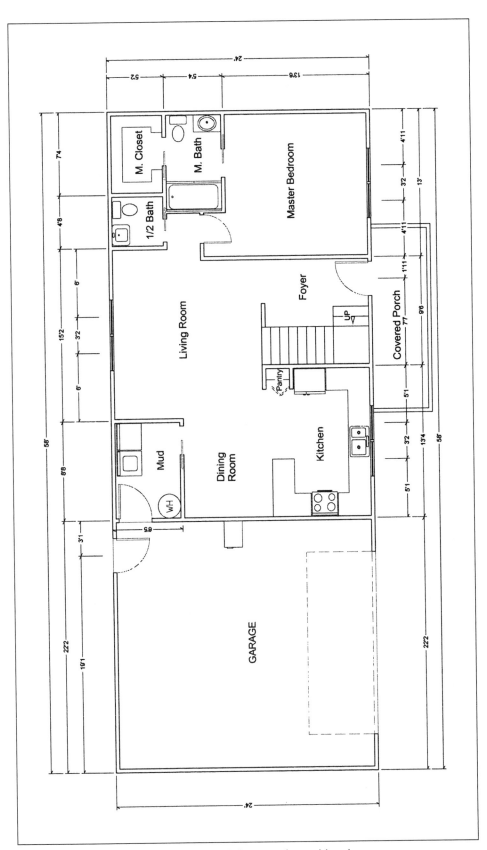

FIGURE 2-18A First-floor plan of a 1,769-square-foot saltbox home.

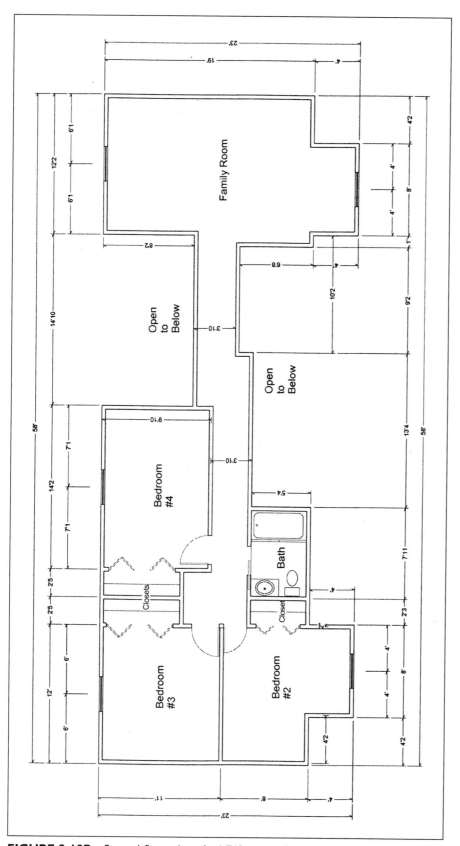

FIGURE 2-18B Second-floor plan of a 1,769-square-foot saltbox home.

This plan is a basic rectangle with loads of curb appeal. The master suite on the first floor and three additional bedrooms upstairs make this the perfect plan for a large family or someone who needs an additional room for an office or for guests. This provides a ton of living on a very small footprint.

Some possible changes are to extend the front porch across the entire front of the house, remove the two-story ceiling in the living-room area, or eliminate the dormers and rearrange the upstairs to save money.

The Multilevel Home

Multilevel homes include bilevels, trilevels and quadlevels. Multilevel homes are economical to build and usually offer more square footage for the money than other designs. By putting half the first story in the ground, costs are reduced when compared to full basements or full-story living spaces over crawl spaces. Multilevel homes are usually harder to resell and fetch smaller prices per square foot than other styles of homes. However, for someone who is trying to wring every last square foot out of a tight budget, multilevels are worth taking a look at. I've chosen a quad-level floor plan as an example of a multilevel home.

The sample plan features four bedrooms, three baths, separate living

BOTTOM LINE
A multilevel home will give you more square footage for less money than other styles.

FIGURE 2-19 Multilevel home.

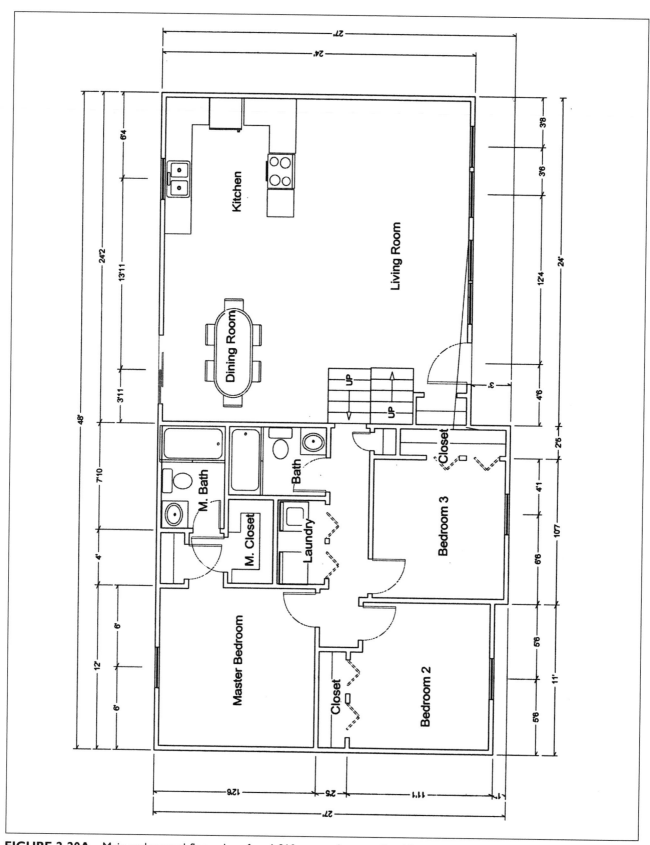

FIGURE 2-20A   Main and second-floor plan of an 1,810-square-foot quadlevel home.

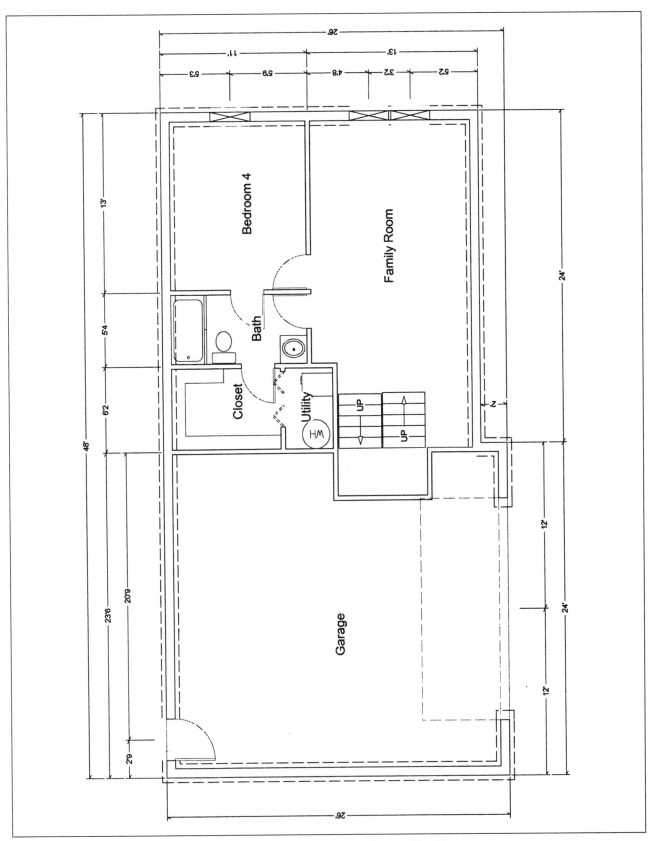

FIGURE 2-20B   Garage and basement floor plan of an 1,810-square-foot quadlevel home.

PROS AND CONS OF MULTI-LEVEL HOMES

Pros	Cons
■ Economical to build.	■ Resells more slowly and usually for less money per square foot than other styles of homes.
	■ Lower level is partially below grade.
	■ You must travel steps every time you enter or leave the home or move from one area of the house to another.

and family rooms, a centralized laundry closet and a two-car attached garage.

A simple alteration would be to add cathedral ceilings in the living and kitchen/dining room areas by using cathedral trusses.

GUIDELINES FOR COST-EFFECTIVE DESIGN

Following are some basic guidelines that I follow while designing a house. However, there are exceptions to every rule. Some things are worth the cost. Deciding what you want to pay for and what you don't is up to you.

- **Keep the corners to a minimum:** When you look at a floor plan, count the number of corners, both inside and outside, on the first-floor exterior walls. The fewer corners you have, the more economical the house will be to build. If you look at the sample floor plans, you'll see that most of them are basic boxes. The ranch has by far the largest number of corners with eight.
- **Use simple rooflines:** The more valleys a roof has, the more expensive it becomes. As you can see from the sample houses shown earlier, a house can still look fantastic without elaborate rooflines.
- **Keep roof pitches at 4/12:** A common 4/12 pitch roof should be used where possible. If you want dramatic lines and pitches, use them on accenting gables or hips only, not on the major body of the roof. The one exception to this rule is if you want usable attic space.
- **Plan exterior dimensions in even feet:** Most materials are purchased in even lengths and sheathing comes in 4' × 8' pieces. By keeping the major dimensions of your designed house to even lengths, preferably divisible by four, unusable left-over material will

FIGURE 2-21   A typical gable roof.

FIGURE 2-22 A typical hip roof.

be reduced.

- **Eliminate wasted space:** Designs should have minimal hallways, dead areas and oversized rooms. A dead area is an area that serves no purpose. Such areas are usually found in and around hallways and where several rooms meet.
- **Avoid custom features:** Unless you can build cabinets yourself for a reasonable price, kitchens and baths should be designed with stock cabinetry and fixtures in mind. Custom cabinetry, built-in features and specialty fixtures can all run up the cost of a home in a hurry. For example, the cabinets shown in Figures 2-23 and 2-24 look similar but the cost of each set was vastly different.

CONSIDER YOUR OPTIONS

When you buy a new car, the sky's the limit when you start talking about options. Chrome wheels, compact-disc changers and moon roofs don't come free, and neither do options in your new home. Balance what you

FIGURE 2-23   A kitchen with custom cabinets; cost is approximately $5,600.

FIGURE 2-24   A kitchen with stock cabinets; cost is approximately $2,100.

need with what you can afford. Below we'll look at porches, decks and patios, garages, landscaping and passive solar design. Covering the plethora of styles and materials you could choose for such optional features would and does fill many books. Consult these resources to increase your knowledge, because by increasing your knowledge of your options, you increase your ability to control the outcome in use, aesthetics and dollars. I'll cover what I typically include and why. I'll also offer some suggestions so you can consider doing some of your own work to save money.

- **Porches:** Porches are nice when they're used and make an attractive exterior for the home. However, covered porches cost almost as much as finished square footage. If a large covered porch is desired, compute your costs and weigh your options. Consider several style and material options and check your local codes to see what is required for a foundation. Concrete porches require continuous foundations, and some municipalities require continuous foundations under any covered porch as well. I almost always try to include some form of covered porch over the front door, but shy away from covered porches on the sides and rear of the house. On the sides and rear, I prefer decks or patios for cost-effectiveness.

- **Decks and patios:** Your options are many. Patio blocks and paving stones come in myriad styles and can be installed without great skills. Poured-concrete patios are inexpensive and very functional. Treated wood decks are very popular and can be tackled by some homeowners, even with little or no experience. Cutting costs in this area is generally a matter of cutting labor costs, so consider doing it yourself.

- **Garages:** Treat garages as garages. They house cars, tools, and myriad other things, but you don't live in them. Garages typically house junk and maybe a car or two, but they sometimes get as much attention as the rest of the house. Finishing the interior of your garage is optional. What you install is also optional. Don't put in what you won't use; 240-volt electrical circuits, large numbers of electrical outlets, paneling, large numbers of light fixtures and washbasins are all examples of nice things to have, but if you have no need for them, don't pay for them.

- **Landscaping:** Fancying up the yard is usually a matter of hard work,

Consider adding a patio or deck after construction is completed to save money on financing costs.

not large amounts of skill. Almost anyone can scatter grass seed and turn on a water hose. Utilize your nursery to help with planting ideas and design. Adding trees, shrubs, retaining walls and flowers shouldn't break the bank. Shop around and utilize the Internet to get your plants at fair prices. Using starter plants instead of fully-grown ones will save lots of money — and you get the thrill of nurturing your plantings as they grow beautifully to their full size. Be sure to check your lot's covenants and restrictions for a planting schedule.

- **Passive solar:** Designing in passive-solar features can be as simple as adding some window space to your southern exposure, using heat-gathering materials on the floor in front of these windows, and designing your overhangs to the right size for your location. There are many good books written on this subject. Passive solar elements can be very simple and cost-effective. Your local library is a great free resource for information. Check it out!

CONSTRUCTION PLANS

To start your project off right, you need to start saving money from day one. This can be accomplished by getting your plans for free or next to free. To get your plans for free, you must design them yourself and be able to make your own blueprints. This may sound like a daunting task at first, but with the right resources it can be done. The key to going it alone is to start with a good template and make some modifications from there. If you don't have experience and training in design, this is the only way to go. I was told by a wise man once, "If you want to be successful, find someone who is doing what you want to do and do exactly what they do." This concept can serve you well when designing a home.

- **Basic plan:** There are many, many resources for floor plans. Your local library, home centers and the Internet are just a few. With the information you've read so far, you should have a good idea of what you're looking for. Search until you find a plan that's close to what you want. I don't recommend using the plan right out of the book. For starters, this would be illegal. But more importantly, you can do better than that. All you're looking for is a starting point. Be sure your plan matches the elevation that you want. By that I mean to make sure that the inside of the home fits the outside.
- **Shuffle things around:** This can easily be done with some graph paper. Lay your rooms out (from your Room Size Determination form in Figure 2-4) to scale on the graph paper and cut them out. Keeping within the parameters of your chosen type and size of

BOTTOM LINE

By adding features later and paying cash instead of borrowing the additional amount on your mortgage, you can save money. For example, a $1,000 deck added later for cash will save almost $2,500 over the life of a 30-year loan.

BOTTOM LINE

For free storage over the garage, have the roof and ceiling stick-framed, leaving the center as open as possible, and sheet the floor yourself with scraps from the job.

BOTTOM LINE

Passive solar design, which can be incorporated very cost-effectively, can save you as much as 30% on your heating bills.

Broderbund's 3D Home Architect is a very user-friendly and affordable CAD program with a great feature that automatically checks plans for potential pitfalls.

house, place the rooms next to one another in various patterns until you find one you like.

- **Putting your design on paper:** If you have drafting skills and equipment, you can draw your prints onto vellum paper and have copies run at the printer. But if you're like most of us, you are better off using CAD software. I prefer Broderbund's 3D Home Architect. This software is very user-friendly and easy to learn with a point-and-click style. It is readily available and inexpensive. Your local library may even have a copy for you to try out. By using this program you can create your own plans. The software even has a feature that will check the plan for potential problems.

- **Review by a pro:** Once you have your plan on paper, it's time to have it checked over for problem areas and code issues. Now's the time to discover design problems, not when you're halfway through construction. You may be able to find someone to do this for free. Possible resources include general contractors, lumberyards, municipality inspectors, municipality reviewers, subcontractors, friends and relatives. I highly recommend that you talk to as many people as necessary until you feel comfortable with your plan. I always show my plans to my individual subcontractors to look for potential prob-

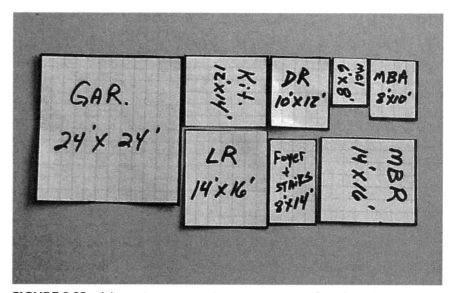

FIGURE 2-25   A layout in progress using rooms cut out of graph paper.

lem areas. In some municipalities you must have your plan reviewed and even stamped by an engineer or an architect. Check in your area to see what's required. If you can't get your plans reviewed by experienced people for free, pay for this service. This is one time when spending a few hundred dollars may save you thousands later.

CHAPTER THREE

QUALITY AND COMPROMISE

Construction perfection, nirvana, the Shangri-la of hammers and nails, how do we define it? It'll vary with each one of us. A cute cottage with no mortgage, a sprawling country estate with a tack barn outside, or a suburban two-story with $50,000 in equity — no matter what your definition of perfection is, you'll have to compromise between quality and economy to make it happen. If we all had unlimited amounts of money to build with, this book wouldn't sell very many copies. We would all build whatever we wanted with no regard for the bottom line. But this is the real world, and we're all dealing with our own very real dollars. To save money, you must learn how to balance quality and economy. I'll guide you through the common pitfalls to avoid and forewarn you of the snares that lie on your path ahead. It is very easy to blow your budget. You may have to change some of your thinking, and you definitely need to learn to take advice with a grain of salt. So read this chapter very carefully. Pull out or copy the checklist found later in this chapter (Figure 3-7) and review it periodically throughout the construction process. It will keep you from making spending errors before you're all done.

KEEPING THE JOB IN PERSPECTIVE

Take a look around and check the quality of the construction where you are living right now. Do you see any errors? Chances are that you will see none. Does this mean there aren't any? Probably not. Put a trained and critical eye on the scene and we'll usually pick it apart. My point is that there is a difference between a job well done and absolute perfection. Here are several things to consider when you're deciding if you can live with a certain product or service or not.

- **Structural integrity:** When deciding on materials or workmanship the first thing to consider is their effect on the strength of the building. For example, if your exterior window and door headers have been specified by the lumberyard to be double 2×12s but the code allows for plywood box headers that you can construct for one-third the price, which do you use? The plywood header meets code and therefore it won't affect structural integrity, so use the box header and save the money. This is really not a compromise on quality. While there may be a perceived value to the 2×12 header because it may look more substantial, there is no real value. The plywood header will disperse the load fine and won't even be seen once the wall is closed up.

- **Visibility:** If an unsightly job won't be seen, is it really a defect? If it passes all other tests listed here, then I say no. Let's say that you have a block covered with mortar on the second row of your foundation. Should you demand that your layer clean it up and insist that you won't accept that kind of sloppiness on your job? The answer is a resounding no. This block passes the integrity question and won't show because it'll be covered when backfilled. Compromise and let this go.

- **Performance:** If an error won't affect performance, is it really a defect? Again, I say no. Let's say that you have a rough opening that is 2 inches too narrow. The door leads to the hall closet, which was supposed to have a 30-inch door. Reframing the door will take considerable time and extra materials and will tear up some surrounding framing. You can demand that the framer fix the opening to meet the plan, or you can let it go and live with a 28-inch door. The 28-inch door will not measurably affect the performance of a hall closet. Compromise and live with it. At a minimum you will have a happy framer who'll remember your fairness when he bids another project for you (or more time and money if you are doing it yourself) and at a maximum you may get a reduction in your bill or some additional work thrown in for no cost. Either way you win.

- **Resale value:** This is a big consideration. I don't recommend playing around with your resale value. However, there are times when small calculated risks can pay off big. Let's say that you can buy a scratched and dented set of cabinets that'll work in your kitchen. The scratches are small and in discreet places. Similar scratching will probably take place in the course of normal living over the next few years. So in five years, when you try to sell the house, these cabinets won't adversely affect the sale. Compromise, buy the cabinets, and pocket the savings.

GLOSSARY

Spec'd
Specified, called out for use. Listed as the common or preferred material for use in a certain application by an architect, estimator or contractor

GLOSSARY

Header
The framing member supporting the load above a window, door or opening. (See Figure 3-1.)

BOTTOM LINE
Plywood headers, when compared to their solid wood counterparts, save money now and later — now by saving two-thirds of the material cost and later by their better insulation, thus saving you fuel dollars down the line.

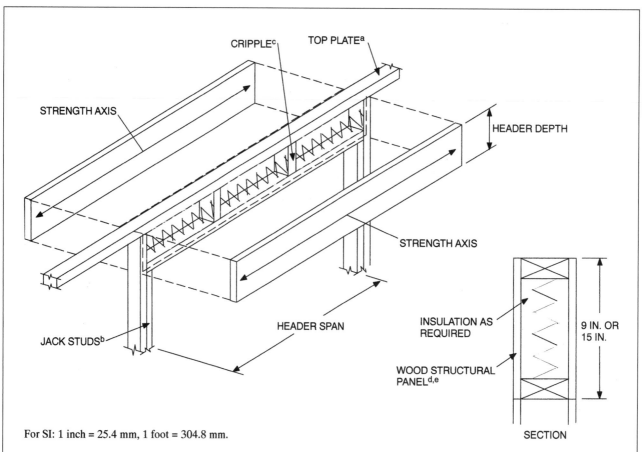

For SI: 1 inch = 25.4 mm, 1 foot = 304.8 mm.

Notes:

a. The top plate shall be continuous over header.
b. Jack studs shall be used for spans over 4 feet.
c. Cripple spacing shall be the same as for studs.
d. Wood structural panel faces shall be single pieces of $^{15}/_{32}$-inch-thick Exposure 1 (exterior glue) or thicker, installed on the interior or exterior or both sides of the header.
e. Wood structural panel faces shall be nailed to framing and cripples with 8d common or galvanized box nails spaced 3 inches on center, staggering alternate nails $^{1}/_{2}$ inch.
f. Galvanized nails shall be hot-dipped or tumbled.

MAXIMUM SPANS FOR WOOD STRUCTURAL PANEL BOX HEADERS[a]

HEADER CONSTRUCTION[b]	HEADER DEPTH (inches)	HOUSE DEPTH (feet)				
		24	26	28	30	32
Wood structural panel—one side	9	4	4	3	3	—
	15	5	5	4	3	3
Wood structural panel—both sides	9	7	5	5	4	3
	15	8	8	7	7	6

For SI: 1 inch = 25.4 mm, 1 foot = 304.8 mm.

a. Spans are based on single story with clear-span trussed roof or two-story with floor and roof supported by interior-bearing walls.

b. See Figure R602.7.2 for construction details.

FIGURE 3-1 Typical wood structural panel box header construction. International Residential Code 2003. Copyright 2003. Falls Church, Virginia: International Code Council, Inc. Reproduced with permission. All rights reserved.

Cultivating a reputation for being fair and understanding will go a long way in helping you obtain reasonable bids.

- **Livability:** If an item or level of workmanship won't adversely affect how you'll live in the house, how can it be a defect? I say it can't. But here's an example of how an error can affect livability. Say that your foundation contractor has placed the service door opening for the garage on the east wall instead of the south wall. You plan on fencing the south side of the house, where you will let your dog in and out. You can either have the contractor move the opening or you can walk outside and through the elements every time you want to let your dog in or out. Insist on quality and have him move the opening.
- **Functionality:** If an error changes the functionality of an item, it is a defect. For example, if your electrician has missed the switch for your garbage disposal, you'll have to open the cabinet and plug the dispos-

GLOSSARY

Backfill
The dirt placed against the foundation once it is completed, or the act of placing the dirt against the completed foundation.

FIGURE 3-2 A typical double 2x12 header.

When installing baseboard trim, inside corners can be handled in several ways. My two favorites are to shim the bottom out or to use corner blocks.

GLOSSARY

Rough Opening
The opening in the framing that allows for the installation of a door or window, or the dimensions of said opening.

al in when you want to turn it on and unplug it when you want it to go off. Insist on quality and have him install the missed switch.

• **Aesthetics:** Beauty is in the eye of the beholder, and I know some people with very big eyes. I don't believe in taking out a microscope to inspect new construction for defects. You can insist on quality without losing your common sense. If you've ever said, "I can't see it, but I can feel it" or "If you stand over here at 4:30 when the light is just right, you can just make it out," you're too picky. Get over it and start being practical. For example, let's say you elected to do the trim in the house yourself. You're having a terrible time getting the inside miters on the baseboard to come out uniformly (this is caused by the bevel on the bottom edge of the drywall). You're halfway through the house when you discover options to correct the problem. Do you go back and rework every corner you've done? This'll cost you materi-

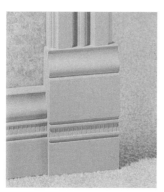

Plinth Blocks
Plinth blocks are used where base moulding meets door casing trim.

Outside Corner Blocks
Corner blocks form a decorative outside corner where base trim meets.

Inside Corner Blocks
Inside corner blocks form a decorative inside corner where base trim meets.

Rosette Blocks
Rosette blocks form a decorative corner where two mouldings meet.

FIGURE 3-3   Inside and outside corner blocks, plinth blocks and rosettes. Illustration courtesy of House of Fara®. For more information go to www.houseoffara.com.

als and time, both of which cost you money. The question then becomes a matter of beauty. If the corners will always be covered with furniture, is it worth the time? Can you consider filling the imperfections with putty or caulk? Is there some other option that'll correct the problem for less money or even free? This problem is one I would address with some common sense, and the answer may be different for different corners. I would not recommend ripping out every corner you've done. If they were that bad, you would have stopped after the first one and sought some professional advice anyway. Pick out the noticeable corners and fix them, then deal with the others as you see fit.

Common sense can go a long way in helping you decide what's acceptable and what isn't. The bottom line is up to you. Refrain from making snap decisions. When in doubt, back away from the situation and get some advice from the pros and maybe even your friends. But always remember that just because your aunt would blow a gasket in a certain situation doesn't mean you have to.

GETTING THE BEST

We all want the best. Most people building new houses insist on it. These people are also paying for it. That's part of the reason that the national average for construction is around $95 a square foot. Knowing when to spend and when to save is a major piece of building for less, as you make decisions I'm going to give you some guidelines to follow.

- **Use the minimum:** If your return won't outweigh your investment, think twice. Find out from your broker or another knowledgeable person whether your costs will come back to you, then use this information to help you decide where to put your money. For example, say that you are considering window options. You can purchase the name-brand unit with the built-in shades and the reputation for $700 each, or you can buy an all-vinyl window and install a vertical blind for $200 total. The vinyl unit is widely used and accepted. It performs as well or better than the expensive one; it just doesn't have the name. While the name brand may create a perception of quality in your home, that alone will not make a considerable difference in your resale value. Buy the vinyl unit and pocket the savings.
- **Skip the upgrades:** Keeping up with the neighbors will put you in the poorhouse. Heat pumps, geothermal heating systems, foam insulation, stone facades, stamped metal ceilings and copper roofs are all nice, but they all have less expensive alternatives. One of the surest ways to blow the budget is to start upgrading. Ten dollars a square

BOTTOM LINE
Rosettes, corner and plinth blocks eliminate the need for miters, making it possible for anyone to install trim and thus saving the labor costs.

GLOSSARY

Miter
Any angled cut needed to fit pieces of trim together to form a corner.

foot sounds like very little, but if you upgrade often and you start adding those overages up, they come to a lot. In chapter nine I'll specify what I use and why, but everything you do and use needs to undergo evaluation to keep the budget in line. Take a look at Figures 3-4 and 3-5. I can't tell the difference between the $44 and the $99 version, and I guarantee you that when you flush the toilet, as long as it works, you won't be able to tell either.

- **Look for savings:** Scratched and dented pieces, closeouts, discount-store offerings and even rummage sales can yield good value. Don't let where your buy an item determine its worth. Treat statements such as "I never buy lumber from _____; it isn't as good as what I get over here" with skepticism. Get the facts. This exact statement has been made to me concerning a couple of local stores, and when I hear it I'm quick to point out that the store they shop in carries a lower grade of lumber than my "cheap" store. "Oh really? I don't believe it!" they usually respond. Most of them still vow that their yards are better, even though I can prove that my yard (Menards)

FIGURE 3-4 A $44 toilet.

FIGURE 3-5 A $99 toilet.

carries a no.1 grade and theirs carries a no.2 grade of lumber.

- **Brand names vs. generics:** You don't have to buy the name brand to get quality. "Oh, I would never use that brand of service panel," the electrician said.

  "Really, why not?" I asked.

  "They're just not as well built; they have a better chance of failure," he replied.

  "How many have you known to fail in the 30 years you've been in business?" I asked.

  "None," he replied.

This electrician means well, and he truly believes what he is telling me, but the facts just don't back it up. This electrician and I have never done business together. He's not a bad guy and he's a heck of an electrician, but he's stuck with a "you have to buy the best of everything or it's junk" attitude that I don't subscribe to. He has a place in the market — it's just not with me. If you hire a sub and he refuses to use what you supply him, find another sub.

BOTTOM LINE

A stud-grade 2x4 from the discount store is the same quality as that from the local lumberyard, no matter what the cost difference is.

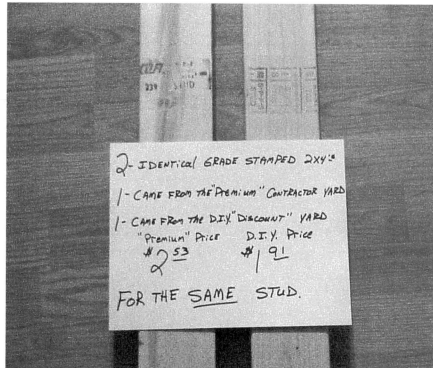

FIGURE 3-6   Two precuts showing a SPF stud-grade stamp. They were purchased from different yards for different prices.

- **Worth:** Don't let what you pay for something determine its worth. Don't let statements such as "You can't buy a decent front door for less than $700" lead you into spending money. I thrill on the bargain found. My father recently purchased a tub-and-shower unit from a salvage store for $139. The same unit sells for $219 at the local discount supplier and more than that through some other local suppliers. If you installed the units in three bathrooms and asked someone to distinguish between the three, they could not do it. I love saying, "That light fixture originally sold for $99 but I got it for $20 on closeout," but I try not to listen to statements such as, "Oh, I just love my whisper-quiet garage-door opener; it's the best on the market. And at $700 it should be." This purchase may make some people feel better when they stand in their garage, but I'm not interested in keeping up with the nouveau riche. I'm usually in my car outside the garage when the door goes up and down, and the $150 opener had a better warranty.

- **Less expensive alternatives:** I'm always leery of the neat and prepackaged "fixes" that are available at your local supplier. Take as an example trim pieces for laminate flooring. I love laminate. It's inexpensive when purchased right, great looking and fairly easy to

❑ Will it be visible? If not, consider the minimum.

❑ Will it affect your resale value? If not, save your money.

❑ Will the less expensive item work the same as the more expensive one? If so, buy it.

❑ If there is no return on your investment, don't spend your money!

❑ Think hard before upgrading. Will you really get your money's worth?

❑ Can you buy a scratched and dented, closeout or discounted item that will fill your needs?

❑ Can you buy the off brand that performs the same for less?

❑ Is there a less expensive alternative? Can you be creative and save a few dollars?

Cut out or copy Figure 3-7 so you can review it throughout the construction process. It will help remind you of the important questions to ask before making any purchases.

FIGURE 3-7   Elements to consider before spending your money.

FIGURE 3-8   This tub-and-shower unit was purchased at a salvage store for 63% of retail.

FIGURE 3-9   Wood transition strip I made myself for $2. The prepackaged alternative was $7.95.

install. However, when you're ready to trim it out, you'll be directed to a neat-looking rack with tons of choices on it. All the trim pieces will be neatly and individually wrapped in a custom-made display rack. These strips work extremely well for their intended purposes and they'll match your floor exactly, but they are expensive. I prefer to make my own from solid stock pieces with my router and table. It takes a little effort to save this money, but it's well worth it.

CHAPTER FOUR

BUILDING CODES

I want you to forget every piece of advice you've ever received about construction. You can't serve two masters. You're either going to follow me and save a bunch of money, or you're going to listen to everyone else and spend it. To build a house for 55 cents on the dollar, you'll have to follow my advice. I'll guide you past the common money-eating pits that most homebuilders fall into during construction. By recognizing and avoiding them, you'll be able to evaluate others' recommendations, decipher where the real value lies, and then determine where your hard-fought-for money should go.

BUILDING TO CODE

There seems to be a code for everything. Even the amount of insulation you install is regulated by a government agency enforcing a code. Whether you love codes or hate them is up to you. When I first started in this industry, I let the codes intimidate me. After all, there were so many, and most of them read like a college calculus book. But when you spend some time with them, you may learn to value them as I do. The codebooks do one great thing for me — they dispel myths about the way "everyone has done it" since the hammer and nail were invented and show me how it *can* be done. When you stand on the code, no one can knock you down, since it's the law. Here are some code issues I use to keep my costs down when I build.

- **Proper spans:** Use the span charts to determine the proper spans for lumber and I-joists. By using the charts in the code book (Figure 4-1) or the manufacturer-provided charts, you can determine what size of lumber or joist is required for your application. For example,

Codebooks are a great resource for the beginning homebuilder.

a no.2 grade Hem-fir 2×8 at 16 inches on center (O.C.) will span 11 feet 4 inches with a 40-pound live load and a 20-pound dead load. Whoa! I know, that's a mouthful, but don't panic. It's not as complicated as it sounds. Your suppliers will tell you the grade and lumber types (e.g., no.2 Hem-fir) they carry, and your building inspector or codebook can help you determine what spacing and loading you need. Don't take the easy road and ask an old-timer to use the common method of joist sizing. You may wind up with an answer such as, "We don't build with 2×8s; we only use 2×10s 'cause they're better." This is not the way to design your house; use the charts and get it right.

- **Span length:** Shorten your spans by adding another bearing point. When building over an area where an extra support won't interfere with living, consider adding a beam to shorten the span, allowing you to use a smaller size floor joist. Let's say you're building a house that's 24 feet wide. If you're placing your joists 16 inches O.C., you can span 12 feet twice with 2×10s and a single beam, or you can span 8 feet three times with 2×8s and two beams. By adding the beam and using the smaller lumber I get a stiffer floor and several hundred dollars in my pocket. Be sure to include the extra cost of the extra beam, including the footing and support, when calculating your cost difference. (See Figure 4-2.)

- **Size with the span charts:** Skip the "let's be safe and go to the next size up" trap. When you're sizing materials, whether it's joists, beams, rafters or headers, don't think outside the span charts. I know several estimators and builders who want to jump to the next size before they have to. If you hear a statement such as, "You could use two 9-inch microlams to carry the load, but I'd use three to be safe," be leery and check the tables yourself. The span charts found in your code book or provided by a manufacturer were calculated by licensed engineers. They don't say that a certain item will span 10 feet when it will span only 8 feet. Use the chart and skip the well-meaning advice of the layman behind the counter, unless he happens to be a licensed engineer. The big determining factor should be the deflection allowed by the code. When sizing materials, this should always be considered. For example, a floor joist is allowed L/360 deflection on the live load. This means that a joist spanning 20 feet

FLOOR JOIST SPANS FOR COMMON LUMBER SPECIES (Residential living areas, live load=40 psf, L/Δ=360)

JOIST SPACING (inches)	SPECIE AND GRADE		DEAD LOAD = 10 psf				DEAD LOAD = 20 psf			
			2x6	2x8	2x10	2x12	2x6	2x8	2x10	2x12
			Maximum floor joist spans							
			(ft.- in.)	(ft.- in.)	(ft.- in.)	(ft.- in.)	(ft.- in.)	(ft.- in.)	(ft.- in.)	(ft.- in.)
12	Douglas fir-larch	SS	11- 4	15- 0	19- 1	23- 3	11- 4	15- 0	19- 1	23- 3
	Douglas fir-larch	#1	10-11	14- 5	18- 5	22- 0	10-11	14- 2	17- 4	20- 1
	Douglas fir-larch	#2	10- 9	14- 2	17- 9	20- 7	10- 6	13- 3	16- 3	18-10
	Douglas fir-larch	#3	8- 8	11- 0	13- 5	15- 7	7-11	10- 0	12- 3	14- 3
	Hem-fir	SS	10- 9	14- 2	18- 0	21-11	10- 9	14- 2	18- 0	21-11
	Hem-fir	#1	10- 6	13-10	17- 8	21- 6	10- 6	13-10	16-11	19- 7
	Hem-fir	#2	10- 0	13- 2	16-10	20- 4	10- 0	13- 1	16- 0	18- 6
	Hem-fir	#3	8- 8	11- 0	13- 5	15- 7	7-11	10- 0	12- 3	14- 3
	Southern pine	SS	11- 2	14- 8	18- 9	22-10	11- 2	14- 8	18- 9	22-10
	Southern pine	#1	10-11	14- 5	18- 5	22- 5	10-11	14- 5	18- 5	22- 5
	Southern pine	#2	10- 9	14- 2	18- 0	21- 9	10- 9	14- 2	16-11	19-10
	Southern pine	#3	9- 4	11-11	14- 0	16- 8	8- 6	10-10	12-10	15- 3
	Spruce-pine-fir	SS	10- 6	13-10	17- 8	21- 6	10- 6	13-10	17- 8	21- 6
	Spruce-pine-fir	#1	10- 3	13- 6	17- 3	20- 7	10- 3	13- 3	16- 3	18-10
	Spruce-pine-fir	#2	10- 3	13- 6	17- 3	20- 7	10- 3	13- 3	16- 3	18-10
	Spruce-pine-fir	#3	8- 8	11- 0	13- 5	15- 7	7-11	10- 0	12- 3	14- 3
16	Douglas fir-larch	SS	10- 4	13- 7	17- 4	21- 1	10- 4	13- 7	17- 4	21- 0
	Douglas fir-larch	#1	9-11	13- 1	16- 5	19- 1	9- 8	12- 4	15- 0	17- 5
	Douglas fir-larch	#2	9- 9	12- 7	15- 5	17-10	9- 1	11- 6	14- 1	16- 3
	Douglas fir-larch	#3	7- 6	9- 6	11- 8	13- 6	6-10	8- 8	10- 7	12- 4
	Hem-fir	SS	9- 9	12-10	16- 5	19-11	9- 9	12-10	16- 5	19-11
	Hem-fir	#1	9- 6	12- 7	16- 0	18- 7	9- 6	12- 0	14- 8	17- 0
	Hem-fir	#2	9- 1	12- 0	15- 2	17- 7	8-11	11- 4	13-10	16- 1
	Hem-fir	#3	7- 6	9- 6	11- 8	13- 6	6-10	8- 8	10- 7	12- 4
	Southern pine	SS	10- 2	13- 4	17- 0	20- 9	10- 2	13- 4	17- 0	20- 9
	Southern pine	#1	9-11	13- 1	16- 9	20- 4	9-11	13- 1	16- 4	19- 6
	Southern pine	#2	9- 9	12-10	16- 1	18-10	9- 6	12- 4	14- 8	17- 2
	Southern pine	#3	8- 1	10- 3	12- 2	14- 6	7- 4	9- 5	11- 1	13- 2
	Spruce-pine-fir	SS	9- 6	12- 7	16- 0	19- 6	9- 6	12- 7	16- 0	19- 6
	Spruce-pine-fir	#1	9- 4	12- 3	15- 5	17-10	9- 1	11- 6	14- 1	16- 3
	Spruce-pine-fir	#2	9- 4	12- 3	15- 5	17-10	9- 1	11- 6	14- 1	16- 3
	Spruce-pine-fir	#3	7- 6	9- 6	11- 8	13- 6	6-10	8- 8	10- 7	12- 4
19.2	Douglas fir-larch	SS	9- 8	12-10	16- 4	19-10	9- 8	12-10	16- 4	19- 2
	Douglas fir-larch	#1	9- 4	12- 4	15- 0	17- 5	8-10	11- 3	13- 8	15-11
	Douglas fir-larch	#2	9- 1	11- 6	14- 1	16- 3	8- 3	10- 6	12-10	14-10
	Douglas fir-larch	#3	6-10	8- 8	10- 7	12- 4	6- 3	7-11	9- 8	11- 3
	Hem-fir	SS	9- 2	12- 1	15- 5	18- 9	9- 2	12- 1	15- 5	18- 9
	Hem-fir	#1	9- 0	11-10	14- 8	17- 0	8- 8	10-11	13- 4	15- 6
	Hem-fir	#2	8- 7	11- 3	13-10	16- 1	8- 2	10- 4	12- 8	14- 8
	Hem-fir	#3	6-10	8- 8	10- 7	12- 4	6- 3	7-11	9- 8	11- 3
	Southern pine	SS	9- 6	12- 7	16- 0	19- 6	9- 6	12- 7	16- 0	19- 6
	Southern pine	#1	9- 4	12- 4	15- 9	19- 2	9- 4	12- 4	14-11	17- 9
	Southern pine	#2	9- 2	12- 1	14- 8	17- 2	8- 8	11- 3	13- 5	15- 8
	Southern pine	#3	7- 4	9- 5	11- 1	13- 2	6- 9	8- 7	10- 1	12- 1
	Spruce-pine-fir	SS	9- 0	11-10	15- 1	18- 4	9- 0	11-10	15- 1	17- 9
	Spruce-pine-fir	#1	8- 9	11- 6	14- 1	16- 3	8- 3	10- 6	12-10	14-10
	Spruce-pine-fir	#2	8- 9	11- 6	14- 1	16- 3	8- 3	10- 6	12-10	14-10
	Spruce-pine-fir	#3	6-10	8- 8	10- 7	12- 4	6- 3	7-11	9- 8	11- 3
24	Douglas fir-larch	SS	9- 0	11-11	15- 2	18- 5	9- 0	11-11	14- 9	17- 1
	Douglas fir-larch	#1	8- 8	11- 0	13- 5	15- 7	7-11	10- 0	12- 3	14- 3
	Douglas fir-larch	#2	8- 1	10- 3	12- 7	14- 7	7- 5	9- 5	11- 6	13- 4
	Douglas fir-larch	#3	6- 2	7- 9	9- 6	11- 0	5- 7	7- 1	8- 8	10- 1
	Hem-fir	SS	8- 6	11- 3	14- 4	17- 5	8- 6	11- 3	14- 4	16-10ᵃ
	Hem-fir	#1	8- 4	10- 9	13- 1	15- 2	7- 9	9- 9	11-11	13-10
	Hem-fir	#2	7-11	10- 2	12- 5	14- 4	7- 4	9- 3	11- 4	13- 1
	Hem-fir	#3	6- 2	7- 9	9- 6	11- 0	5- 7	7- 1	8- 8	10- 1
	Southern pine	SS	8-10	11- 8	14-11	18- 1	8-10	11- 8	14-11	18- 1
	Southern pine	#1	8- 8	11- 5	14- 7	17- 5	8- 8	11- 3	13- 4	15-11
	Southern pine	#2	8- 6	11- 0	13- 1	15- 5	7- 9	10- 0	12- 0	14- 0
	Southern pine	#3	6- 7	8- 5	9-11	11-10	6- 0	7- 8	9- 1	10- 9
	Spruce-pine-fir	SS	8- 4	11- 0	14- 0	17- 0	8- 4	11- 0	13- 8	15-11
	Spruce-pine-fir	#1	8- 1	10- 3	12- 7	14- 7	7- 5	9- 5	11- 6	13- 4
	Spruce-pine-fir	#2	8- 1	10- 3	12- 7	14- 7	7- 5	9- 5	11- 6	13- 4
	Spruce-pine-fir	#3	6- 2	7- 9	9- 6	11- 0	5- 7	7- 1	8- 8	10- 1

Check sources for availability of lumber in lengths greater than 20 feet.
For SI: 1 inch = 25.4 mm, 1 foot = 308.4 mm, 1 pound per square foot = 0.0479 kN/m.
a. End bearing length shall be increased to 2 inches.

FIGURE 4-1 Floor joist spans for common lumber species. Chart courtesy of International Residential Code.

Use the codebook or the charts from your manufacturer to properly size your framing. An approximation by other means is not good enough.

GLOSSARY

Microlam
A generic term used for most manufactured beams. Examples are laminated veneer lumber, commonly called LVL, and Paralam, known as PSL.

is allowed to deflect, or sag, just over ⅝ inch under normal loads. If you want a more solid floor, you'll have to adjust your spans or pay for larger size joists. When it comes to headers and roofs, I stick strictly to the span charts; with floors, I shorten the spans as outlined earlier in this paragraph.

- **Use the rated sheathing:** This concept ties in with the last one. The worst abuse usually comes with roof sheathing. Most people want to oversize the roof sheathing because it deflects terribly when walked on. This leads to the deduction that it's weak and will sag over time. I disagree, and the people with the degrees agree with me. The discrepancy arrives from the fact that a man standing on a roof presents a live load. If he weighs 180 pounds, he is placing a 180-pound live load on the sheathing. If the code requires a 20-pound live load, the man is nine times over the rated limit. Under this stress, of course the sheathing is going to deflect. But roofs are not meant to support men day in and day out. They are meant to support shingles, wind and snow. Using this test of a roof's structural strength is unfair. Sheathing is rated by the American Plywood Association (now the Engineered Wood Association) or another agency for roofing and flooring spans. Each sheet has a stamp (see

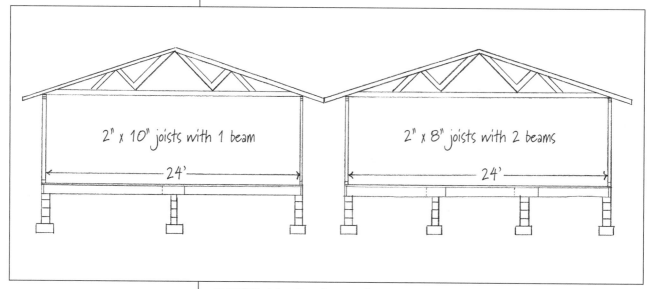

FIGURE 4-2 One drawing shows one beam carrying the floor; the other shows two beams carrying the floor.

FIGURE 4-3 This stamp, from the back of a sheet of OSB, shows the sheet's span ratings.

GLOSSARY

OSB
Oriented strand board. A manufactured sheathing made from wood strands. It is a common substitute for plywood. Also referred to as waferboard and oxboard.

GLOSSARY

Deflection
The amount a framing member is allowed to sag, stated as length over a given number. For example, a 20-foot-long joist allowed to deflect at L/360 would be calculated as 20 (the length of the joist in feet) x 12 (to convert feet to inches) ÷ 360 (the given number) = .67 (the amount of allowed deflection stated in inches). The stated number converts to approximately ⅝ inch. The above joist could sag ⅝ inch under normal loads and still meet the code.

Figure your return on investment before spending extra money unnecessarily.

Figure 4-3) that gives the rated span. I use ⁷⁄₁₆-inch OSB on my roof spans up to 24 inches O.C. because it's rated for them. Oversizing — or maybe I should say overthickening — your sheathing will cost you a lot of money.

- **Don't make changes:** Stick to your plans. Don't get talked into doing it now while you're building "because it's easier." You know how you live and what you need, and you designed your house around these needs and the code. There are times when thinking ahead can save you some trouble down the line, but in general I don't build for possibilities. For example, "I might buy that welder someday, and I'll need a circuit for it" or "Eventually, I might want to put a ceiling fan there, or "I might as well do it now while the wall is open." In my experience, most of these "I mights" just don't happen. Circuits can and do get added to existing houses every day. It may not be as easy as adding a circuit to a new house while it's being built, but it isn't impossible either. Save your money now, and if an "I might" arises that you want badly enough, you can still get it when the time comes.

- **Don't go for energy efficiency:** Skip the "super" heating and cooling systems. Geothermal heat pumps and high-efficiency furnaces are all great, but skip them if the return isn't there. When you can see — on paper, calculated for your specific example — where you'll get your money back for upgrades, please use these devices. However, in my experience, I haven't been able to get the numbers to work in my favor. The biggest reason for this is that I don't plan on building a "final" house anytime soon. I haven't settled in a house for more than four years, and I always plan to move every two to four years, at least for the near future. When I build a home that my family will stay in for the long haul, I'll seriously consider such a heating system. But for now I know that my dollars in won't equal dollars out. However, if you can show where you'll save money over the long haul, definitely use the more energy-efficient systems.

Follow these guidelines to keep your house to code. Decide for yourself if and when the need to go over and beyond what's required arises. Never forget that you should go over for only two reasons: a practical use specific to you or your family, or when a dollar in will result in more than a dollar out. When in doubt get another opinion, take it with a grain of salt, and then decide what's best for you.

COMMON TRAPS

There are several very common traps that have cost homebuilders countless dollars. They seductively pull you in with their siren song or they're so sneaky that you don't even know you've been caught. But the key to avoiding the snare is the same as it is with any trap. You must know where it is and have an alternate route to get around it. It sounds simple enough, and it is, but it's also so easy to forget. To arm yourself against these money wasters, read this chapter very carefully. Commit the words to memory and review the end-of chapter checklist (Figure 4-4) often. Copy it or tear it out and keep it with you. If you read it before making decisions, it'll save you from the money pits that you will encounter.

- **Beware of small additional costs:** "I'm spending a hundred grand on this house; what's an extra thousand?" If these words ever escape your mouth, one of us has failed. When money ceases to be important to you, it will flee from you. This can happen when you look at bids: "Honey, Uncle Joe's plumber is only $1,000 higher than this other company and Uncle Joe really likes his guy." It happens when you're shopping for materials: "Jim's Lumber Yard was only $1,000 higher on the lumber package, and they're so much more personal than the superstore." It happens all the time, and people are spending thousands upon thousands of dollars unnecessarily. I'm not saying I haven't ever gone with a higher bid, because I have. But when I do, you can bet there's a darn good reason and that it doesn't happen often.

- **Beware of "needs":** "You can't build a new house without _____!" Now fill in the blank. If the item you filled in isn't required by the code, you don't have to have it. You may think you do, but when you're installing it because everyone else says you have to, you're wrong. I've heard all kinds of statements to this effect: "When you're spending the money on a new house, you might as well go ahead and put in a three-car garage. You can hardly sell a house without one anymore," and "When I built, I just went ahead and ordered the custom cabinets. You just have to have a John Doe kitchen to sell a home in this market," and "If I was ever going to build, I'd install a skylight in every room; they're all the rage these days." Now, if you really want or need a particular item and it's in your budget, by all means put it in. Just don't let keeping up with the neighbors separate you from your hard-earned cash. Remember, your goal is to build for 55 cents on the dollar, so hold on to your money.

- **The tool trap:** "If I'm going to install the siding on the house, I have to have a new saw." This one's tough, especially for us guys. We love

BOTTOM LINE
For every $1,000 borrowed, you'll repay $2,394 on a 7% loan amortized over 30 years.

FIGURE 4-4   A right-angle drill commonly used by plumbers and electricians.

the chance to get a new tool, and the cooler the tool, the harder it is to resist. If we wire a house, we need new wire strippers; if we install the furnace, we need a new tap and die set for the pipe; if we plumb the new house, we have to have that right-angle drill. There are countless tools and gadgets out there to make working on a house easier. Some of them are absolutely necessary and absolutely expensive. Try everything possible to avoid the trap of buying every tool you'll need. Tools can be borrowed, rented or leased. If you can't pay for the tool on this job — if it will cost you more to rent it than to buy it — consider an alternative. And don't consider only the cost; remember that you'll have to store it after you're done with it. If you buy all the tools you need to build, not only will you go broke, but you'll have to park your car outside because the garage will be full of tools.

- **Spending your savings:** "I saved $500 on the foundation, so I can spend an extra $500 on windows." Wrong! Your entire budget will work because the ups match the downs. For every item you bring in under budget, there'll be one that comes in over budget. It's a constant battle to keep your costs down. You'll win some battles, lose others, and hopefully in the end you come out where you wanted to be. For example, on the last house I built, I had specified the concrete at around $2 a square foot. I can usually get it done for

BOTTOM LINE

When doing it yourself, don't forget to calculate the cost of renting or buying any tools or equipment you'll need to complete the job.

this price and even had a guy committed to the job, plus a backup if he failed. Everything's fine and dandy until it comes time to pour. I call the first guy two weeks before I'm going to need him (I always try to give my subs as much notice as possible), and he crawfishes on me. OK, on to the second guy, who just hurt his back and will be down for at least six weeks. So I end up paying over $3 a foot for the job. For the happy ending, I hadn't spent saved dollars from other portions of the project, and the whole job came in on budget. If I had blown the saved money when I first had it, I would've blown the whole budget.

GLOSSARY

Crawfish
A term used in the industry to describe someone who is backing out of a deal.

- **Skip last-minute changes:** You'll lie awake at night wondering if you should move the kitchen wall over 6 inches or not. You can't sleep. How can you live with the kitchen if you don't move that wall? Don't laugh. This happens all the time. It usually starts with the statement, "I've been thinking." Do your thinking back in chapter two when you're designing the house. Don't start rearranging walls once they're up. This takes materials, labor and time — all of which cost money. You're going to make a couple of mistakes, some of which may include moving that wall at the last minute, but don't drive yourself crazy with them. Most people would change something about their house if they could, and almost all people who build houses are on their third or fourth one before they get it the way they want it. I know that anything I design will be closer to what I want than anything I can buy. I learn from each house I build, so with every new one I get a little closer to the perfect home.

- **Don't be upsold:** "It's only $50 more for the better one." Everyone will try to get you to spend your money on the "better" one, or the higher grade or the thicker this or the faster that. Don't let them talk you into it; stick to what you've specified. There's always a "better" grade, but that doesn't mean that you have to have it or that the lower grade is not any good. Think about it this way: a Chevy is a fine car, but a Cadillac is better, but a Lamborghini is better, and so on. The point is that a Chevy is still a fine car even though there is a "better" one, and most good materials are the same. The big factor is usually the warranty. Many times the less expensive line has the same warranty as the "better" one, and sometimes the cost difference outweighs any longer warranty you may get with the upgrade.

To keep your dollars, stay close to them. Don't let someone get to you by calling you a tightwad or miser; you should wear those badges with pride. Let them have a little laugh at your expense; you'll be the one laughing all the way to the bank when your house payment is half theirs. Then, when

BOTTOM LINE
The bottom line is usually more like the bottom hilly road — full of ups and downs. This price goes up while this other one comes down. The idea is to maintain the average so your project comes in on budget.

 If the entry-product has a lifetime warranty, why upgrade? Good examples are vinyl siding and faucets.

BOTTOM LINE

Some warranties simply aren't worth it. For example, you can buy a toilet for $44 that comes with a one-year warranty. You can buy a different toilet for $99 that comes with a five-year warranty. The replacement parts to rebuild a toilet if it fails cost about $8. The "cheap" toilet would have to fail almost twice a year every year for the four-year difference in warranties before you would lose money.

1. Don't upsize framing from what the code book or the span charts tell you to use.

2. Use the rated sheathing.

3. Don't add extras once you start.

4. Skip the super systems and the upgrades.

5. Every $1 you spend can cost you $2.40 over the life of your loan, so save every $2.40 you can.

6. Don't listen to the family, neighbors, subs or anyone else when they try to get you to spend extra money.

7. Don't buy that new tool unless you can't do the job without it. Then see if you can borrow it or rent it for less.

8. If you've saved on part A, don't blow your savings on part B. You may need it for part C.

9. Don't buy the upgrade without a very good reason.

10. Hold tight to your money, or it will flee from you!

FIGURE 4-5   Checklist to use when shopping for materials.

you're packing your bags for that week-long trip to Cancun, and they ask you, "How in the world can you afford a trip like that?" you can reply with a sly smile, "Oh, I don't know, maybe I'm just a little miserly."

Pull out or copy Figure 4-5 and keep it with you when you go shopping or make decisions on what to put where. Read the advice and keep it in the front of your mind when deciding where to invest your money. Remember, a lifetime warranty is as long as you'll get or ever need.

CHAPTER FIVE

FINDING AND WORKING WITH GENERAL CONTRACTORS AND SUBCONTRACTORS

O h, I love these guys. They can and will be one of your primary reasons for success — or failure. This man (as we'll call him or her) can be your best friend, or the source of your nightmares. If he's good, he'll be worth his weight in gold. Keep him, cherish him. Don't be afraid to buy him lunch, or a beer, whichever he prefers. Talk to him about his business, his wife, his kids or his dog. I don't care what you talk to him about, just make sure it's what he wants to talk about. Remember, the sweetest sound to a human being is his own name. Do whatever it takes to get the break on the bid, get the work done on time and get it done correctly. Finding him may be the hardest part. I'll walk you through how and where to find a good contractor. Then we'll move on to your working relationship. I'm going to fill you in on a decade and a half of experience, so read this chapter well; it's one of the most important in the book. I wasn't foolin' when I said contractors can make or break your project. Read on to learn how to use them to make your project the success I know it can be.

DISTINGUISHING BETWEEN GENERALS AND SUBS

Before we can discuss the hows and whys of contractors, we need to establish the difference between a general contractor and a subcontractor. Each of these contractors serves specific purposes. The general contractor plays a role kind of like the general manager of a baseball team. He doesn't actually swing the bat, but he makes sure everything is in place so the bat can get swung. The subcontractor is more like the batter. He's given a specific task, at which, hopefully, he is very good, and he carries

General contractors are commonly referred to as generals or GCs. Subcontractors are commonly called subs.

out that particular task. The key is to have the game well organized, so the outcome is good. Let's pinpoint the differences between these two types of contractors.

Pinpointing the Difference

- **Subcontractors usually do one thing:** For example, typical subs include masons, electricians, plumbers, painters, roofers and heating contractors (plus a multitude of others). These contractors perform only the individual task they were hired for.

- **General contractors are in charge of the whole project, or large portions thereof:** For example, let's say you've hired a GC to shell your project. He would then hire and supervise workers and/or subs to do the foundation, framing, roofing, siding, window and door installation, concrete, decks and possibly landscaping on the project.

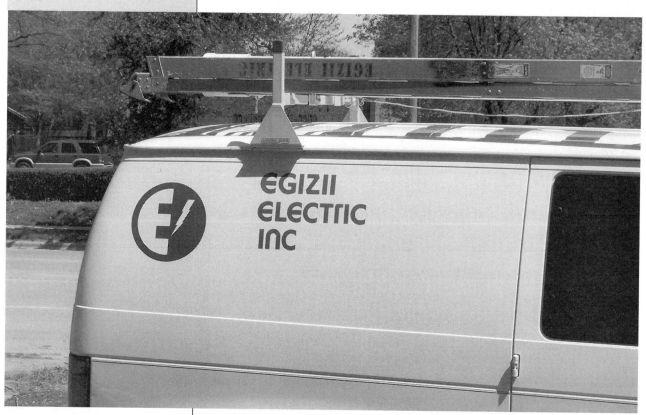

Figure 5-1   The contractor's van designates that the company is an electrical subcontractor.

Figure 5-2 This contractor's truck designates the company as a general contractor.

- **General contractors hire subcontractors; subs don't hire generals:** As stated previously, a general may hire subs to do all or any portion of the work he is required to handle. Some GCs have personnel on staff to complete all phases of their projects; other generals may not have any employees at all. The latter contractor hires subs to do all of his work for him.
- **Generals can be subs, and subs can be generals:** Don't assume that because a contractor is only subbing the siding work on a job that he isn't capable of running the whole show, or that if he is running the whole thing he won't consider doing just a portion of another project. Contractors can and do play different roles on different projects.

BOTTOM LINE

By hiring a general contractor to shell your project rather than complete it, you can save 50% of the fee.

Hire a general contractor only for jobs or portions thereof that you can't handle on your own.

 The whole project is only as complicated as its individual parts. By breaking the whole down into manageable pieces it won't seem so overwhelming.

GENERAL CONTRACTOR COMPARISON CHART

Contractor's Name	Insurance, including worker's comp.	Similar projects completed	References, 3 minimum	Price

FIGURE 5-3 General contractor comparison chart.

WHEN TO HIRE A GENERAL CONTRACTOR

When you're the owner of a project, the buck stops with you. If that responsibility is too much, hire a general. When you're first starting out, it's advisable to have someone looking out for you. Does that mean you should automatically run out and hire a full time GC? Not necessarily. When determining if you need a GC, consider all of the following.

• **Can I do some research and run part, or most, of the job myself:** If you can research the project and handle it yourself, you won't need a full time GC. For example, let's say you feel comfortable handling the framing, siding, roofing and electrical in your new house, but the foundation and plumbing have you feeling a little shaky. Hit the library and do some research on foundations, plumbing and the responsibility of the GC with regard to these projects. Then, if you hire strong foundation and plumbing subs, you should be able to handle the rest. Remember, building a house is only as difficult as the individual projects that must be done to finish the whole. Don't let uncertainty in one area keep you from doing the whole; just get the help you need in that area.

- **Can I hire a GC to consult with me instead of running the whole show:** By hiring an experienced GC to consult with you once or twice a week, you can save a considerable amount. Let's say you're not comfortable handling everything without a "safety net." Don't throw in the towel and hire a full time GC just yet. Can you find one who will consult with you on an hourly basis a couple days a week? By visiting with him on the jobsite at the middle and the end of each week, he can help you plan ahead and avoid costly mistakes. He can also check the work that's been done and provide valuable insight to keep your project running smoothly. This way you can run your own project, but feel confident knowing that a seasoned pro is helping to keep you on track.

- **Can I track a job and learn what steps it takes to complete a house:** To learn the process of homebuilding, track someone else's job from start to finish. Watch the job daily from the very start to the very end. Ask questions of anyone who will talk with you. Watch what's going on during each stage of construction. Keep a log. Keep track of when materials and subs show up. Note what they're doing. Collect a business card from each sub. Explain that you're planning to build and ask if they'd be interested in giving you a bid. Now pump them for information. They'll be more than willing to talk for the possibility of future work. Learn all you can from them about the job at hand, then apply that knowledge to your own job.

Eliminating the GC can provide up to half of your savings on a project, so consider the option seriously. For first timers, I would highly suggest tracking a job or hiring a consulting GC to educate you. A job can run smoothly or be a mess; it's up to you to direct it the way you want it to go. I personally think of a project as a symphony. The jobsite is the auditorium, the subs and workers are the musicians, and I am the conductor. Now my job can sound like a smooth and beautiful piece of classical music or it can sound like a punk rock frenzy where the instruments get smashed and the music and vocals are indistinguishable from the sound of a garbage grinder. Whether it sounds like music or noise, the responsibility lies on my shoulders. That's why the job well run can be so thrilling.

BOTTOM LINE

By eliminating the general contractor altogether you can save 5% to 15% on your project. That equals $15,000 to $25,000 savings for every $100,000 you would have spent.

BOTTOM LINE

By consulting with a general contractor instead of hiring him full time, you stand to save $11,000 to $21,000 on each $100,000 you would have spent.

GLOSSARY

Consult

To advise without taking control or responsibility. For example, a contractor may consult with you on a project without being under contract for the project's outcome.

HOW TO FIND CONTRACTORS

Finding the perfect contractor is like finding the perfect mate. You can find him almost anywhere, but it's not easy. He may be the guy down the street, or he may be from a completely different town. Just like finding your mate, you may have to do some "dating" before you find that special one. You can use the yellow pages, like most people, or you can be more creative. When looking for contractors consider all of these ways I've found them before.

- **Word of mouth:** Word of mouth is the best advertising because it comes from someone who knows. They've either worked directly with or know someone who's worked directly with the contractor. If this type of reference comes from someone you trust, consider it well. If it happens to come from someone you don't trust, try to take it in stride. I don't rule out a contractor because of his association with someone I don't trust, but it puts me a little more on edge than I would be otherwise.

- **Social gatherings:** Finding a sub at a social gathering is great. You get a chance to meet them personally before conducting business. You can observe the beast in its natural environment, so to speak. Whether it's a business, public, religious or private gathering doesn't matter; you'll get at least an inkling of his basic background by his affiliations. I'm not saying to base your entire decision on his associations, but this at least gives you a little heads up. I like finding subs here because it typically means we have mutual friends, acquaintances, business ties or beliefs. While this doesn't guarantee a good working relationship, it often means a good start.

- **Other jobsites:** If you need a roofer (or other sub), and you see one working, stop and talk to him. By visiting a sub on his job, you'll get an insight as to how he'll behave on yours. Observe how he's working. Check out the quality of what he's doing. If you like what you see, and you want to talk price, ask him for a by-the-piece figure. Write it down. Or better yet, get him to write it down.

- **Other contractors:** This can be a valuable source of information if they'll share. Some contractors don't want to give up their secrets, while others will spill everything they know. Most good, reliable and inexpensive small contractors don't stay small for long. Word gets out and they get busy, big and expensive in a hurry. So one contractor may not want to share information on another for fear of him getting big and expensive. But I've been given leads on several great subs by other contractors.

When you find a small contractor who still does some of his own work and he checks out, hire him.

FIGURE 5-4 Jobsite signs are a good way to locate contractors.

- **Friends, family and co-workers:** This way ties in with word of mouth, but I wanted to point out these particular sources of information. These are people you know well, so you have a reference point to start from. I've heard we're only six people away from knowing everyone on the planet, so you should have at least some link to all the good contractors in your area. The trick is to find the link. To do this, talk to everyone you know, and when the chance arises, even talk to those you don't know.

- **Yellow pages:** This is the last place you should look for contractors. But I have, on desperate occasions, found them here. It's impossible to judge a contractor from a yellow pages ad. Anyone can place an ad, large or small, in the yellow pages. A big ad doesn't mean you'll get a big, financially solid contractor; it just means the guy advertis-

BOTTOM LINE

Small contractors with low overhead typically charge less than large contractors with large overhead.

es his services. If you do resort to this source, check out many of the listings. Most contractors give free estimates, so take them up on their offer.

By looking in all of these places you should be able to find the subs you need to get the job done. Be sure to talk to anyone who will listen about what you're looking for. Take the provided information and sort through it to find the diamond in the rough. Diamonds are out there, it's up to you to search. I like small contractors with low overheads. If a guy drives a Cadillac and has a great big beautiful office, someone is paying for it — don't let it be you. I'm not saying you can't get a deal from the big guy, but in my experience, the little guy has come through for me again and again. When dealing with the small guy, you may have to be flexible on payment. Don't be afraid to be accommodating, but don't ever pay out totally until the job is done to your and the building inspector's satisfaction. I don't mind buying materials or making partial payouts, but I always retain enough to have the job finished by someone else in case of disaster.

TECHNIQUES TO BRING DOWN COSTS

The ways that pay, and how to apply them. I use a variety of methods to bring down the bids I get from my subs. I'll show you how to manage yourself and your subs to keep everyone honest and aboveboard. To develop a relationship with a sub is a great thing. It means you kept up your end, and he kept up his. By maintaining these postures, you'll have a reliable source of help at a decent price for many years to come. Never think that you won't build again. Once you've built a home and lived in it a while you'll want to do it again. Even if you swore you wouldn't, you will. There are too many reasons to do it, and not enough reasons not to do it. Let's forget the pride, self-esteem and sense of accomplishment you're going to get, and boil it all back down to why you're reading this book: Money! Almost anyone can make money when they build, but if you apply what you've learned here you'll make a boatload of it. That alone will make you think twice about stopping.

So whether you're building, or building again, use the following techniques to save money.

Keeping Him In Check

• **Get bids by the piece, not by the whole job:** Get bids per block, per square foot or per linear foot wherever possible. I have blocks, concrete, roofing, siding, soffit, fascia, framing and floor coverings bid this way. I keep my prices down by taking the guess work out of the contractor's bidding process. He knows if he installs X amount of material, he makes X amount of money. No surprises for him or for me.

- **Buy the materials for the sub instead of letting him supply them:** When a contractor has to bid materials for a job, he is going to make sure he doesn't run out. He'll always bid extra materials to make sure he doesn't get stuck having to buy more material than he bid, and to insure he has adequate money to finish the job. By supplying the material yourself, you'll pay only for what's used.

- **When you first talk to a potential contractor, get him to give you a per-piece price then and there:** Whenever I'm talking to a new contractor I always get them to give me some figures. I will demand it if he wants to do something I bid by the piece. There's no point in wasting his time, or mine, if he isn't in my price range. But more importantly, there'll never be a time when he wants my business more and is trying his best to impress me than right now. He'll be inclined to give me his best price at our first meeting, and you can bet I'll hold him to it when it comes time to go to work.

- **For first time bidders, always try to negotiate the price:** Remember, you have received a bid, not a contract. I have saved thousands upon thousands of dollars by negotiating down bids. I've used the promise of future work to bring down bids. For example, after receiving a bid, ask the contractor if he'd be willing to come down any if you give him a shot at your next project. Even if you build only part time, this still works. Or, promise him some great exposure of his work for a discount. Use this when you have friends or family who are considering building in the near future. If he does your project well and on budget, you'll show the work off to others and recommend him. If I'm using a new contractor with a new product, I always try to narrow the margin a little. Contractors with new products (or a product that's new to you) will almost always drop their price some to get your business.

Keeping Yourself In Check

- **Don't feel like you have to hire the best:** Hiring the best is like buying the best. Brand names are great for recognition, but use them only when they'll return dollars on your investment. In other words, your "best" subcontractor's name will not be stamped all over your house. When you go to sell it in a couple of years, the important thing is that the work is done and functions properly, not who did it. Paying more for the same work just so you can say such and such a contractor did it won't make you money; it'll cost you money. To keep the bottom line down, stick to your lowest competitive bid.

GLOSSARY

Square Foot
A measure that equals an area of 1 foot x 1 foot.

Lineal Foot
A measurement used for running feet. A wall that is 8 feet high and 20 feet long has 20 lineal feet.

Square
100 square feet or an area 10 feet x 10 feet.

BOTTOM LINE
If you have a prime location, ask for a discount for letting your contractor place signs in your yard. This works especially well when you're at the entrance of a developing subdivision or on a major thoroughfare.

When you are supplying materials for a sub, make sure that you are on site often to keep track of their use.

- **When getting bids, don't come across as picky or hard to please:** Every contractor I know has raised a bid because a homeowner appeared hard to please, and almost every contractor I know has refused to bid a project simply because they didn't want to work for a particularly "cranky" customer. By being understanding, and sometimes even flexible, you'll get lower bids and save money. For example, let's say your sub doesn't want to include debris cleanup and removal in his bid. Everyone else included it in their bids. His bid is $500 less than the others. It'll probably cost your family a couple of hours on a Saturday and $5 in gas to throw the debris into the pickup and haul it to the dump. Dump fees are $45. Do you demand he clean up the property like everyone else was going to do? Do you make sure he understands you want every scrap removed from the house and the yard? No! Save the $450.00 and clean up the mess yourself.

- **Be on site as often as possible:** You can't run a jobsite without ever showing up. Don't get in the habit of not stopping by for days at a time. You don't always have to be there when your subs are working, but at least stop by at the end of each day. It's much more cost-effective, and it will save a lot of headaches if you catch a mistake, or a misunderstood directive, early. Once the job is done, it may be too late. For example, the lumberyard has delivered the wrong style of doors on Monday. The contractor begins installing them on Tuesday morning. Your first visit of the week is on Wednesday when you get off of work. When you arrive, you discover that every one of the doors has been installed. Now you'll have to pay the contractor to remove the wrong ones (which are used and can't be returned), buy the right ones, and pay him again for reinstalling them. What a costly mistake! And don't think you'll get the lumberyard to pay for it since it was their mistake; won't happen. You'll have signed a statement saying you'd have someone check the load upon delivery or that you'd accept it by default. If you had shown up on Monday after work and checked the load, everything could have been fixed before it turned to disaster.

- **Don't make constant changes. The time for making changes is past:** Changes cost time and money, both of which you're trying to

BOTTOM LINE

Offer to do the cleaning and removal of debris for your subs. By spending a little time picking up yourself instead of paying his workers $27.50 an hour to do it, you'll save money.

save. Once a job is done, leave it done. The dollars that get wasted on moving walls, sinks and closets is astronomical. I can tell you from experience; most contractors don't like changes. They've made their schedule and have everything figured in; when you make a change it throws them off track. They more than likely won't be happy and the bill will reflect that unhappiness.

- **Don't be afraid to split jobs:** I've been known to hire two contractors for one job. I don't do it often, but if it works for me and for them, then why not? For example, I've had one contractor hang the drywall, and another one finish it. The finisher I was using was having troubles with his hanging crew, so I hit the grapevine and found a crew to hang it, and he finished it for me. The total price came in a little higher than I was used to, but lower than if I had to go to another contractor altogether. This concept will work well for you if you can do part of a job yourself, but not the whole project. For example, you may want to frame your floor and walls, but don't want to do the roof. You can find someone to do the roof and still save a bundle over paying someone to frame the whole house.

Review the negotiating techniques from chapter two before trying to lower a bid price. Don't be afraid to be creative. If you can show an added value or cost savings to your subs, expect something in return. Not everyone will want to deal with you, so don't be pushy; but you'll never get what you don't ask for. Sometimes saving money is as easy as asking for it.

FREE ADVICE FROM THE PROS

Knowledge is power. Consultants make a great deal of money by providing advice. People in some disciplines of construction are very tight lipped when it comes to the "secrets" of their profession. They will not share that information with their own apprentices, let alone the customer. But, to properly execute a stage of construction, you have to arm yourself with as much knowledge of that stage, and its related stages, as possible. So, how do you get the knowledge without paying for it? You simply go to the people who aren't charging for it. Try these sources for free know-how.

- **Retailers:** When you want basic information about a product and its installation, get help where you buy it. This works well in most places. You may have to weed through a couple of employees to find the knowledgeable one, but keep going until you find him or her. In today's world of large homebuilding supply chains, you may have trouble finding someone with experience, so go to the manager. Most managers have more time and training than the typical floor helper.

BOTTOM LINE
By splitting a job in half and doing the half you can handle, you can save on labor costs. For example, you might hang your drywall but hire a contractor to finish it.

GLOSSARY

Delivery Statement
A statement on a delivery agreement that puts the burden of inspection on you. A typical example states that if you or your representative cannot be on site at the time of delivery, you waive any and all rights for claims on the invoices that are delivered. In essence, you have to be there to inspect the load or you accept it as is.

- **Other homeowner builders:** Don't forget your peers when getting advice. Even if this is their first home, they can give you some insight into the trials and tribulations they've had and some sound advice about how to avoid them. Talk to these people about scheduling, balancing work and after-work projects, things they've done well and things they'll do differently next time. Learn from their mistakes and mimic their triumphs. Take the technical advice they give you, then research it with the experts. You'll get more value from their experiences while building than from their technical expertise. For example, Joe, your co-worker who built his first house last year, can warn you of the mistakes he made with the building inspector and his subs, but I would check his advice on materials and their applications with a pro. Joe may have some useful input on technical matters, but you should always confirm it with the experts.

- **Building inspectors:** Most building inspectors will consult with you over the phone, and some will do on-site consultations. Before calling your local inspector to your site, make sure there isn't a fee for his trouble. If there's a fee, try to find your answers elsewhere, or handle your questions on the phone. Unfortunately, code interpretation can vary from one place to the next, so if you're in doubt about a particular situation, it's wise to consult with your own inspector. If your inspector is unavailable, or uncooperative, you'll have to talk to someone else who knows how he handles your particular situation.

- **Manufacturers:** This resource is my favorite. No one knows more and is more up to date than the manufacturer. They'll generally go above and beyond the call of duty to help you use their products. They're especially helpful when you're learning about a product you haven't used before. When I installed my first radiant heat system (see Figure 5-5) the manufacturer was indispensable. Since radiant heat is not widely used, the salesperson at the retailer was lacking in the expertise I needed to install the system. But the manufacturer stepped in and was instrumental in achieving proper installation. Without their help, I surely would've blundered. The great thing is, the price for all of their valuable help was zero dollars!

- **Online:** In today's world, we can't forget the Internet. This resource can be overwhelming at times, but it can also provide much needed information. I love to use it when researching new products and for obtaining design ideas. The wealth of available information is staggering, but without a staggering price. You can find articles on almost everything. The Internet brings new meaning to the term "let your fingers do the walking."

Some areas have only one building inspector for the whole project, while others have separate inspectors for each discipline.

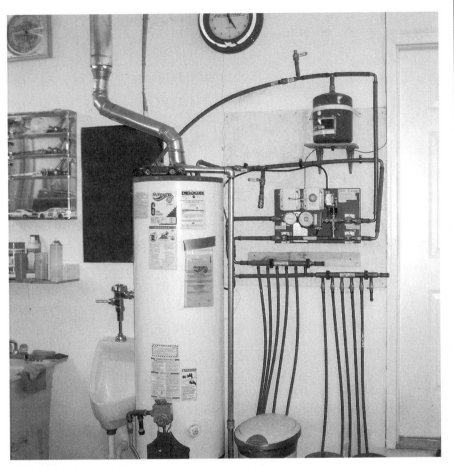

FIGURE 5-5 A radiant heating system used to heat a garage.

Use every available resource when looking for, negotiating and consulting with contractors. You never know where the diamond in the rough is hiding. And don't be intimidated. After all, if you're running your job, you're officially a general contractor yourself.

GLOSSARY

Discipline
A particular trade or field of expertise. My area has four major disciplines that require separate inspectors: plumbing, HVAC, electrical and structural.

GLOSSARY

Radiant Heat
A heating system composed of tubing placed in the floor or wall and a pump that circulates heated fluid through the tubes. The heated fluid heats the surrounding area, which in turn radiates heat into the room. (See Figure 5-5.)

BOTTOM LINE
Don't forget to shop online for materials. Many bargains are there waiting to be discovered.

CHAPTER SIX

REDUCING LABOR COSTS

Half of every dollar you spend on new construction goes to labor. By cutting down on this one expense, you can save tens of thousands of dollars. You can do this in several ways. I'll highlight the ways I've used and point you in the right direction. I'll show you how to get others to work for you for cheap and even for free. Use all your resources and call in favors if necessary, but get some warm bodies wherever you can to help you lower your labor costs. Be sure to check out all of the following resources.

- **Buddies:** Everyone has some pals, mates, chums or whatever you call your friends. When you need a helping hand, don't be afraid to ask for it. Think back to when you helped Joe and Amy move or when you babysat for Jim and Judy so they could go out on their anniversary, and get those favors returned. If you don't have an outstanding list of favors you've done for others, you still have some friends who'd be willing to help if you just ask them. I always try to offer something in return. My buddies will work for beer and/or lunch. What will your friends work for?
- **Bartering:** I have a friend who is a mechanic. He's worked on my vehicles for years. In 2002 I built him a new house. When the occasion arises, we barter for our services. I've also bartered with a well driller and a backhoe operator and almost cut a deal with a veterinarian. The key is to determine what you do or what you have that might be valuable to someone else. Don't be afraid to ask someone if he might be interested. When I asked the vet if he was interested, I was only joking. But his reply was, "I love to barter!"
- **Learners:** I've had people offer to help just so they could learn a lit-

Don't be afraid to ask someone to barter.
Professionals of all kinds may take you up on
your offer.

tle about construction. It never ceases to amaze me how many people are fascinated by construction, and I'm not counting my two-
year-old's fascination with equipment. These adults and young
adults may include someone who's looking to build, remodel or add
on; a teenager who might be considering construction as a career; or
a homeowner who wants to know more about his house. The key to
obtaining these workers is to get them on site. Don't tell them to
come out so you can work their tails off; just get them on site *and
then* put them to work.

- **Bystanders:** When you build, you'll inevitably wind up with people
who come by just to "check up on you." They may be bored, they
may fit into the previous category or they may just be neighborly.
When people hang out at my sites, I put them to work. Hand me this,
hold onto that, grab that end, or anything else they can do. You'll
weed through the gawkers and get to the ones with real interest
quickly by making them work. Just don't let them slow down or halt
production. If you stop to talk to everyone who shows up, you'll
never get any work done.

- **Neighbors**: Many an individual builder has been helped by a friendly neighbor. After all, you'll be living next to each other. Neighbors
can help in so many ways. I've had them clean up, mow the yard,
pitch in on big tasks, provide electricity and water, loan tools, supply
drinks and allow access to bathrooms. Always meet the neighbors
early into the project. Go say "hi" and extend a friendly hand. Talk a
while and get to know them a little. It's never a bad idea to start off
right with your neighbors; you never know when you'll need them.

- **Relatives**: A reluctant brother-in-law who just happens to be a
plumber may be swayed with some bartered babysitting. Once again,
you should tap every resource you have to get the job done for less.
Most of the relative-provided labor I've had is free. But when I'm
paying for it, I make sure to get the "relative rate." After all, Uncle Joe
should do more for you than he would for a complete stranger,
shouldn't he?

- **Church:** Parishioners are a great help. I've given and received help
with block laying, roofing, siding, framing, electric work and more
from fellow church members. Not only do they work for free, but

BOTTOM LINE
When someone visits my job site, I put them to work. By doing this I cut down on the number of people interrupting my work, and I get some valuable help from those in a position to provide it.

BOTTOM LINE
By bartering, I gained $2,500 worth of goods for my personal residence. My out-of-pocket expense was $0.

BOTTOM LINE
A neighbor who will keep watch over your site while you're absent can help prevent vandalism or theft. I love having a retired couple or someone who works second shift next to my sites.

FIGURE 6-1   Blowing debris from your job site should be cleaned up ASAP.

they usually work hard. You may also find some skilled and/or licensed help from this source as well. You may happen to attend church with a plumber, electrician or heating contractor, or someone who works for one of these. Word spreads fast about who's doing what in most churches, especially small ones. Tap this resource network for what you can.

Every house I've ever built has had some free labor put into it. Search the sources I've listed for help. Don't count anyone out until you've asked. Some people may be reluctant to volunteer, but they may come through for you if you ask. Once again I recommend talking to everyone you know to look for possible leads; they can come from anywhere. Don't turn away any help that's offered, even if it comes from an unexpected source. If someone is offering, he is obviously ready and willing to pile in and give assistance.

Consider forming a work swap group with other owner-builders. Not only will you get extra help; you also get to tap into their knowledge and list of valuable resources.

SKILLED HELP AT DISCOUNT RATES

An electrician who works for half price? I'll show you which contractors to consider for discounted rates. Most of the time they don't advertise, so you'll have to use every resource you can from the section in chapter five on how to find contractors. But keep talking and you'll find them. They come in many shapes and sizes, and most don't fit the usual description of being successful, but over the years they've saved me a ton of money. Being a small operation, doing only one house at a time, opens up opportunities that the big guys don't always have. Construction is an industry where costs don't always go down as you get bigger. I've found it's easier to get a deal on one roof, for example, than on ten.

- **The retired guy:** Finding a retired plumber, electrician or heating consultant who still works a little on the side is great. Every once in a while, he'll find you. When working on my father's house, a pair of retired plumbers approached me to see if they could bid the plumbing. My dad is a retired pipe fitter, so he knows his way around

FIGURE 6-2   Small, part-time contractors usually don't advertise. They may not be in the yellow pages or have signs on their trucks.

BOTTOM LINE

I've saved 52% over the going rate by using part-time contractors. Because they have little or no overhead, they usually charge much less than a large contractor.

plumbing and was doing this house himself, but you can bet I wrote down their names and phone numbers for future use. These gentlemen, in their effort to sway me before they knew that my dad was a pipe fitter, practically guaranteed me a better rate than I'd find anywhere else. If I had been interested in using them, I would have asked for a ballpark price then and there, as discussed in chapter five.

• **Part-time contractors:** I love these guys. You can get all the experience without all the overhead. I especially like the guy who works alone or a husband-and-wife team. These contractors can generally work cheaper than full-time guys. The reasons are many: no employees and thus no employee payroll and tax burdens; no overhead since they work out of their homes and their trucks; they make the bulk of their living from other sources and concentrate on the jobs that are small and overlooked by the big guys. For example, I've used part-time electricians and a husband-and-wife plumbing team. Both contractors did excellent work at a fraction of what I would have paid a full-time contractor.

• **Help out a licensed guy:** Consider working with the skilled help on your house and maybe other projects. Let's say you go to church with Nancy, a licensed plumber. She would love to help you on your house, but she's behind schedule and one of her customers is going to go ballistic if she doesn't get her shower by Monday. This means Nancy has to work on Saturday because she can't get any of her guys to work. The solution? Maybe you can help her on Saturday so she has to work only half a day, and then she can help you lay out your job. She'll get you started, and you can begin laying out pipe and cutting holes so that she can come in and work with you on Wednesday to tie it all together. By doing the basic stuff, you can cut down the amount of time your skilled labor has to work. This also cuts down the amount of time you're paying them to work.

• **Build in the slow season:** By hiring when contract jobs are scarce, your costs should come down. I've seen many, many contractors reduce prices and fight hard for bids when they aren't busy. They'll do whatever they can to keep their employees occupied, so this tactic works to everyone's advantage. They get to make payroll, and you get a lower price. You can build in the winter when construction slows down, or if you can be flexible in your scheduling, you can let a contractor use you as filler work when he needs it. Always consider the savings against the loss of time — and therefore the cost of the lost time — before deciding on this course of action. It's served me well over the years, but more by chance than by choice.

Always check your subcontractors' insurance, including worker's compensation insurance, before signing a contract with them.

- **The laid-off worker:** When a person is laid off, times can get tough. When they do, some people will pick up a hammer to make ends meet. I know several guys who were in construction before landing a "good" factory job. When the factory lays them off or has a shutdown, they turn back to their construction skills to earn a living or make some extra dough. Since these fellows have very low overhead and usually concentrate on one particular portion of construction, their prices are generally reasonable. A word of caution when using a part-timer: always check their insurance, including worker's compensation, before signing a contract.
- **The making-a-living guy:** There's always a small contractor who's just getting by. He usually drives an old pickup and lives in an older house that he's done some remodeling on. His business never seems to grow, and he is often out of work. He may even fill in for other contractors as a sub when he has been too long out of work. In my experience he's either good at what he does and just not a brilliant business person or he's just not very good at what he does. He may have some traits and maybe some quirks that most people don't like, or maybe he's hard to deal with. I won't deal with all of these guys, but you can find good ones. One of the good ones I know has been doing this for his whole life and he's good. He's just not personable, and he does absolutely no advertising. He's very reasonable, and once you get him on the job, he works quickly. If you can find a contractor similar to this guy, hire him.

There are a ton of small guys out there. I love them because they save me money and I deal directly with the person who's actually doing the work. When I deal with a larger contractor, I never know who's going to be there driving the nails; it could be a different guy every time. I know that if a problem arises, I can call the owner of the bigger company and get satisfaction, but I prefer the small guy. I can call one guy all the time and know that my words are heard correctly firsthand. I can't count the times I've seen the story get twisted by the time it goes from me to the big company's boss to his foreman at the jobsite. This can and does cause problems, and problems almost always cost somebody money.

BOTTOM LINE
By doing simple things for your skilled help, such as drilling holes, picking up materials, pulling wire or laying out pipe, you'll lower your overall cost dramatically.

GLOSSARY

Pulling Wire
Drilling holes in studs and pulling electrical wire from one outlet box to another without making any of the connections.

GLOSSARY

Worker's Compensation
Insurance required by law that covers employees when they are hurt on the job.

FREE AND LOW-COST EQUIPMENT AND TOOLS

If you bought every piece of equipment and tool you'd need to build a house, it would break the bank. I'm going to tell you where to get tools for free or at low cost. Remember that saving money is an everyday occurrence. The old trap of "it's only a few bucks" can add up quickly. Use every resource you've got to save your money. By avoiding purchase and/or rental costs for tools and equipment, you'll save money and lower the ever-critical final total on your project.

- **Borrow what you need:** This concept has saved me many hundreds of dollars on a single project. Instead of buying that all-important tool for your very limited needs, borrow it. I recently borrowed a right-angle drill and bit set. The tool was critical for getting the job done well and on time. The cost of purchasing the tool and the bits would have been close to $400, but I needed them only for a couple of days. By borrowing what I needed, I saved the rental fee and the cost of buying the bits — not to mention the cost having to buy it all. Other contractors are a great source for tools and equipment. I try not to impose, but most guys are helpful if given the chance. You may need to pay back the favor or offer something in return, but decide where your value lies. Buying a $1,300 aluminum brake for one job is nuts. It's simply not feasible to buy high-cost tools. Your alternatives are to borrow or to rent. I've rented tools and equipment before but prefer the free road when I can find it.

- **Free equipment:** I've used free equipment from many sources. I built a house for a friend who had a friend who worked at a major rental dealer. My friend's friend had access to equipment as part of his employment. We enjoyed the use of a backhoe, scaffolding, man lift, drywall lift and skid steer—all at no cost. That was the exception, not the rule, but there always seems to be a way to gain access to some equipment for free or at a reduced cost. Contractors working in the area can often be counted on for cheap or free help. For example, I've had sand and gravel moved by neighboring contractors for both free and next to nothing. Once I asked for the help when I saw a worker using his skid steer, and once a guy just saw me working hard with a shovel and felt sorry for me so he came over with the skid steer and moved the rock for me. I've received help from neighbors in the same way. Tractors and other equipment are offered and appreciated on a regular basis. Think of whom you know and if they'd be willing to help you out. After all, you don't build a new house every day.

FIGURE 6-3 A man lift or JLG is a mobile piece of equipment with a basket used to lift workers and materials. Equipment courtesy of Sunbelt Rentals.

FIGURE 6-4 A skid steer, commonly called a Bobcat. Equipment courtesy of Sunbelt Rentals.

GENERAL RULES OF THUMB

There are certain taboos to avoid when building and some common-sense things you can do to save money. I see them missed on jobsites on a regular basis. They are money wasters, and some procedures are just plain unsafe. By using the right techniques you will bring down costs and keep your jobsite safer for your workers and for yourself. When you build your new home and you're trying to bring down costs, be sure to follow these rules of thumb.

- **Don't pay until the work is done and inspected:** Take it from a guy who's been burned. Never pay out fully until you and the building inspector have approved the work. I don't mind making partial pay-outs based on progress, but I don't pay out completely until I *know* the job is done to my satisfaction. A contractor is a lot more willing to fix any deficiencies if you're holding his money than if he already has your money. He who holds the money is in control. I'm not advising you to hold out on a guy. I get good bids partly because I pay out in a timely manner, not because I take advantage of situations. I expect good work, but I'm not going to hold a $3,000 check from a sub for a $50 deficiency. I might hold the amount I think it would cost me to fix it or have it fixed, but no more than that.

- **Keep the site clean:** This is hard to do sometimes, especially when you're working only part time. One of the primary causes of a messy site is a quick exit at closing time. The whistle blows and you drop everything and let it lie where it falls as you run out the door. Take a little time to put things away and clean up debris. Not only is a dirty job site dangerous; it's costing you valuable production time. If you're spending half your time maneuvering around the debris while you're working, it's costly. Take a few minutes every day to remove debris and place it somewhere other than in the middle of your work zone. I also place the tools in one spot, the same spot, at all times. I can't count the hours of time wasted looking for tools. If you put them in the same spot every time, you'll know exactly where to find them next time.

- **Don't overpay for trash removal:** Don't order a roll-off for the job site and have it emptied every week unless you have to. An alternative is an old pickup truck. It can be a great tool for hauling materials and debris from and to the site, thus saving you Dumpster and delivery fees. Another alternative might be to find someone who wants your scrap lumber, or another outlet for your trash. For example, I have a subcontractor who keeps a Dumpster at his shop at all times. It gets emptied once a week, and he pays the same amount for

FIGURE 6-5 Tools, bags of materials, extension cords and debris make it almost impossible to set a ladder anywhere in this room without hitting something.

the service whether it's full or not. Half the time there's nothing to empty. When he's working on my site (which is also his site since he's working on my project) he takes all my refuse back to his Dumpster. Another idea is to fill up one of your sub's dump trucks, if he happens to be going to the dump anyway. You'll pay for the extra dump fees, but you'll save gas and time.

- **Don't pay for cleaning:** I save money on bids by cleaning up the debris from my subs. By not making them responsible for cleanup, I can avoid paying their labor rate of $27.50 or more an hour. I also save by being creative with the waste. For example, I once worked out a deal for the removal of two large piles of scrap drywall for approximately $13. You can negotiate this after you have bids that include debris removal and disposal, or you can get bids that don't include the service; either way will work.

- **Follow proper work order:** By keeping your mechanical work in order, you'll save time, money and headaches. Once your house is closed in, you'll begin work on your mechanicals. Always follow this order: heating and cooling, plumbing, electrical so that you can work from the least flexible application to the most. Moving a heating duct is a lot more complicated and costly than moving an electrical wire. It's easy to get talked into changing this order if one of

GLOSSARY

Roll-off

A large Dumpster that is delivered by truck. The bed of the truck is raised, and the Dumpster rolls off the truck and onto the ground.

your subs has a scheduling dilemma, but stick to your guns and keep the tasks in order. When you get past painting and you're ready to begin trimming and installing cabinets and floor coverings, talk to your subs to see what order they want to follow. Some guys are very particular about this and others aren't, so check. Personally, I prefer to set the cabinets and trim over vinyl, ceramic and wood floors and trim over carpeted floors, but your subs may disagree with me on what the proper order should be. Some subs like to install carpet after a house is trimmed out, while others want to install the trim after the carpet is installed. Check to see what yours prefer.

FIGURE 6-6 Don't let your job site look like this. Debris can be a real productivity killer.

FIGURE 6-7   Electrical, plumbing, heating and siding materials on site all at once.

- **Complete one task at a time:** I hate to see a job where the mechanicals are underway before the framing is complete. Or to see drywall being installed before the mechanicals are done. Once you start a task, finish it before moving on to the next one. You have everything handy for doing one job — why would you want to put the tools away and begin another, just to have to drag everything back out later to finish the first one? When jobs overlap, jobsites begin looking like Figures 6-7 and 6-8. This site is not only unproductive; it's dangerous. Problems also occur when too many crews are on site at once. If your workers are constantly bumping into other workers, you have too many workers on site. Rearrange your schedule and alleviate some of the congestion.
- **Free cable installation:** Several companies offer free installation of cable or satellite systems. Call your local providers to see what they offer. Determine your commitment, if any, before signing any deals.

BOTTOM LINE

If you don't own a pickup truck, consider buying an old beater truck for your job. If purchased correctly, you can use the truck on your project, then sell it when you're done for the same amount you invested. By having your own truck to haul materials and debris, you won't have to pay others for this service.

GLOSSARY

Mechanicals
A term used for the systems in your house. They include electrical, plumbing, heating and other systems.

I also recommend being on hand when the installation is done so you can have your outlets put where you want them. Also check to ensure that wires are properly supported. They should have a staple within eight inches of the box and be supported every four feet by a staple or similar anchor.

By following these simple guidelines, you'll save time, money and headaches on your next job. How your job site runs is up to you. Even if you have a GC, you should still take an active interest in how things are going. Don't assume that someone else will cover your back; cover it yourself. Being on site and checking progress daily go a long way toward achieving success. By catching mistakes *before* they become problems, everyone will walk away happier and with better results than if things get out of hand.

FIGURE 6-8   Electrical, plumbing and heating work collide without proper scheduling.

CHAPTER SEVEN

DO IT YOURSELF

There is a first time for everything, and in construction it's no different. Before you offhandedly dismiss the possibilities of what you can do, read this chapter. Saving large amounts is work, and to save large amounts you'll have to do it yourself. Right now, with whatever experience you have, I'll point you in the direction of savings. Not a smoke-and-mirrors tactic such as suggesting that you insulate your house to save $200 — I'm talking about big savings on big items. I'll show you the way to do much more by yourself than you ever thought possible with your current skills.

- **Carpet:** If your rooms are no wider than a typical piece of carpet, commonly 12 or 15 feet, you can install the carpet in your house. The trick is to use carpet that doesn't need stretching or seaming. To do this, buy carpet with the pad already attached and keep all seams at doorways. You'll simply cut the carpet to fit the room, tape it down, and install ready-made transition strips in the doorways (see Figures 7-1 and 7-2). There are no special skills needed. I recommend laying the carpet before you install the trim; this allows you some margin for error on installation. By doing this yourself you can save $4.50 a square yard.
- **Laminate flooring:** Laminate floors are not only beautiful — they're tough. It's a great choice for flooring if you have kids, pets or both.

Always wear ear and eye protection while completing your DIY tasks. Many tools can cause severe damage to hearing and eyesight even in normal use.

Never get talked into doing your own insulating to save money. You can have it done by pros for almost the same price as you'll pay for the materials. Concentrate on the tips I show you that actually save dollars.

And with today's glueless laminate, installation is easier than ever. If you can use a circular saw and a jigsaw, you're in business. The flooring actually floats over your subfloor, so there's no nailing involved. You simply click the pieces together like a jigsaw puzzle. The hardest parts of installation are getting started and cutting around doors and walls. I recommend installing the trim and doors after the laminate. By installing these after the floor, you'll gain a decent margin for error. The last quote I received for installation was $18 a yard. That's almost twice the cost of the product and shows what you stand to save by doing it yourself.

- **Foundation:** Don't stop reading yet. A crawl space can be installed without laying all the block. This is done through the miracle of surface bonding. All you do is dry-stack the blocks and trowel on the cement. (See Figure 7-5.) You'll have to do some research into the process, but it doesn't take the skill of a block layer. I have a buddy who doesn't consider himself skilled at all and isn't in the trades. He wanted a retaining wall installed and needed to do it himself to save money. I suggested he try surface bonding. He was skeptical at first,

pad attached to carpet

FIGURE 7-1 Installing carpet with the pad attached requires no stretching of the carpet, special tools or skills.

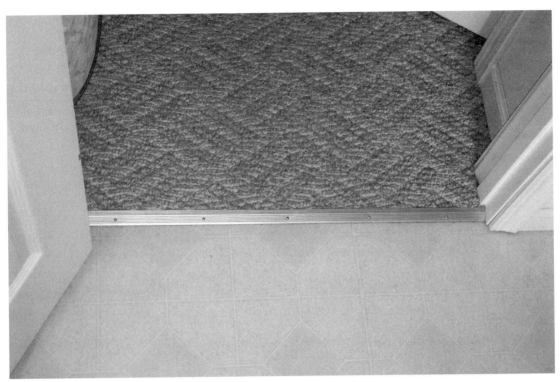

FIGURE 7-2   Ready-made transition strips help make carpet installation easy.

FIGURE 7-3   Laying snap-together laminate flooring is a project that many home-owners are tackling themselves with great success.

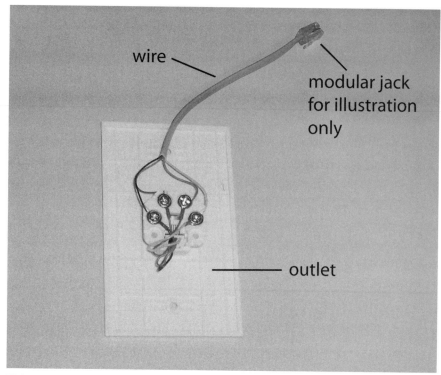

FIGURE 7-4   Wiring for phone service is easy, thanks to color-coded wiring.

BOTTOM LINE

By surface-bonding the foundation block yourself, you can save 50% over a subcontractor's bid. This will shave thousands of dollars from your bottom line.

but I loaned him some tools and started him in the right direction to find information on the process. Now he has a beautiful retaining wall that he constructed himself — and savings in the bank. By constructing your own foundation you can save thousands of dollars.

• **Phone and cable:** Installing the phone service to your house is considered a snap by most people who have done it. Simple phone systems, meaning single-line service like most homes have, are run on a single wire made up of four color-coded strands. The outlets can be purchased very inexpensively at your local home center. For single-line service, during the electrical rough-in simply install a standard electrical box everywhere you want a phone outlet and run the phone wire from the starting point to the first box. Then connect all your outlet boxes together by running another wire from the first box to the second, the second to the third, and so on. When you're trimming out the electrical, connect the wire to the outlet by matching the color-coded wires to the color-coded terminals on the outlet. Plug your phone in once your service is connected, and you've got a dial tone. By doing this yourself you save paying an electrician or phone installer around $45 an hour. Cable installation is similar, but you should be able to get this done for free by calling your local provider or a satellite company. (See chapter six for details.)

- **Paint**: I'm always flabbergasted at what painters charge. I know they're good at what they do and will probably do a neater job than I will — I always end up with a few little imperfections — but when I get their bids and see how much I stand to save, I accept the little imperfections gladly. Ninety percent of my imperfections will wind up behind a picture, shelf or piece of furniture anyway. One secret to a good paint job is decent paint (including the primer) and decent applicators (rollers and brushes). I say "decent" because I definitely don't buy the most expensive ones, but I've learned the hard way not to buy the cheapest ones either. If you go a step or two above bottom dollar, you should be OK. I have friends who swear by airless sprayers, but I've never had much luck with them, and any touch ups done with a brush stick out like a sore thumb. If you're a novice painter like me, stick to the old-fashioned way and roll, roll, roll it on. You can save $0.69 a square foot — that's $441.60 for every 12'×16' room in your house.

BOTTOM LINE

By buying better roller covers and paint brushes, you'll get more use for every dollar spent. The cheapest covers and brushes don't perform well and fall apart in no time at all. You can save cleanup time by wrapping your rollers and brushes in airtight plastic bags between uses rather than cleaning them.

FIGURE 7-5 A bag of surface bonding cement with an illustration showing how blocks are bonded.

GLOSSARY

Nursery
A retail establishment that grows and sells plants, trees and shrubs for landscaping.

Review the suggestions for getting free labor in chapter six to find help for do-it-yourself projects.

GLOSSARY

Construction Loan
The loan given while building is going on, usually paid out in partial sums called draws. This loan is converted to a mortgage after construction is complete.

GLOSSARY

Fill Sand
Rough sand used to fill in and level the area under concrete slabs. Large amounts are sometimes required under the garage floor and porch slab.

BOTTOM LINE

If you have a truck, pick up your own fill sand. By doing so, you'll save the $70 plus per load for a dump truck and a driver to deliver it.

- **Landscaping.** I consider anything other than seeding the yard an extra. I highly recommend that you pay for any extra landscaping out of pocket after you're done with construction and have converted your construction loan to a mortgage. Once you're in the house, you'll have a better feel for where you want shade trees and how you use the yard. You can then design your landscaping around how you live. However, if you're in a subdivision that requires it or you really want it now, do it yourself. Get your shovel out and follow the directions on the plants. Use fertilizer and plant spikes as recommended. The key to this is the same as anything else you plan on doing yourself: if you don't know all about it, learn from those who do. Your nursery will be more than happy to explain everything you ever wanted to know about plants and where you should put them. Use this resource to guide you through the what and where of plants. Then consider buying starter plants instead of grown ones. The savings will be large.

- **Shoveling:** When you have fill sand delivered, consider moving it yourself rather than paying for equipment and an operator to do it. By spreading the fill the old-fashioned way with shovels and rakes, you can save a fair amount of money. I get my wife and my kids out there with me, and we go to town. With several shovels and rakes flying, we make short work of a pile of sand. It turns into a family affair, with my little ones doing more playing than working, but we have some fun with it. It's hard work, but by using our backs instead of renting equipment, we save $65 an hour. If you don't need a large quantity of sand, go pick up the sand yourself. This will save considerable money over having it delivered.

- **Cleaning:** I try to never pay a contractor to clean up and remove debris. Don't pay his men $27.50 an hour just to clean and drive to the dump. Use the free labor resources discussed in chapter six to do this. The only time I pay for this service is when a sub insists, or when I can barter the service out inexpensively. This is one of the times when an old truck comes in handy and can help save you some dough.

- **Trim:** The key to trim is eliminating the miters. Anyone can make a straight cut with a miter box. It's easy whether you're using an electric miter saw, like the one in Figure 7-7, or an old-fashioned miter

Sold On 12/15/2003

Direct Gardening
Division of House of Wesley
1704 Morrissey Drive
Bloomington, IL 61704
USA

Phone: 1-309-662-7943
Fax: 1-309-663-6691

Payment	• #### #### #### • Expiration Date:		
Item Number	**Description**	**Order Quantity**	**Extended Price**
6752	Lily-of-the-Valley Tree	2	$4.96
5103	Walk-On-Me	6	$3.00
6891	Willow, Weeping	2	$1.95
6857	Hydrangea, Tree	2	$2.00
6814	Phlox, Creeping	12	$3.76
5745	Red Bud Tree	2	$4.51
	Free Gifts as Earned		*Free*
	Planting Instructions Handbook	1	*Free*
	Tax		$1.76
	Packing & Processing		$7.95
		Total Due	**$29.89**

OUR SHIPPING POLICY

Orders placed for Holiday Wreaths before Nov. 28 will be shipped the first week of December. Orders placed by December 15 for Wreaths & Gift Certificates will be shipped for delivery before Christmas.

The winter months are a great time to plan your garden and reserve your plants for next spring. We continue to take orders through the winter and will ship according to proper planting time and availability of the stock. We will contine to ship hard goods throughout the winter. Expect nursery stock to arrive next spring.

As a general rule, we begin shipping nursery stock in early March to the southern states and warmest climates first. As weather and climatic conditions permit, we begin shipping to other locations. We wait to ship sensitive houseplants and other greenhouse plants until after April 1, or until weather permits. Seeds usually begin shipping in February.

OUR ONE YEAR GUARANTEE

If you are not satisfied with any item you order from us, simply return the item and the ORIGINAL SHIPPING LABEL, with the correct postage affixed, within 14 days from the time you received it, for a REFUND of the purchase price. In addition, if within one year of receipt of your order any item does not live, it will be replaced FREE just by returning your ORIGINAL SHIPPING LABEL along with your written request.

FIGURE 7-6   When landscaping, consider buying inexpensive starter plants from places like www.directgardening.com to save money.

FIGURE 7-7 The electric miter saw I use for cutting trim.

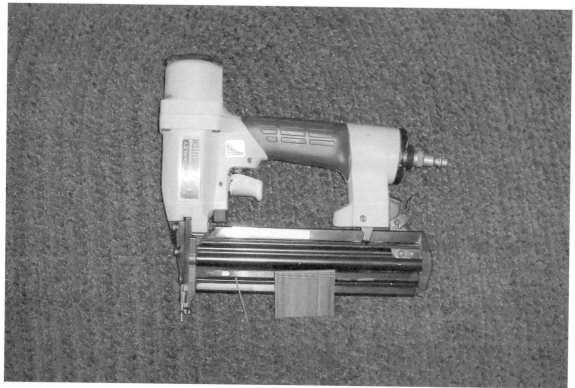

FIGURE 7-8 A brad nailer used to install trim. One brad (nail) and a band of brads lie against the nail slide.

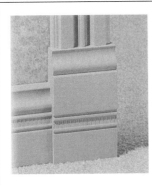

Plinth Blocks
Plinth blocks are used where base moulding meets door casing trim.

Outside Corner Blocks
Corner blocks form a decorative outside corner where base trim meets.

Inside Corner Blocks
Inside corner blocks form a decorative inside corner where base trim meets.

Rosette Blocks
Rosette blocks form a decorative corner where two mouldings meet.

FIGURE 7-9   Inside and outside corner blocks, plinth blocks and rosettes make trim installation easy. Illustration courtesy of House of Fara®. For more information go to www.houseoffara.com.

box and back saw. A simple straight cut is all you need to make when using rosettes, plinths and corner blocks (see Figure 7-9). By using these ingenious blocks all the miter cuts can be eliminated, which makes the installation a snap. A new electric miter saw can be purchased, if you can't borrow one, for less than $100. The cost is well worth it because you'll save thousands by doing your own trim. Another tool that makes this installation even easier is a brad nailer like the one in Figure 7-8. This handy tool keeps you from having to hand-nail your trim and will prevent mashed-in pieces and maybe some mashed-in fingers. When you install your own trim, you'll save $1.58 a linear foot on base and $1.71 a linear foot on casing. When you figure an average house has 1,500 linear feet of trim, this means you'll save $2,467.50 just for hanging the trim, not including the money you saved if you do the staining or painting as well.

- **The usual:** This covers all the things people think of doing to their own houses. It includes (but is not limited to) siding, roofing, framing, window and door installation and drywall. I won't cover these in depth because you know whether you want to do them or not. I would applaud you for tackling any of these projects. With the exception of roofing, which I won't do, all are well worth your effort and will save you money. Research the installation, get the help and answers you need, and go for it.

It takes guts and a willingness to make a mistake or two to do it yourself. But by tackling some of these projects, you'll save big money. I've shown you ways to make these projects manageable, even for those with little or no experience. Be sure to educate yourself before starting, and don't be afraid to get help if you need it. Splitting jobs is often useful in these areas. For example, maybe you want to install your laminate flooring and carpet but plan to hire someone for your ceramic tile, or you want to have your interior doors hung but intend to install the trim yourself. Don't be afraid to get creative; doing it yourself is critical to saving major dollars. The smaller your house, the more you'll have to do to come out ahead. The larger the house, the more you can get away with not doing, but where's the fun in that? You'll want to proudly pipe up when someone tells you how beautiful your laminate floors are and claim, "Yes, we love them. By the way, did I tell you we installed them ourselves?"

THE JOBS I DON'T DO

There are a few jobs I see people being pushed to do on their houses in the name of saving money that I just won't do. I can't justify tackling these dirty, hard jobs that save so little when I could spend my time doing jobs that are less dangerous and save so much more. Any of the tasks previously listed in this chapter are a much better way to spend your time. Read my reasons and decide for yourself.

- **Insulation.** When I discovered years ago that I could have insulation installed for about the same price as I could buy the materials, I quit installing it myself. In fact, I kicked myself for not finding out sooner. The hours I spent itching and fighting pink fiberglass could've been spent doing something that saved more and was much more enjoyable to do. The first time I calculated the difference between doing it myself and having it done, the resulting difference was around $150. I had been spending days sweating and itching for $150! Learn from my mistake, and have this done for you.

- **Roofing:** This is another task I should've stopped doing years before I did. Not only is this job dangerous, it's just back-breaking! This by itself wouldn't stop me from doing something, but roofing doesn't save all that much either. Think about it: I can install shingles for around $15 an hour (my rate is low because I don't do it often and I'm slow at it), or I can install the siding on the house for around $45 an hour. The decision is easy. I can carry a 3-pound

When considering which projects to do yourself, always give preference to those that save the most money.

piece of vinyl siding up a ladder or an 80-pound bundle of shingles, and I get paid three times as much to carry the light piece of vinyl. I have shingles installed for $25 a square. The last roof I had installed cost me $525 for labor. It would've taken me a week to install. In that time I was installing the radiant heating system for the garage, which saved me thousands of dollars.

• **Gutters:** I often see people buying all the parts and pieces to put on their own gutters. While this isn't really difficult, it just doesn't pay well. The parts and pieces will cost almost as much as the $2.05 a foot to have seamless gutters installed. The seamless gutters look and perform better, and I don't have to touch them.

These are the three jobs I won't do anymore because they just don't pay. My time can be used in much more valuable ways. When determining what to do and what not to do, always do the things that would cost you the most otherwise.

BOTTOM LINE

Blown cellulose costs just hundreds of dollars more for installation than fiberglass batts and will return money on your investment with better performance. Consider the upgrade for your new home.

FIGURE 7-10   Blown cellulose insulation is an upgrade from the normal installation of fiberglass batts.

FIGURE 7-11   My homemade siding table cost $30 to build. The commercial model sells for $600.

MY FAVORITE JOBS TO DO

There are two jobs I would highly recommend you do if you think you have the skill or can find someone who does. If you paid for these two tasks at the going rates, they would account for almost 20 percent of your total cost of construction. They come with a built-in checks-and-balances system to ensure you do the job properly. I know many owner-builders who've done one or both of these tasks with great success. Some enlisted the help of a family member with knowledge of the trade, while others simply read a book and then did the job. The bottom line is that they all saved huge amounts by doing it themselves.

- **Plumbing:** Most people would never consider tackling a job like this. After all, it takes a four-year apprenticeship just to get a license in this profession. Besides, they don't know how to sweat a joint, and water leaks are just plain scary. I understand your doubts; I've had them myself. But when I saw how much money I could save by doing this work on my own house, I got over my fears. I had to. When I started out, I couldn't afford to pay someone else to do it for me. So

I got the advice I needed and did the job. I have an owner-builder friend who started with no experience. I built him a house in 1990. He watched what we did and said, "I can do that!" He's since built several houses. In the last house he built for himself he did his own plumbing. When the inspector came out, he asked, "Who did this?" My buddy sheepishly answered, "I did," thinking something might be wrong. The inspector answered that everything was perfect and wanted to know how my friend did it with no experience. My friend answered, "I read a book from the library." To this day the inspector thinks my buddy's pulling his leg, but it's true. You can do more than you think you can if you put your mind to it.

- **Electrical:** I see many owner-builders wiring their own houses. In fact, I've seen a guy with absolutely no experience install the service entrance on his house. The basic principles of electricity are not complicated. The hardest part of this job is keeping up with the codes. In today's world we must install GFCIs, arc fault breakers and more smoke detectors than ever before. But the fact remains that basic electricity is simple to understand; it gets complicated only when you try to string it all together. If you'll break it down to its basic parts and study it one branch circuit at a time, it'll start to make sense. Almost anyone can hang a nail-it box, drill some holes for wire, pull a wire through those holes and install a basic outlet — and that's a good start. Do the research or get some help from someone who knows, then save a ton of money by doing it yourself.

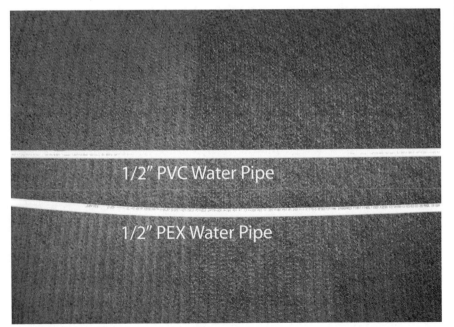

FIGURE 7-12   A short length of PEX pipe and a short length of PVC pipe.

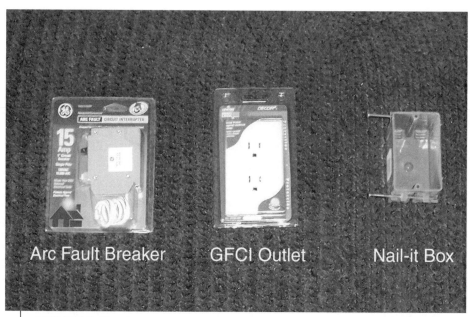

FIGURE 7-13 Common items used to wire a house include: an arc fault breaker, a GFCI outlet and a nail-it box.

Before you dismiss tackling these two projects, let me remind you of the checks and balances that come with them. You'll pay for these checks even if you have someone else do the work. They're called inspections by the code official. If the inspector is doing his job, you'll have a qualified safety inspection before you're done. I'm not saying you should take no thought about safety when you wire or plumb your house just because the inspector will catch it if you do something wrong. I'm just assuring you that another set of eyes will look at your project for you. These two jobs are highly regulated by municipalities. Most municipalities require a professional installer to have some type of license to conduct the work. But in most places you don't have to be licensed to complete the work on your own home. When you're calculating the cost for your job, get bids for the plumbing and electrical. Now take the bids and calculate how much of it is for materials and how much of it is labor. You'll quickly see why I recommend that you do these jobs yourself.

GLOSSARY

Service Entrance
The assembly where the electricity enters the building. This assembly includes the meter base, grounding rod, weatherhead (overhead service only) and conduit. The electrical company's wires connect to your own at this assembly.

CHAPTER EIGHT

HOW TO BUY MATERIALS

Everybody loves bargains, and I'm going to tell you where to find them. I'm also going to describe techniques I use to bring down costs. Materials make up a large portion of your overall costs. Always remember that a dollar saved is a dollar earned. I've said it many times throughout the course of this book, and I'm going to say it again: keep saving money at the forefront of your mind, or your dollars will flee from you. If you fall into the trap of using the easiest or quickest way to buy materials, chances are it won't be the least expensive way. For you husband-and-wife duos, pick out which one of you will be responsible for the information in this chapter and make sure that person reads and rereads it. If you abide by it, you'll be well on your way to your goal.

- **Shop on Sunday:** I place all my major orders on Sunday. At Menards, where I do the majority of my shopping, sale ads run from Sunday to Sunday for two weeks at a time. This means that Sunday is the only day I can take advantage of three sales at once. My wife's job is to check our receipts from the prior two weeks' purchases to see if anything we bought at regular price is now on sale. For whatever she finds, the store issues us an in-store credit for the difference in price. By doing this, we get the sale price on all items that have been in five of their biweekly flyers. I pay sale prices for approximately 70 percent of everything I buy at this store. Check your local store's policies on sales and purchases and schedule your buying accordingly to take full advantage of every sale you can.

- **Buy in advance:** If you see a great deal, buy it now. This works well when you can pay cash or if you can take advantage of a free credit offer. It often seems that super sales don't coordinate with the timing of our construction needs. Two things I always consider when buying in advance are where to store the materials until they are needed, and whether interest charges will exceed the amount saved on the purchase. You don't want your jobsite full of materials you aren't ready to use, so be sure you have a place to put the item where it will be out of the way. Some stores will hold items for you, but make sure they'll hold your purchase until you need it. Next, you have to consider the cost of paying the money out now. If you're borrowing the money, there's always interest to compute, and if you're using a 0-percent credit card, make sure there aren't any fees involved. Unless you pay cash that you've stored in a shoebox under your mattress, there's always a cost, so compute carefully to make sure you're saving more than you are paying.

- **Buy direct:** Some times you can save money buying directly from the factory or a wholesaler. The Internet is a great resource for such purchases. For example, I've bought carpet directly from a mill in Dalton, Georgia. I placed the order, the carpet came in two weeks, and I saved some money compared to buying it locally. I've also purchased tools directly from the manufacturer. Sometimes when you can't find what you want or need locally, you can find it on the Web.

- **Utilize chain stores:** I've heard every reason under the sun for not buying from the big guys: *They sell closeouts*; *the service is terrible*; *no one there knows what they're doing*; and — my personal favorite — *the lumber is junk*. Three of the four reasons are at least partially correct. But let's not lose sight of why you're reading this. Your goal is to save money, so before you dismiss the big "cheap" store, let's address these reasons one at a time. *First, closeouts:* what's wrong with a closeout? I love closeouts. They're brand-new, undamaged goods that come with a full warranty — they're just cheaper! *Bad service:* unfortunately, this does happen, but saving money is work. So, when you get bad service (and you will), walk away from the unhelpful person and find someone who is helpful. If you're having trouble, find the manager. I always get to know the managers of the individual departments anyway. There is always one on duty, so I can get the help I need when I need it. *Unknowledgeable staff:* this also can be a problem occasionally. There's always a time when no one seems to

When you prepurchase materials, many stores will hold the purchase for you until you're ready to use it. This keeps you from having to store it yourself.

If you can't find what you want locally, search the Web. Many specialty stores, wholesale locations, warehouse outlets and factory-direct stores can be found this way.

know what I need, but that's OK. When this happens, I just go to another source for my information. This can be another contractor, a code official or, more often than not, the manufacturer. The manufacturer is more up-to-date and knowledgeable about the product than anyone else, so I end up getting better information when it comes from the source. *Junk lumber*: this is a fallacy. The only difference between the two studs shown in Figure 8-1, besides the price, is that the Menards stud was marked "select" and was a much better-looking piece of lumber. Always check the grade and species of the lumber you're buying. If the same grade is carried at the home center as at the contractor's yard, buy it from the home center and save your money. Grade and species are the only measures I use, other than price, when buying lumber. The bottom line is that I save a ton of money by shopping at the big store, so I'm going to continue to shop there as long as they stock quality material and keep the prices down. I advise you to do the same.

BOTTOM LINE

Salespeople at the big chain stores, such as Menards, Lowe's and Home Depot, often lack experience. By taking the time to find the more knowledgeable ones, you can get the help you need and still save money.

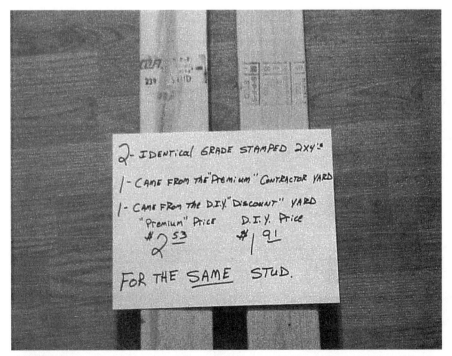

FIGURE 8-1 Two precuts showing a SPF stud-grade stamp. They were purchased from different yards for different prices.

When you need in-depth information about a product and its installation, go to the manufacturer. No one is more knowledgeable or up-to-date on application procedures.

BOTTOM LINE

By holding stores to their price-match guarantee, you can save 10% or more, even off sale prices.

- **Money-back guarantees and rebates:** When there's a rebate on an item you've purchased, send it in. I've read that only people in the Midwest do this, but why is that? They're holding your money — go and get it. If Joe owed you $1, most of us would drive halfway across town during rush hour to collect it. But let a company offer a $20 rebate and all we have to do to collect is mail it off, we won't do it. Take advantage and get every rebate you're entitled to. Most large stores have some type of "low price guarantee," assuring that if you find a lower price, they'll give you an extra 10 percent off. When you're purchasing materials, take them up on their offer. Our area has a Menards and a Lowe's that are only a quarter of a mile apart. It's easy to stop in to see which has the cheaper price and make the other give me the lower price plus the extra 10 percent off.
- **Bargain areas and closeouts:** When you're building a house, you'll be in the lumberyard frequently. On your visits swing through the bargain areas and closeout aisles. You can find some great deals here.

FIGURE 8-2 The $300 window I purchased for $50 on closeout.

For example, I've purchased doors for 50 percent off that only needed the jambs reattached, and I've found $80 faucets for $29, just to name a few of many, many items. There are two keys to getting the great deals here. The first is to check these areas every time you're in the store. The second is not to be afraid to negotiate the price down. The prices on most of these items are arbitrarily set by an employee. If you can give them a good enough reason, they'll lower the price. I often use multiple purchases as the reason to get the prices down. For example, I might pay the asking price for the door if they'll throw in the cabinet for nothing. This works well when you know the person, usually the manager, who has the ultimate say on the price. If you've come to know the managers, this becomes easier. When you're buying a whole house from them, they're eager to keep you happy.

- **Salvage outlets:** You can find some wonderful bargains at the "scratch and dent" store. You may even get lucky and find some matching sets for your bathroom. For example, a friend of mine was building a spec house and wanted to jazz up one of the bathrooms without spending a lot on matching colored fixtures. He went to the salvage store and found a tub, toilet and vanity top in seafoam green. He ended up with a beautiful color-coordinated room for about the same price that he would've paid for standard white fixtures. My friend's story illustrates the only time I recommend that you buy colored fixtures — if you can find them for about the same price as white and you really like the color. Otherwise, the cost is just too astronomical and you're stuck with that color forever. I recommend that you put the color in the room, not in the fixtures. You save money initially on the fixtures, and you can redecorate without having to pay for new fixtures just to change the color of the room.

- **Market fluctuations:** Sheathing and drywall are commodities. Very few people think of them this way, but they are. Recently, prices for OSB (oriented strand board, a popular wall and roof sheathing) tripled in a very short period of time. It only took a few months for $\frac{7}{16}$-inch OSB to go from under $5 a sheet to almost $15 a sheet. I've seen drywall prices do the same thing. The reason is simple: supply and demand. While it's impossible for the layman to predict when the price of individual items will spike, you can still avoid the yearly peak in pricing. To do this, you merely build when most others aren't. I've seen lumber prices rise every spring for many years. Everyone wants to hop out at the first sign of spring and start swinging hammers. I advise you not to do this. Wait until things slow

BOTTOM LINE
Don't accept the marked price. When buying in bargain areas with closeout prices, always try to negotiate a better deal.

BOTTOM LINE
You can save as much as 46% off new prices by shopping the salvage store. Recently, my father purchased two new tub and shower units: one for $138 from the salvage store, the other from the lumberyard for $239. Once these are installed (one upstairs and one downstairs), no one will be able to tell which is which.

GLOSSARY

Spec House
A new house built on speculation. These homes are built by developers and are not presold. The developer is speculating that he can sell the house for a profit.

BOTTOM LINE

When I encounter rising material prices (such as the recent tripling in price of oriented strand board), I seek out and use alternative materials when possible to help keep my project on budget.

down, at least a little. You'll not only miss the usual rise in prices, but you'll stand a better chance of getting cheaper prices from your subs if they're not swamped with work like they are during the spring rush. I like starting a project around August or September. I can get the outside done while it's still moderately warm and finish the inside while things are slow in the business.

- **Contractor's discounts:** If you're playing an active role in the construction of your home, technically you're a contractor. And if you're a contractor, there's no reason you shouldn't get a contractor's perks. Some contractor's yards will give you a discount, while others will give you free deliveries, but they'll all do something for you if you're recognized as a contractor. For example, I have a special rate with one of my suppliers, and I'm a member of the Contractor's Club at Menards. Being a member of this club gets me free deliveries on all orders over $1,000. Being a contractor also opens doors to some contractors-only stores. Be sure to get recognized as a contractor so you reap the benefits.

- **Fixtures.** I don't let my subs supply fixtures. Why do I want to let someone else buy something for me and then charge me extra for it? There isn't a sub out there who will be as careful with my dollars as I am. Most of the time they're making a markup on the fixtures, as well they should for providing and warranting them. I prefer to buy them myself, take the responsibility of dealing with the manufacturer in case of a warranty issue, and save my money. Some subs insist on installing only fixtures that they provide themselves. If I run into a sub like this, I find a new sub. After all, it's my job site. If he's going to work for me, he has to work my way, not his. Find subs who'll work with you, not dictate the way things are going to be.

- **Buy off brands:** In an e-mail I received from the folks at Early To Rise, Michael Masterson said, "Looks to me that you can get good-quality anything for a fraction of the going rate, so long as you are willing to ignore brand names. Of course, you've got to develop good judgment." I agree with him wholeheartedly, especially the last part. When comparing products to the name brand, use your good judgment. Ask yourself: Will it perform like the name brand? Does it look similar? Is the warranty similar? Could a layman distinguish between them if both products were side by side and the labels were removed? Why should I pay more for the name brand? Once you've answered these questions, you'll have a clearer picture of which product to buy. I use the old saying, "If it looks like a duck and quacks like a duck, it must be a duck," and buy the similar item when it's comparable.

It's your job site — don't forget it. Don't let your subs dictate how work will be done. Take control and have them work the way you want them to work.

- **Don't shop for convenience:** I watch builders and homeowners spend two to five times what they should for an item just because they don't want to be inconvenienced. This concept has made millionaires of some convenience-store owners, and it works well for the soda and cigarette market, but don't buy your building materials this way. When you're working and you need a widget but you don't have one, you have two choices: stop working and go get a widget, or work on something else until you can get a widget. I use the second option. Don't immediately hop in the truck, drive to the nearest store, and buy a widget. Chances are the nearest store is not the best place to buy a widget. I suggest you work on something else and wait until your next planned visit to the best place to buy a widget, and then buy the widget. Maybe the widget costs only $1.50 at the nearest store. That's not so bad, right? Wrong! The best place to buy the widget sells it for $0.79. That's 48 percent less! OK, $0.71 isn't going to blow the budget. But spending 48 percent extra on anything, for any amount of money, will quickly shoot holes in your budget, especially if it becomes a habit. My best advice is to plan ahead and have the widget when you need it. But when you find yourself without it, wait until you can buy it at the right place; don't run to the nearest high-price outlet to pick one up.

AN OUNCE OF PREVENTION

Here are a couple of ways to prevent your money from leaving you. I've seen these simple concepts ignored on job site after job site. Ignoring them drives up the cost of construction and can add many dollars to a project's bottom line. When you visit your site, which you should do daily, make sure these principles are being followed. Don't allow your money to trickle away.

- **Return unused material:** It sounds simple to take back what you don't use, but often it just doesn't get done. Something else always has priority. You may be busy siding the house or plan to do it next week. Excuses like these cost you money. The returnable items get damaged or forgotten, and the money you paid for unused material is lost forever. What's worse is that you'll repay every lost dollar more

BOTTOM LINE

When comparing lumber bids from suppliers, always include delivery prices. Ask if they provide free deliveries.

I save all scrap lumber pieces that have the potential for future use. That means anything over 2 feet long. Why cut up new lumber when you can use a scrap for nothing?

BOTTOM LINE

Don't drive all the way across town to pick up one item, even if it is less expensive — you'll spend more money on gas than you're saving. Instead, wait until you can place a sizable order and have it delivered (for free).

BOTTOM LINE

Put returnable material in your vehicle as soon as you know you won't use it. Return it during your next trip to the store. Material that lies around will get damaged, lost or forgotten before you can get your money back for it.

GLOSSARY

Layman

Someone other than a professional; a person with only basic knowledge of the trade.

than two times over by the time you pay off your mortgage! Return all unused material promptly. You'll be at the store often anyway; just get in the habit of taking all your returns with you. I load them in my truck when I know they're no longer needed. Then when I'm at the store, I pull them out and stop at the return desk before I start shopping.

- **Use all material.** Save usable scrap material. This is another simple concept that often is ignored. Be wise with material usage. I've seen hundreds of 12-foot pieces of lumber ruined when all that was needed was a 2-foot piece, and I've seen entire sheets of plywood cut into for one 12-inch strip. Both of these small pieces could have been retrieved from the scrap pile. Don't cut up a 12-foot piece of 2×4 when you only need a 3-foot piece and your scrap pile is full of 4-foot scraps. Material usage is easy to monitor when you're doing your own work, but much harder when you're having it done. Don't abandon pieces large enough to be reused. I've seen large sheets of OSB (oriented strand board) thrown in the Dumpster because a worker was "too busy" to reuse them. Keep usable scraps handy and when you need a small piece, you can grab it off the scrap pile. When I have a job site cleaned up, I tell my cleaning crew (usually my wife and/or kids) which sizes to keep and which to pitch. You'd be surprised at how much "scrap" we end up using and how many times I haven't had to halt production to get something from the store because it was sitting there for free in my scrap pile.

Use the techniques from this chapter when you're buying and using materials. Don't listen to the neighbors or your subs unless they're helping you save money. Think about functionality and price; forget the brand name. Keep in mind that once a product is installed, the brand name almost never shows. The entry-level product or one step up that looks like the name brand and has the same features and warranty is the one to use. Remember, if it looks like a duck and quacks like a duck, it must be a duck.

CHAPTER NINE

BUDGETING

It's do or die time. This is where we separate who'll save huge dollars from who'll save just a few. If you do everything you can to follow the guidelines in this chapter, you should come in on budget. I've developed them to keep my budget in line while I'm building. I'll list them so you can follow in my footsteps. Don't let the naysayer tell you it can't be done, because I do it all the time. If you follow my advice from the preceding chapters, you'll be able to find prices similar to what I list, depending on your area. You may not be able to match all of them, but you'll be able to beat some even if you have to pay more for others. The point is that prices fluctuate. You should come out with the same averages by spending less on some items and more on others. That's how my costs vary so little from project to project. By being aware and taking advantage of bargains when you can, you'll average out over the entire project. I don't flip out when I get high bids on one item. I'll certainly bust my butt to try to save money on this particular item, but if the attempt fails, I'll look to save on other items to even out the costs. These are only guidelines; how much you spend is in direct correlation with how much you save. You're the only one who should determine what your money is worth and what you should spend it on. Splurge where you want and scrimp where you want. Once again, it's all up to you.

- **Plans:** I don't pay for plans or designs; I do it myself. I've never been satisfied with any ready-made plans, and I don't budget for architects, so I have to do it myself. I draw my plans on 3D Home Architect, a CAD program produced by Broderbund, LLC. I always discuss my designs with my HVAC man, Ed Cary of Fleetmaster Mechanical, Inc., before finalizing the plan to ensure that he can

Always have your plans checked by your heating, electrical, plumbing and framing contractors to ensure affordable design. The time to find out about potential problems is before you begin work.

configure my heating and cooling system within the plan as drawn. I do all other checks myself. You should consult with all your subs or experts for suggestions and to ensure affordability. Be sure to check your structure, HVAC, plumbing and code design parameters before beginning construction.

- **Temporary power:** You'll need a temporary power source. I have a convertible temporary power pole that alternates between overhead and underground service. I built it myself from a plan I was given by my local power company. You can do the same, or you can have an electrician build one (I don't recommend this due to the added labor cost), or you can borrow one. The last option is your best, not just because it's free but also because you don't have to store it when you're finished using it. The cost to hook up to power is determined by your local power company.

- **Excavation:** Once you know what type of foundation you're using, you need a hole. I have my crawl spaces dug for $450 and I pay $1,000 for basement holes. I have the area for the house excavated and the sod scraped from the garage and porch areas. My backfill prices have varied. When I can hire a part-time guy, I've had it done for $150, but when I can't I've paid up to $450.

- **Footings:** I always do my own footings. I've tried other ways, but none seem to work. I form my house footings with ⅞₆-inch OSB and *hand-cut* stakes. I dig my garage and porch footings by hand with a spade. By doing this I save money on excavation, fill sand, blocks and block laying, but pay more for concrete for the footings. It's a wash, but I get a more solid base for the concrete slabs in the garage and on the porch by not using so much fill. If I need a lot of fill, I have it delivered; when I can, I send my wife out with the old truck and have her pick it up. Using bolt cutters or a sawzall, I cut rebar stakes to set the depth of the hand-dug footings. I have the concrete delivered at a cost of $65-$70 a cubic yard.

- **Foundation walls:** I've built primarily over block crawl spaces. They're economical because I do them myself. If you can get your money back, basements are worth the trouble. If you haven't done a foundation before, don't dismiss the possibility of doing it yourself

BOTTOM LINE

Don't buy ready-cut stakes in bundles. Cut your own from scrap lumber. If you don't have any scrap available, visit any job site and ask to raid the scrap pile. If you can't do this, buy furring strips and cut your stakes out of them.

FIGURE 9-1 My temporary power pole is convertible for use with overhead or underground power.

Backfill

The excavator creates a hole larger than the foundation (the extra is called the overdig) so the workers have room to erect the foundation. Once the work is done, backfill is placed in this hole, to fill it up and level the yard around the house.

without checking out chapter seven's section about how to do it. When I do pay for block, I pay between $1 and $1.50 per block for labor. I split my material order between two or more suppliers to get the block, mortar, sand, foundation vents, anchor straps or bolts, foundation windows, window wells and window-well covers at the best prices. I don't damp-proof or tile my crawls, but I do on basements. I use 4-inch sock tile for drainage and black-fibered foundation coating to damp-proof my basements.

- **Floor beam:** When beaming over a crawl, I keep supports close and spans short for beams and joists. I use a dimensional lumber beam over block piers in this application. When beaming over a basement, spans lengthen and I'll use microlams where I can and a steel beam if necessary. If you're not versed in how to size your beams and they aren't covered in the code, have a pro do this for you. Undersizing could cause dangerous trouble over time.

- **Floor:** When flooring over a crawl space, I use dimensional lumber at 16 inches OC for framing. I don't install bridging. When flooring over a basement, I'll use I-joists or floor trusses at 19.2 inches on center if the budget allows. I use ¾-inch floor sheathing in OSB or plywood nailed and glued to the subfloor. I don't buy the most expensive adhesive I can buy; I typically use PL-400 because that's what my supplier carries and the price is reasonable. The only upgrade I would consider in this area might be the sheathing. I've considered using high-performance sheathing, such as Advantech, to

FIGURE 9-2 Several sizes of I-joists. Courtesy of Louisiana-Pacific Corp.

Sizing structural beams and headers should be left to a professional. Undersizing can cause structurally weak points and possible sagging or failure, and oversizing spends unnecessary dollars.

keep the joints from swelling when the floor gets rained on.

- **Stairs:** I use 2×12 dimensional lumber for stair stringers (sometimes called horses). I use bull-nosed particleboard treads and 1" × 8", no.3-grade pine for the risers. This assumes that they'll be carpeted. For other finishes, you'll have to be creative and get your raw materials as cheaply as possible.
- **Walls:** I use 2×4 studs at 16 inches on center for my wall framing. I'll use plywood box headers in load-bearing exterior walls (see Figure 3-1) when I'm doing the framing myself and double 2×12 headers when I'm paying someone to frame for me. For non-load-bearing

GLOSSARY

Bridging
Metal or wood strips placed from the top of one floor joist to the bottom of another to prevent the joist from tipping and to share loading. They form an X between the joists when viewed from the side.

FIGURE 9-3   The stringer, tread and riser on a typical set of stairs. Notice the 2x4 spacer that holds the stringer away from the wall for easy drywall installation.

FIGURE 9-4 This is a 2x4 stud wall at 16" on center and a trussed roof at 24" on center. Note the OSB corner and insulated sheathing on the wall.

GLOSSARY

Insulated Sheathing

Any type of sheeting that can be used to replace OSB on side walls of houses. Types commonly used are impregnated asphalt fiberboard sheathing, foil-faced sheathing and extruded polystyrene.

GLOSSARY

Housewrap

Commonly referred to as Tyvek®, it is a paper-like material used to wrap the exterior walls of a house before siding is applied. Originally promoted as an air barrier, it is now recognized primarily as a moisture protection.

walls, interior and exterior, I use double 2×4s on edge. I use ¹/₂-inch OSB on the corners, and I prefer to sheet the whole wall with OSB. However, with recent price increases, I've reverted to an insulated sheathing for the wall except the structural OSB corners. I use house wrap, the least expensive I can buy, not for air infiltration but to provide some protection from moisture that comes through the siding. Although I've never used 15-lb. felt paper as a house wrap, I may on my next project. According to an article in the August 2000 issue of the *Journal of Light Construction,* there is no significant difference in moisture protection between most wraps and felt, and the felt is much cheaper.

• **Roof:** I use manufactured trusses at 24 inches on center when I'm using a roof pitch under 6/12. Over the trusses I use ⁷/₁₆-inch OSB with an H-clip for sheathing. When I exceed a 6/12, I stick-frame the roof using dimensional lumber 16 inches on center for rafters. This is so I can use the open area underneath for living space or at least for storage. I use ⁷/₁₆-inch OSB sheathing over the rafters; the clip is now optional. When I pay labor for framing, I get it done for $3-$4 a square foot for living areas and $1.75-$2.25 for garages and covered porches.

- **Roofing:** I use 15-lb. felt and a minimum of a 25-year shingle. I don't have a real preference between fiberglass and asphalt shingles as long as they're over 225-lb. a square. I use both three-tab and architectural shake shingles. For curb appeal I always use the fake shakes on any pitches over 6/12. I don't have a favorite brand of shingle; I buy the least expensive one that meets my minimum requirements. I prefer ridge vents to mushroom vents. I usually buy the least expensive shingle-over ridge vent I can. I pay $25 a square foot for labor on pitches 6/12 and under, and $35 on steeper pitches to have shingles installed.
- **Windows:** I use Ellison or Simonton windows. I order vinyl, white, double-hung windows with low-E glass, argon gas and built-in J-channel. Depending on your area, you may or may not be able to find these brands. If you can't, do some research on what's available.

3-Tab Shingle Board   Fake Shake Shingle Board

FIGURE 9-5 A three-tab shingle and an architectural shingle.

I pay $180 for a 3'× 4' window. When I want larger units, I have singles mulled together to form doubles or triples. Window installation is included with the price for framing.

- **Exterior Doors:** I use prehung, steel-insulated entry doors. I spend anywhere from $180 to $500 on the front door, depending on the overall value of the house when completed. A 1,200-square-foot ranch does not require the same door as a 3,500-square-foot two-story. All other entry doors are purchased as inexpensively as possible. I buy a good-quality entry door that has an adjustable threshold and magnetic weather stripping. For a patio door I prefer insulated steel French doors. I don't spend over $600 for a patio door. If I can't find a decent French door, Anderson makes a nice vinyl slider for around $600, so I'll use that. I splurge a little on the front door handle; all others I buy inexpensively ($15-$20 for a lock and deadbolt combo). I recommend that you have all the locks keyed alike so one key fits every lock. Entry-door and patio-door installation is included in the price of framing.
- **Siding:** I use vinyl siding. I buy it from either a large chain store or my contractor's outlet. I don't buy the extra-thick type; I prefer the

FIGURE 9-6   Shingle-over ridge vent.

Always have all your exterior locks keyed alike. This will allow one key to fit every lock, so you have to carry only one house key for all your doors.

Soffit Panels

Frieze Runner

Siding Panels

FIGURE 9-7 The siding is run behind the frieze moulding on the eaves. This eliminates the need for "J" channel and finish trim.

basic siding. Thick sidings are harder to work with, are more brittle in the cold, and leave too large a profile on lap joints. Almost all vinyl comes with at least a 50-year warranty, and that's all you'll ever need. The only criterion I have for vinyl, other than price, is color. I buy the least expensive type I can in the color I want. I run my siding behind the frieze runner on the eaves instead of cutting the siding and installing a piece of finish trim and J-channel. When I pay to have siding installed, I pay $70 a square.

• **Soffit and fascia:** I use vented aluminum soffit and fascia cover in white. I buy the least expensive I can find. I tack the frieze runner against the house with siding nails, cut the soffit to length, tack it to the bottom of the subfascia with aluminum nails, and wrap with a pre-bent fascia cover. I always use white trim on my houses because colors get expensive. You can add color by painting your steel entry doors and adding inexpensive stock shutters from the superstore. When I pay for soffit and fascia installation, I pay between $1.50 and

BOTTOM LINE
By running the siding behind the frieze runner on the eaves (see Figure 9-7), not only is the installation easier, but you save money by not having to buy J-channel and finish trim.

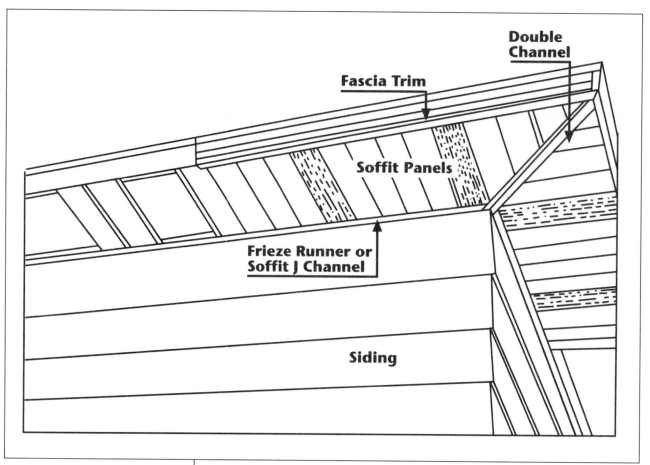

FIGURE 9-8   Diagram showing the components of a soffit and fascia system. Illustration courtesy of Gibraltar Building Products, Appleton Supply Division.

$2.25 a linear foot.

- **Gutters:** I have seamless gutters installed. I always use white to match my soffit, fascia and windows. I pay $2.05 a linear foot for materials and installation combined.

- **Heating and cooling:** I use an HVAC man who installs Goodman furnaces and air conditioners. I have him install 92-percent efficient furnaces and standard air conditioners. The only reason I install high-efficiency furnaces is that his price is better than I get elsewhere for 80-percent furnaces. I also get a five-year parts and labor warranty, so I know that if I have any trouble, I can just pick up the phone and he will fix it, no charge. I can't give you a normal price for heating and cooling systems. I always bid materials and labor because I don't want to mess with it myself. Get several bids and compare what's offered.

- **Plumbing rough-in:** I use the least expensive plumber I can find who's licensed. I have copper water lines and PVC waste lines

PVC flue

FIGURE 9-9 A high-efficiency furnace looks like a regular unit. Look for the PVC flue used on high-efficiency units to tell the difference.

installed. I let the plumber provide the rough-in material only; I provide all fixtures. When I'm doing the plumbing (only on my own houses) I install PVC or PEX water lines and PVC waste lines. I prefer these lines to copper because they're much more user-friendly and I think PEX is a better product than copper. I use the least expensive water heater I can find that has a decent warranty. (There are only a few manufacturers of water heaters in the country, so the multitudes of brands available are coming from the same few

GLOSSARY

Romex®

A multiple-wired electrical conductor in which each strand is individually sheathed and the multiple strands are collectively sheathed. This type of wire is the standard for most residential construction and is used commonly in 12-2 and 14-2 configurations.

GLOSSARY

Type-X Drywall

Commonly called firecode, this type of drywall has tiny fibers in it that give it strength and determine its fire rating. In residential construction, $5/8$"-thick type-X drywall is typically used on ceilings.

sources.) When comparing water heaters, be sure to calculate the venting material and installation of the vent and flue. It costs much more to vent a standard water heater than it does a high-efficiency or a power-vented heater. I always install white plumbing fixtures because of cost. I recommend putting color in your vanity top, walls and floors. This way you can remodel without having to change fixtures. I install one-piece tub/shower units that I buy at the superstore for around $219. I install the least expensive toilet I can for around $45. I don't install shower doors; I leave the shower curtain and rod up to the owner. I can't give you a standard price per unit because I have my plumbing bid by the project. This is one area where you should get as many bids as you possibly can and do your best to find a part-time contractor. Find a retired guy or an on-the-side husband-and-wife team to keep your costs down.

- **Electrical rough-in:** I haven't paid anyone to install electric systems for so long that when I see a bid, I know immediately why I do it myself. I use plastic nail-it boxes, Romex wire, the least expensive GFCIs (ground fault circuit interruptors) and arc faults I can find, the least expensive 200-amp service panel (breaker box) and the least expensive service-entrance wire I can get. When calculating costs for service panels, don't forget to figure in the cost of the breakers. If the panel itself is $20 less but the breakers (including arc faults) are $2 more per breaker and you need 35 breakers, you'll lose money on the whole project. I install inexpensive bathroom vent fans. When I've asked for bids on electrical installation, I've had whole projects bid with the sub supplying rough-in material only; I supply all fixtures. Check all your resources for part-time and retired contractors when getting bids, and get as many as you can.
- **Insulation:** I have cellulose blown in the walls and ceiling of the house. I prefer it, even though it is higher in price (installed) than fiberglass, because it is a better-performing product. I pay 25 cents a square foot for cellulose and installation combined.
- **Drywall**. I install $1/2$-inch drywall on 16-inch-O.C. walls and ceilings and $5/8$-inch type-X drywall on ceilings that are 24-inches O.C. I don't hang or finish drywall unless it's absolutely necessary — if I can't get anyone to do the job in my time frame or the prices I get are ridiculously high and I refuse to pay them. However, I usually find a bargain drywaller. I supply the drywall and let him supply the finish material. The going rate is 65 cents a square foot for labor and finish materials, but I've beaten that by 52-percent by shopping around.
- **Paint:** I use USG primer, made for bare drywall, and a decent grade

of paint. I don't buy the cheapest paint I can because it doesn't cover well. I prefer Valspar and Dutch Boy when they're available. I do my best to keep the cost at $10–$15 a gallon. I buy a couple of steps up from the cheapest rollers and brushes without buying the best. The inexpensive ones won't last and they do a poor job. When I've gotten bids on paint, I've had the painter bid materials and labor. I recommend that all builders paint their own houses unless they're physically unable to do so.

- **Interior doors and trim:** I install prehung six-panel colonial doors and primed, finger-jointed trim. I've used split jamb and regular jamb doors. I've purchased these doors from the superstore for around $35 and at the contractor's yard for around $70. Both doors performed the same. The key to keeping a door working well is sealing (painting) it on all six sides. Once installed, the trim joints should be caulked with a good-quality paintable caulk and painted. I install inexpensive door hardware from a number of manufacturers. I usually buy the least expensive lock sets the superstore has that don't look cheap. I know that's a bad way to describe them, but in my opinion as long as they don't look cheap, they're fine. I usually spend $5–$7 for passage sets and $7–$9 on privacy locks. I've paid to have doors and trim installed only once, and that was because I found a retired contractor with spare time and he gave me a great price. If you're bidding this out, get many bids and look hard for the part-timer. To do it yourself, consider using rosettes and plinths (see Figure 7-9).

- **Cabinets.** I install Kitchen Kompact cabinets in Richwood Lite Cathedral. This is a box cabinet with raised-panel oak doors and solid rails. I design the kitchen to accept these cabinets in the sizes available. I get a great-looking kitchen for half the cost of custom cabinets. I've installed both custom kitchens and box-cabinet kitchens, the kitchen I received the most praise for was a box-cabinet kitchen. (See the comparison between the two in Figures 2-23 and 2-24.) These cabinets run approximately $75 a linear foot for uppers and lowers combined. I install laminated counter top in a no-drip edge style. I pick from the least expensive standard colors available. When I've bought custom cabinets, installation is included with the purchase price. I've never paid someone to install box cabinets for me. If I were to try to find someone to do this, I would search out a trim carpenter and get as many bids as possible. Of course, I would use my grapevine to find the best price possible.

- **Bath Cabinets:** I install vanities that I buy right off the floor at a superstore. I find the least expensive one I can that has some draw-

BOTTOM LINE

When bids on an item are too high and I've done everything I can to bring them down, but my budget can't stretch to accommodate the increase, I'm forced to pick up my tools and do the job myself.

GLOSSARY

Split jamb

A door jamb, on a prehung door, that is split down the middle. The jamb can be separated and installed as half from one side of the opening and half from the other. The two halves are milled to fit one inside the other.

FIGURE 9-10   A six-panel colonist door trimmed with finger-jointed pine trim.

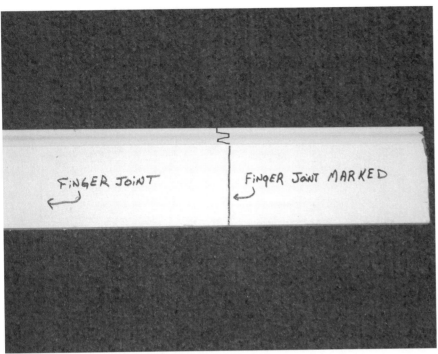

FIGURE 9-11   A section of primed finger-jointed trim showing where the joint is spliced together.

ers and solid-panel doors. I try to match up a medicine cabinet and light bar without buying matched sets. I spend around $165 for a 30-inch vanity, $100-$150 on a medicine cabinet, and $20-$30 on light bars. I buy one-piece faux marble tops for $50-$75. Your electrician should install the light bar, and your plumber should install the vanity and top; that leaves you (or someone you pay) to install the medicine cabinet. An alternative to the medicine cabinet is a plate-glass mirror. I trim out the bathroom with inexpensive towel bars and toilet-paper holders. I don't install soap dishes because I don't personally like them.

• **Floor coverings:** I install laminate flooring, carpet, ceramic tile and vinyl flooring. I buy my laminate for $1-$1.25 a square foot and a medium grade of underpad. I don't buy the ready-made transition strips that come with laminate flooring; I make my own or buy less-expensive metal transitions. I buy carpet remnants when possible and $7/16$-inch rebond carpet pad unless I've bought carpet with the pad already attached. I keep the cost of my carpet to $15 a yard including carpet, pad and installation. I install carpet directly over the subfloor. I buy ceramic tile for $1 a tile (12" × 12") or less and install it over the least expensive underlayment I can find that's recommended for tile. I buy vinyl flooring and plywood underlayment

GLOSSARY

Underlayment

The smooth subflooring installed under floor coverings such as vinyl and ceramic floors. Examples are BCX plywood (a plywood with one smooth face) and cement board (a sheet underlayment used under ceramic tile).

FIGURE 9-12   Quiet pad for laminate flooring.

and keep the cost at $21 a yard or less for the vinyl and installation of both vinyl and underlayment. I provide the underlayment material rather than having the flooring supplier provide it.

- **Electrical fixtures:** I put my money where it will be seen and nowhere else. I buy outlets in contractor packs for 34 cents each and light switches for 45 cents each. Covers are typically 19 cents each. I usually spend about half my light-fixture allowance on the dining room, kitchen and foyer lights. The allowance is typically $350-$400. I buy cheap two-packs of lights for the halls and the bedrooms for around $10. I buy an inexpensive ceiling-fan and light combo for the living room for $30-$100. I buy inexpensive exterior lights for the front of the house for $15-$25 and I buy $3 exterior lights for the back of the house. I buy a $5 fluorescent fixture for over the kitchen sink. I buy a range hood with a light for $30. Installation of electrical fixtures is included in the total electrical price.

- **Plumbing fixtures:** I spend $150 on my kitchen sink and faucet. I buy chrome single-handle faucets with pop-ups for the lavatories for $35-$50. I buy single-handled anti-scald tub/shower faucets in chrome for $75. I buy the cheapest laundry box I can get (see Figure 9-14). I buy laundry tub sinks for $30 and spend $30 on the faucet for them. Installation of plumbing fixtures is included in the total plumbing price.

- **Fireplaces:** I install vent-free gas logs and fireboxes with pre-assembled surrounds and mantles. I keep the cost for the entire package at $1,100 or less and I install them myself. I buy these from the contractor's yard or directly from the fireplace store, whichever is cheaper.
- **Closet trim:** I install wire shelves myself, using the least expensive I can buy.
- **Interior stair railings:** When I just need a handrail, I buy unfinished fir railing from the superstore and the least expensive brackets I can find. When I need a finished guardrail, I buy the least expensive spindles I can find and install a decent oak handrail. If you don't install these yourself, it'll cost you a lot to hire a decent finish carpenter. Before rejecting any possibility of doing it yourself, know this: I have a lawyer friend with no carpentry experience who installed a finished oak guardrail, complete with turned spindles, in his house. It was one of the best jobs I've ever seen. He researched how to do it, borrowed some tools, and jumped right in. This is another area in which I spend money only when it will show. If your staircase descends directly into the front-door foyer, dress it up. But if you're installing a railing in a staircase that will be used only by the kids, be practical and save your dollars.

FIGURE 9-13 A $5 light fixture.

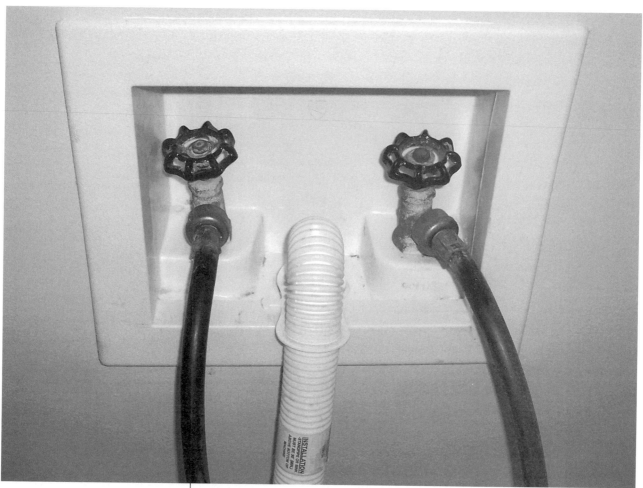

FIGURE 9-14 A laundry box.

- **Overhead garage doors:** I install white raised-panel steel doors, insulated and noninsulated. I buy them from the superstore. I don't use the specialty garage-door places because of cost. I buy extension-spring and torsion-spring doors. Many people prefer torsion-spring hardware for their doors, but I've had better luck with tension-spring doors. I buy the least expensive opener I can find for the size of door I'm installing. I pay $75-$100 for door installation and $50 for opener installation.

Try to follow these guidelines whenever possible, improving on them when you can. Remember, the bottom line is more like the bottom hilly road: you're going to have ups and downs. The idea is to be cognizant of your dollars at all times. You will save on some items and lose on others, the bottom line should balance out on average. The practices in this book will save you money no matter where you live, but exact prices will vary according to your location. The higher the cost of construction in your

FIGURE 9-15   A fireplace comprising a gas log, firebox, surround and mantle.

area, the more money you stand to save. The goal is to come it at 55 percent of the going rate. By keeping close watch on your money and following my advice, you can do it.

BOTTOM LINE

To save on an electrical installation, consider having an electrician do the rough-in installation, then install the outlets, switches, light fixtures and covers yourself. The wires will be staged during rough-in, making the trim out (installing of the fixtures) simple.

CHAPTER TEN

THE SIX-YEAR MORTGAGE-FREE PLAN

'm going to show you how, in six years, you can be mortgage-free and have $181,818 in equity in a new house that you've built. The process takes work and some sacrifice on your part, but nothing worth having comes free. If you want the prize at the end of a race, you must train and run the race with all your concentrated effort. Reaching this goal is much the same. You've taken the first step by reading this book. Now you must put what you've learned and will continue to learn into action. After all, a dream without action is just that: a dream. However, a goal, when combined with action and hard work, can become reality.

NECESSARY ASSUMPTIONS

In order to describe a process that can work for as many locations as possible, I will have to make certain assumptions. Here's what I've assumed to put together this model.

- You can find an acceptable building lot or site for $30,000.
- The going rate and value of a finished new home are the same as the national average for new construction, namely, $95 a square foot.
- You'll follow all my advice and build this house for 55 percent of the national average of the cost for a new home.
- You complete construction on each new home within six months.
- You can get a permanent mortgage at 5.5 percent interest.
- You can sell each home for a 7-percent Realtor commission and pay less than $2,000 in closing costs.
- The value of the real estate in the area where you build is increasing at the rate of 5 percent per year.
- You're starting with no money.

Don't worry if your scenario isn't exactly like my model; you can still follow my advice and save money when you build. You'll simply have to adapt the model to fit your situation.

THE PLAN

Follow the steps below to achieve your goal.

- Secure financing for construction.
- Purchase a building lot for $30,000 or less.
- Construct a new home for a cost of $100,000. (Your new home will be valued at $181,818 because you built it using my techniques.)
- Secure a final mortgage at 5.5 percent and amortize it over 20 years.
- Live in and maintain your home for two years.
- Sell your home for $200,453 through your agent of choice. (Your home's value will have increased over two years.) Your profit improves if you can sell the house yourself, which I've done before.
- Pay off your mortgage of $122,446. (The balance decreased due to your payments made over two years.)
- Take your equity of $63,975 and put it toward a new lot and new home construction.
- Secure construction financing for the new house in the amount of $66,025 ($130,000 total cost minus $63,975 equity made from sale equals $66,025 needed to finish construction).
- Construct a new home for a total cost (including equity invested and money borrowed) of $130,000.
- Secure a final mortgage at 5.5 percent and amortize it over eight years. (Your house payment will be the same as before.)
- Live in and maintain your new home for two years.
- Sell this home for $200,453 through your agent of choice, or by yourself if you can.
- After closing you will have $129,490 cash to build your next home mortgage-free.

In less than six years you've become mortgage-free and you own a new home worth $181,818. Enjoy your new-found "free" cash! Just think of what you could do with the mortgage money every month if you don't have to send it to your banker. Would you travel? Or would you invest? Maybe save for the kids' college? Imagine the possibilities, then put my plan into action so you can get there. What are you waiting for?

CHAPTER ELEVEN

THE SUCCESSFUL MIND-SET APPLIED TO CONSTRUCTION

When it comes to attitude, positive is the only kind that leads to success. It doesn't matter whether you're talking about building a new house or tackling some other project, you must have the right mental attitude or you'll surely fail. The rules don't change because you are doing the plumbing in your house instead of getting that report to your supervisor by Friday at 3:00. You still have to determine what's needed and figure out how to deliver it. The right attitude will help you do this better and enjoy the journey from start to completion. The reverse is also true. If you approach your task with a bad attitude, your performance will suffer and you'll dread the journey. I have completed projects, and seen them completed, with both attitudes. I can tell you from experience that the right attitude will make an extraordinary difference in how your project turns out.

This chapter is a little different from the rest of the book. Everything else we've talked about has been applicable only to construction, while this chapter can be related to other aspects of life. I'm going to explain the effects of attitude as they apply to construction. The examples will be construction examples. You may choose to relate them to other portions of your life, but that is up to you. I'm not Dr. Phil; I don't claim to be. But I do know how much your mental attitude will control the outcome of your project, good or bad. I know what will make a construction project work, and what will make a mess of it. Some attitudes can screw things up in a hurry, while some will tear a project apart little by little. I'm going to tell you the good attitudes you need, and offer some advice on how to avoid the bad attitudes you don't.

While reading this chapter you may notice that some of the potential pitfalls sound like things you think you'd probably do, or like ways you think that you'd react to a given situation. Don't let this scare you. Remember that you can control yourself and your reactions to any situation. You don't have to react automatically. By realizing that problems will arise and by being prepared for them, you can save a world of troubles. Every project has — and will continue to have — its problems. Some may be minor; others may be major. But it's not the problem that usually wreaks havoc on the project: it's the reaction to the problem that counts. Read on to learn effective ways to react.

MENTAL PREPARATION

"Chance favors the prepared mind."
— Louis Pasteur

I've talked about preparation in other chapters, but in this one I'm going to discuss mental preparation. There are as many ways to prepare for what's to come as there are readers of this book. I'm going to list the ones that work for me. You may find some that you like, and you may find some you don't. I may not even list a way that works for you, but this is not meant to be all-encompassing. It's merely a list to suggest things that have helped me. The goal is for you to be prepared so your project can run as smoothly and economically as possible.

If it sounds a little like I'm preparing you for battle, it's because *I am*. Not the blood and guts stuff the movies are made of, but the real-life battle for your money. You will be bombarded daily with information, advice, advertisements, billboards, radio ads, newspaper ads, magazine articles and Web sites, all of which are designed to get into your wallet. Your job is to keep your dollars in your wallet, while everyone else is trying to get them out. To keep them in, the right mental attitude is crucial.

E-mail/Newsletter

I get several e-mail newsletters, daily and weekly, that help me keep my mind ready for success. While they're not directly related to construction, they've helped me tremendously in preparing for construction. They've helped me avoid the pitfalls of blaming everything on everyone else, and helped me realize that when things go wrong, it's my fault. After all, I'm running the job. By realizing this, I've learned to focus on fixing the problem instead of on worrying about who's responsible for the problem. This practice gets the problem solved faster, at less expense, and can salvage a good working relationship that might otherwise be lost. This can

GLOSSARY

Barrel Vault

A ceiling that is curved, as if you were standing inside of a very large barrel, as opposed to cathedral ceilings, which are straight slants.

BOTTOM LINE

If you're interested in free guidance and counseling on your success, see Appendix A.

only be done by attacking just the source of the problem, not the person behind the source.

Research

You cannot do what you have no clue *how to* do. This doesn't mean you have to be an expert. It simply means that you must learn as much as you can before you start. You're taking a great step in reading this book, but don't stop here. Read all you can about what you're going to do. Talk to people. A person can't become a lawyer, a doctor or a skilled carpenter overnight. It takes time. Before a carpenter or plumber or architect becomes a master, he'll have decades in his field. Obviously, you don't want to take decades to build your house or your addition, and that's OK. You don't have to be a "master" to tackle most projects, especially if you keep them simple. If you've never framed a roof and ceiling assembly before, I wouldn't go out and try to tackle a barrel vault for your first project. But if you'll research it and maybe tackle a simple roof first, you can be ready for a barrel vault in no time.

Follow Their Lead

To prepare yourself for your journey, consider tracking someone else's project. Find a new house or remodeling project, and follow its progress from start to finish. Befriend the contractor that's running the job or, preferably, the homeowner. Make a log of the trials they face and the progress they make. Pay attention to the unexpected problems that arise. No doubt there will be scheduling problems, worker problems and code problems. Watch how the person running the project reacts to them. Is he or she overreacting? Underreacting? How could the problem have been handled better? Was there an easy solution that was overlooked? These are the questions you ask yourself as you watch. When you see a problem, put yourself in the other's shoes and think about how you could've handled the situation better. Doing this exercise will help you be prepared when the same situations arise on your own jobsite.

Warming Up

When we exercise, we warm up first. Why not do the same thing to prepare for a large project? Start with something smaller and more manageable to help you prepare both mentally and developmentally before attempting a larger project. If your goal is to build a house, start with a room addition. If your goal is a room addition, start with an interior remodel. By "warming up" you'll get a taste of the flame before jumping into the fire. You'll learn by doing and making mistakes, the way we all do,

"Things don't just happen, things happen just."
This quote is from Jim Rohn's weekly e-zine.
To learn more about this free publication, see
Appendix A.

but on a small scale to start. An Olympic high jumper doesn't set the crossbar at its highest level to start. He sets it lower and then moves it up after he clears it. The same approach will work well in construction.

If You Train Forever, You'll Never Get in the Game

Move forward with your preparations. I've seen people worry so much about whether they're ready or not that they never get started. They simply continue to get ready and never actually achieve readiness. Don't fall into this trap. You'll never be totally ready. You must be willing to make a mistake. It is impossible to cover all the bases to make sure nothing goes wrong. Simply be prepared, and don't panic when something does go wrong. Things go wrong on *every* jobsite. Remember it's not the problem that messes things up: it's how the problem is handled that really determines the outcome.

Get Ready to Shake a Leg

You must be willing to do the legwork necessary to get ready. You'll need financing, material lists, bids, plans, subs, permits and time to complete your project. If you dread these responsibilities, or think you're incapable of handling them, your preparation work won't get done or they won't get done to the best of your ability. As a result, you'll start your project off on the wrong foot. Make a list of what you need to accomplish before you begin. Now set those items up on a time schedule. Estimate how long you need to complete each task. Set expected dates for completion. Now tell yourself you'll stick to the schedule. Tell yourself you know you can get it done. Then do it. Set a periodic date, every couple of days or once a week, to check your progress. Mark off what you get done and determine whether you're on schedule to finish by your expected date. Make adjustments as necessary; you'll learn to juggle items to get things done on time. For example, your schedule says to get the plumbing bid and then the HVAC bid, but the plumber is out of town until Friday and you can meet the heating guy on Wednesday. Flip the two items, since doing so won't affect the outcome; that way you won't waste time waiting for the plumber. This exercise is great practice for when you begin building or remodeling. You'll have the mindset and a pattern to follow to keep your project on time.

Worrying about your project too much causes more problems than not worrying enough.

BOTTOM LINE

I routinely get better prices than my peers because I refuse to accept the "normal" price and the "normal" way of doing things. You can too if you keep telling yourself: "I can do this for less," then search until you find a way.

Bringing Out the Bargain Hunter in You

Promise yourself you'll find a better deal. Be true to your promise and delight in the bargain found. Don't accept high prices; search until you find a lower one. Talk to people, search the web, or get creative and figure out a less expensive way to do something. But don't give up. Convince yourself you can do it. Believe you can do it, and don't quit until you do. Say to yourself, "I know I can find or do this cheaper. I'm not paying $_____ to get it done." Then figure out how to do it for less. Refuse to accept what others tell you. I've heard, "That's just what it costs" many, many times. But I don't take someone else's word for it. I will find a better, less expensive way. *I know I will*, and I routinely do. You can too, if you'll only *realize you can*.

Question Everyone

When someone tells you something has to be this way, question it. When the plumber says you have to use copper water lines, question it. When your electrician says you have to use the expensive supply store, question it. Question when anyone tells you, "You can't do that," or "We always do it this way, so you'll have to too." I even go so far as to question the code official. After all, they're only human and they can't remember the whole codebook. Get in the habit of asking, "Why?" Always ask why when you don't like the answers to your questions. Don't strike up an argument; simply find the answer to your question yourself. Allowing yourself to follow the crowd will get you the crowd's price. Seek out the better-priced way, supplier or contractor to save your money.

Be A Rock

Tell yourself you're rock solid, that you won't stray from your allowances. Period. Don't consider it for a minute. If it's over your budget, don't even start to look at it. If you do, pretty soon you'll be ordering it and you'll shoot down your budget. It happens all the time. You, or your spouse, eye the perfect Berber carpet for the family room. The only problem is that it's $28 a yard and your budget is $15 per yard. But, you (or your spouse) *really* like it. It would look sooooo perfect! And before you know it, you've bought it. The key here is to be a rock and *don't start* looking at it if it's over your budget, period. Just walk away and look at what you *can* afford before you talk yourself into the purchase.

Fear and Doubt Can Cripple You

If you're like most of us, you'll let fears and doubts creep into your brain. First, you'll tell yourself you're not qualified to handle your project. Then doubts will set in about whether you can really complete it or not. Then the doubts turn to worry, and the worry manifests itself in a self-fulfilling prophecy of things going wrong. Fear and doubt must be checked at the door. It's OK to have these feelings if you don't dwell on them. You must believe you can, and will, complete your project. To do this, accept the fact that things will go wrong on your project. They go wrong on *everyone's* projects. Just know that when they do arise, you'll handle them to the best of your ability. Don't be scared of problems; be ready for them. Remind yourself that things will happen, but that they can't control you unless you let them. Instead of spending your time worrying about them, relax until the time comes to handle them. Know that you will handle them. I've seen more problems caused by someone worrying about potential problems than by anything else. If you drive yourself crazy worrying about how to stop every little problem that might arise, you'll cause them to start happening. I've seen it time and time again. Let things flow, and be ready when things happen. Save your mind by allowing yourself to worry only after a problem occurs. You can't address what hasn't happened yet, so don't drive yourself (and everyone else) crazy worrying about it.

Save Money by Having the Right Mind-set

Having the right mind-set is crucial to saving dollars. If you adopt a lazy attitude and begin to buy things the easy way, or if you adopt an "I'll do it like everyone else" attitude, where you do things a certain way because everyone else does it that way, you'll spend more money than you should. Write yourself a note that says: "How have I saved money on my project today?" Now put a copy of it on the dash of your car, on your mirror at home and on your desk at work. When you read it, make these promises to yourself: *I will stick to the plan, I will search out bargains, I will find the cheaper way*. Then, stick to your promises. Keep telling yourself you can. Don't let fear or doubt keep you from accomplishing your goal of saving lots of money.

ROLLER COASTERS ARE FUN BUT WE HATE SPEED BUMPS

When you're at the top of that large drop on a roller coaster, you're prepared for the fall. It can be different, however, when you hit an unexpected speed bump — even a little one — we panic. The difference lies merely in being prepared. If you're prepared, nothing can surprise you. When you're not prepared, anything can induce panic.

The first section of this chapter told you to be prepared for anything. When you ride a roller coaster, you're prepared for quick turns, high speed and even some lulls in the action. You know your stomach is going to jump into your throat at times and that you're going to have to suddenly change direction and speed. It doesn't matter whether you go right, left or down, because you're ready for anything. When you're ready to start your project, I want you to take the same attitude. Mentally prepare yourself for the ride. If you'll do this, I promise that, just like with the coaster, when the ride is over, you'll race around to the end of the line to do it again. I'm going to describe the mental attitudes you'll need to make the ride fun. After reading about them, keep them in mind as you progress through your project. Make it a point to reread them if you feel yourself beginning to lose control or get worried. Then grab the handrail and enjoy the ride.

Don't, Don't, Don't Panic

If something goes wrong, you'll want to panic, especially when you're just starting out. You must curb this anxiety. Not only is it unhealthy physically, it can destroy your project. I've stated before that worrying too much causes more problems than not worrying enough, and I'm saying it again. Most problems have simple solutions if you'll search them out. Keeping a level head is of utmost importance. You're the "Captain of the Ship," so to speak. You direct your project. You set the course. You are responsible for its success or failure. But you can't pilot the ship if you're in a panic. You must be able to look at things rationally to arrive at the best solution. You may not always like what needs to be done, but get through it, calmly, for the benefit of all involved — especially yourself. Remember, troubles should not come as a surprise.

Love Your Dollars

I'm not preaching greed, but you should wince every time you spend a dollar. If you freely spend your money and still sleep soundly at night, you'll blow the budget every time. I want your mind to constantly fight the spending of dollars. Always search for the less expensive way. I want you to be cre-

Writing notes is a great way to keep from forgetting things you need to remember. Carry a small notepad and jot down important info.

FIGURE 11-1   Berber carpet is a favorite among many homeowners.

ative in saving money. Ask yourself, "Is there a cheaper way? What other materials could I use to save money? Can I get the same look without spending so much?" I constantly tell myself that there's a better way. I search it out and implement it when possible. When it's not possible, I simply don't do it if it's not in the budget and not absolutely necessary. You should think the same way to keep your dollars in your wallet where they belong.

Move Quickly, But Don't Hurry

Successful projects run on schedule. The tighter the schedule, the better. When your project sits for weeks or months, it usually costs you money. However, pushing to get things done may cause problems which can cost even more money. Establish a schedule that will keep things running smoothly, but don't rush anything or anyone. Suppose you're on your HVAC rough-in and the heating contractor won't be done for two more days, but the plumber wants to come now. Don't rush in and send the plumber without consulting the heating guy first. If you have a situation like this, talk to everyone involved to avoid problems. If your heating contractor sees problems, either solve them or wait before sending in the plumber. Usually there is an easy way around this situation. By talking it through before initiating any changes, you'll avoid potential blowups and the need to redo any work that was done out of order.

Think It Through

Snap judgments usually turn around and bite you. When you're faced with a problem, take your time and think it through before deciding how to handle the situation. Even if the solution seems simple and it appears that it won't cause any problems, take your time. I try to be amiable in most situations, but I've regretted saying, "Yeah, no sweat, I'll take care of it" more than I care to admit. Sure, it might make someone else happy, but I end up paying the debt I've created by dismissing things quickly without thinking them through. No matter how experienced you are, anything that takes work needs to be thought out. Material, time, labor and coordination all need to be considered before making a decision. The key is not to rush. It's better to put things on hold for a short while than to make a snap decision that sets you back a week because it wasn't properly thought through.

Talk Over Tea

Your attitude when communicating with anyone concerning your project should be the same as it would be if you were chatting with a friend over tea: calm, unassuming, fair and honest. You want all negotiations to

BOTTOM LINE

Before making decisions, ask yourself these questions: Is there a way to do this for less? Are there less expensive materials I could use? Can I get the same look without spending so much?

Communication is the key to jobsite success. Discuss everything with everyone involved. Get everyone's input up front to avoid problems.

end in a win-win situation. I treat each of my subs as I would a friend, and I expect the same from them. They usually give me a good deal and perform well. I don't expect to pay the same as someone they don't know and haven't done business with, but I want them to make money so they'll want to work for me again. I expect both sides to be flexible and willing to work together to finish the project. This can make for long and profitable relationships. This rapport doesn't develop overnight, but you should start to form it immediately. Don't let yourself get lured into the appeal of making a quick buck by sticking it to someone when you can. It may save you a little money now, but it'll cost you ten times that amount down the road. Always be ethical in your dealings.

Finish What You've Started

It's easy to talk ourselves into leaving that last little bit undone. We're anxious to move on to the next step and it would be so easy to finish up later. *Don't* talk yourself into this habit. Make yourself finish what you've started, and finish it completely, before moving on. Chastise yourself for trying to leave things undone. I know it seems easier to do it later, but later will never come. If you start leaving those little things undone, you'll be sitting at the kitchen table drinking your coffee months after completion, and it'll hit you: "I never went back and put the joist hanger on that rafter!" And it'll be too late to do it. Or even worse, you'll start leaving larger and larger portions of projects undone until you find you're framing, plumbing and wiring all at once. Don't do this; finish what you've started before moving on.

You Can Do It

Don't talk yourself out of tackling a project because it's your first time. Everyone has a first time. You have to believe you can do it. You have to be willing to begin and work through whatever problems arise. You won't expand your horizons if you do only what you already know how to do. To tackle something new, you must be willing to begin with the knowledge you have and learn as you go. To help you accept that you can do something new, set up a support system. Let's say you're thinking of plumbing your new room addition, but you've never done it before. You've researched how to do it and consulted with the plumbing inspector so you know you can do your own work, but you're still unsure of your ability to do the project correctly. In this situation, why not arrange to have a pro to come in and help you through any trouble spots that may arise? Or maybe you want to get things close and have him come in and help you finish. This type of safety net can ease your fears, allowing you to take the risk of doing your own work to save money.

Don't Get Lazy

When things are going smoothly, it's easy to get lazy and complacent and start slacking off on the supervision of your project. You'll start telling yourself, "There hasn't been a problem yet, so why do I need to go check on things today? I've got other things to do." Don't let this happen. You should visit the site daily when possible, and at least three times a week if you can't go every day. It doesn't take long for things to start going wrong. If you catch problems early, the solutions are usually easier and less expensive than if the problems go on for long periods of time. Another temptation is to stop checking a sub's work if you've worked with him before and he's performed well. You should check all the work on your project, even if you have a history with the contractor. Stay diligent in your supervision; don't take the easy way and start assuming things are all hunky-dory.

Keep Your Cool

The best thing you can do for yourself is to keep from stressing out. I've watched people make themselves nuts over things that don't matter much. I've driven myself, my wife and my workers crazy by losing my temper. Simply make a decision, and then live with it. If you do something that you don't like later, it's almost always changeable. You're going to move something, pick something or add something that you wish you hadn't, no matter what. There is no 100% guarantee that you'll like everything you do. But since these things are bound to happen no matter how much you stress about them, relax. Realize that everything will be OK. Even if you've already moved the furniture in, if you *really* can't get used to the color of the living room, you can always repaint.

WRAPPING UP

When your project nears completion, avoid the temptation to let your guard down. Don't start relaxing until you've seen everything through. Don't start moving in until you're done. I personally have been guilty of this before. It's easy to let yourself get in a hurry and start changing around the proper order of things. Don't do it. Make a promise to your-

The end of a project is no time to start slacking off. For a successful project, stay diligent to the end.

self that you'll follow my next few points down to the very end and that you won't give in — no matter how much you want to. It's hard to resist when you're so close to your goal. You can almost taste the end. You'll dream about what you can do now that you won't be so busy "constructing." At this point, you'll be very vulnerable. Read the following advice and apply it when you're trying to talk yourself into a bad thing.

Don't Stop Short of the Finish Line

I've seen houses that have been lived in for years that are still unfinished. Oh, they're livable, but they're still not 100% complete. There may be some trim that's not put up, or a room that never quite got finished, or maybe it's that extra feature that was planned but never installed — but there's always something. Set your mind against this. Your mortgage company may even do this for you: Many have adopted policies where they won't convert your construction loan to a mortgage until the house is 100% completed. Even if your mortgage company isn't enforcing this policy, you should, if for no other reason than the fact that anything left undone will hurt your home's appraised value. And if your home doesn't get appraised, you may not get your mortgage.

Don't Rearrange the Schedule in an Effort to Finish More Quickly Than Is Practical

I was building a custom home in 1990 and we were nearing completion. The homeowners were in a hurry to move in and were pushing me to complete the house ASAP. While I was doing what I could to accommodate them, I was still within the time frame of the contract and I wasn't yet working weekends. So, I was very surprised one Monday when I walked in and all the floor coverings were installed. And to make matters worse, their furniture had been moved in! I estimate it took me two extra weeks to complete the house because I had to work over the new floor coverings and around the furniture (not to mention the residents). Don't do this to yourself or to your contractor (because he will surely charge you for it). Follow the proper order until you're all the way done. As you near the end, it's easy to let your judgment slip and talk yourself into alterations. You'll tell yourself, "Oh, it won't take that much longer to install the electrical outlets and fixtures with the flooring in," or "We can move in without the sidewalks." These situations may work out OK, but

Changes are bad. Last minute and end-of-project changes are worse.

they're not ideal. How will you feel when you break that glass globe and put the big tear right in the middle of your new linoleum? Or when you get 3 inches of rain and the electrical inspector tracks in mud on your wife's new white living room carpet.? Just tell yourself no, and do things in the proper order. You'll be glad you did.

Don't Start Thinking at the End

If you start thinking about what you've already done, inevitably you'll want to make changes. Changes are bad, and last minute changes are worse. When you start changing things in the end, you run a greater risk of having to return materials already purchased or on order. You also have a much greater risk of delaying your completion date. At this point, it's best to focus on the prize. Don't let your mind wander to things you've already completed; keep it on things that still need to be done. By concentrating on the tasks that remain, you'll keep from second-guessing things you've already done. You can't evaluate the final project properly until you move in anyway. If you allow yourself to start worrying about something now, you may talk yourself into making a change that doesn't need to be changed at all. The way something looks and feels when it's empty may be completely different from how it looks and feels when it's full of you and your furniture. Leave things alone until you've used them. Then you can make a proper evaluation and determine whether anything is worth changing.

The Job's Not Done Until the Paperwork's Done

At this point, you should turn your attention to making sure your ducks are in a row. Make sure you've paid everyone who needs paid. Make sure you have lien waivers or contractor's affidavits on file. Make sure all accounts have been paid in full. Since you've been returning unused items as you go (as I advised in chapter eight) you don't have to worry about returning a bunch of items. See that the jobsite's left clean. That means hauling off or disposing of all of the leftover scraps, boxes and paper from your fixtures and cabinets.

If you're like me, you think paperwork is a pain. It's easy to postpone it or leave things undone until somebody starts asking for it. Don't fall into this trap. It's easier to do the paperwork as you go than to go back and try and piece it together from what you can remember. Tell yourself at the start that you'll do it as you go along, and then stick to that decision. Don't stop until it's all done.

Now, when everything's done, you can move all your things in and relax. If you've followed all the advice in this book, you will have completed your project at a total savings of 45 percent. So sit back, grab the remote and dream of your next project. I know you'll want to start on it soon.

CHAPTER TWELVE

WHY REMODEL?

The first question you should ask yourself is, "Why should I remodel my home?" There are as many answers to this question as there are readers for this book. Everyone's answer will be slightly different. Maybe you need more space, maybe you want to update your home's look. Maybe you want to change the way you use parts of your home. Remodeling a home is a great way to add equity without having to uproot and leave friends and neighbors behind. I'm going to show you how to remodel and put more money on the equity tree without adding dollars to the mortgage. The key to accomplishing this is knowledge. That's what this book is for: to help you gain the knowledge you need to reach your goal.

The more you know, the more successful your project will be. You don't want to jump into a project only to learn that you could have done it much smarter — or that you shouldn't have done it at all. You don't want to say, "If I'd only known _____." The blank can be filled in countless ways. Some are foreseeable, and others are not. Since I'm not a psychic, I'll stick to outlining some of the foreseeable situations you should consider before remodeling. Before we start looking at logical reasons to consider a remodeling project, let's take a minute to talk about illogical logic. I'm not trying to be coy; I simply know that for some people, tackling projects that don't seem to make much sense financially make sense to them for other reasons. If you're one of those people who knows exactly what you want, and doesn't care whether your project makes financial sense, you can skip this section and move ahead to the section on Life Adjustments. This section is written for the rest of us, people who are trying to determine where to put their dollars for maximum return — or at least, how to break even. The only reason I ever put more money into a home than I expect to get back out is if I determine that my personal gain (in convenience, functionality or beauty) is worth more than my financial loss. I say "loss" because if I put $1,000 into a remodeling project, I expect to get $2,000 back when I sell the home; otherwise, I wouldn't have invested the money and time — unless the project offers some unusual, intangible value. Let's look at some points to consider when deciding whether to remodel.

• **Will I get my money back, or not?** Will the going prices in your area support the needed return? If you live in a post-WWII tract-house subdivision where the average cost of a home is $75,000, you won't get your money back if you install a $20,000 custom kitchen with marble counter tops. Your project should be in line with the style and value of homes in your immediate area. There are a few exceptions to this rule, but very few. See sidebar 1-1, "Covenents and Restrictions" for a way to distinguish your home from your neighbors without driving the cost of your house above the ceiling of the market.

• **Will I live in the house long enough to reap a return?** When considering a project, determine whether you'll see a return on your investment while you're still living in the house. For example, say you want to install new windows. The energy-efficient ones with low-E glass and argon gas cost 20 percent more than regular windows. You're going to live in the house only one more year, so you'll not realize enough energy savings over that year to make up for the extra 20 percent you spent. New windows with unseen extra features such as low-E glass and argon are unlikely to add significantly more to the resale value of your home than new windows without such features, so save your money and put in the standard windows.

• **Can I buy a home with the features I want for less than I can remodel my current home?** If you can buy a home that already has what you want, and you can buy it for less than your mortgage plus the cost of improvements, you should consider the purchase. Let's say you really need a fourth bedroom and you're considering adding one. Your mortgage plus the remodel totals $100,000. However, you can buy a four-bedroom house similar to yours for $85,000. In this case, you should consider the purchase over the remodel.

• **Can I build a new home with the features I want for the same or less than I can remodel my current home?** Most people never even consider this an option, but it always is. This book has already shown you how to build a new home for less than you might expect. You must weigh the pros and cons of remodeling vs. building to determine which is the bet-

Consider using custom materials sparingly to distinguish your home from others in the area without overimproving it. For example, install small sections of brick or stone only to the front of your home.

ter option for you. I find that by putting my reasons on a piece of paper, listing the good and the bad, my decision usually becomes much easier. Just remember: you get nothing back until you put something out.

• **Will the project return dollars when I go to sell the house?** I don't put dollars into a house without knowing that I'll get them back. I often see people dump tens of thousands of dollars into projects that won't return their money. Some examples of this include installing high-priced floor coverings or expensive light fixtures, replacing roofs that aren't bad, replacing vinyl siding or aluminum soffit and fascia when the originals are in paintable condition, replacing windows when the old units are still in fair or better condition, hanging wallpapering and redecorating. These are all nice things to do to a home, but don't invest in them thinking you'll get your money back out, because you won't. They may help your house sell more quickly, but that's it.

• **What additional costs will be incurred if I add on?** If you're thinking of adding on, consider these additional costs. Will your existing furnace and air conditioner handle the added space? If you're adding bedrooms or bathrooms, will your existing water supply, sewer and septic system be able to handle the extra load? Is there sufficient space to add the room(s) and still stay within your zoning setbacks? Are there any underground or overhead utilities that will have to be moved? What will the building permit and inspections cost? Can you add the room(s) without blocking light, ventilation or egress currently needed for the existing house? Will your electrical system support the added load? How much will your real estate taxes increase? Issues such as these can add "hidden" costs to room additions. (Specifics concerning these issues are discussed later in the book.)

• **Will the remodel affect the structure of the house?** If you're going to remove all or part of any framing in the house, make sure you're not removing load-bearing points or assemblies. This can include walls, posts, ceiling joists, floor joists and rafters. If you remove bearing assemblies, the load they carried must be transferred to the footings in a new way. Disregarding this is dangerous. I see this issue ignored by the unwit-

BOTTOM LINE
You'll lose dollars if you overbuild for your area. For example, if you spend $30,000 for brick veneer when 99% of the homes in your area and price range have vinyl siding, you won't get your money back when you sell the house.

ting because they don't know they're doing something dangerous, but I also see it ignored by those who should know better simply because correcting or replacing the bearing can be expensive — but it must be done. If you're not experienced with loading design, consult a pro when considering a project. Be sure to calculate in the cost of any structural reconfiguration.

• **Are there historic district regulations to contend with?** If your home is in a historic district, there are rules that you'll have to follow in order to make any changes to your home. Make sure you check these rules before beginning any work to avoid the cost of having to redo something that doesn't comply with your district's rules.

Consider these items when determining whether or not to remodel. Most projects I see tackled by homeowners will return some of their investment, but if you're going for a maximum return, keep reading. By the time you get to the end of this chapter, you'll be armed with enough information to determine whether you can get your money back. You'll also know how to determine whether you'll reap a huge profit for your effort. This, as they say, is the bottom line.

LIFE ADJUSTMENTS TO CONSIDER.

There are always inconveniences with any construction project. Although these are inevitable, being prepared for them will soften the blow. It's hard to picture exactly what might occur when you've never done something like this before, so I'll be your guide and lay out the things you should be prepared for when tackling a remodeling project.

• **The mess:** Construction can be messy, but the mess can be controlled. The idea is to keep the mess confined to the area where the work is being done. First, isolate the work area from the rest of the house with zip walls. You can purchase ready-made, easy-to-use versions of these, but I recommend buying a $3 roll of plastic or poly (aka Visqueen) to erect your own barrier. I also recommend sealing off heat registers and cold-air returns to keep dust from getting into your HVAC system. Frequently clean and remove debris from the site. Keep all reusable scraps but pitch the rest.

• **Utilities and facilities:** Determine what utilities will have to be interrupted and how you're going to live without them. For example, suppose

GLOSSARY

Ceiling Price
The maximum amount you can expect to get from a house in a particular area.

Don't remodel your existing home when you can buy or build a house with exactly what you want for less money.

FIGURE 12-1   A $5 light fixture.

FIGURE 12-2   A more expensive light fixture that looks virtually the same as the $5 fixture above.

BOTTOM LINE

Before investing money in your home, check with your realtor to see if you'll get your money back when you go to sell the house. Many common home improvements won't return the money spent on them.

you're moving the electrical service from the utility room to the garage. To do this, the power to the entire house will have to be turned off at some time. Schedule the time conveniently to make sure this doesn't create any serious problems. If you're remodeling your bathroom or kitchen, take into account the down time involved when fixtures and appliances cannot be used. For example, let's say you're remodeling the only bathroom in the house and the stool will be unavailable for two days. You'll need to arrange for other accommodations in such cases.

• **Inconvenience:** Life would be so simple if everything just happened automatically, if everything were available at the mere mention of its name. But, I also believe it would be boring as all get out. Your remodeling project is no different from anything else in life: if you want it, you've got to go out and get it. No one else will do it for you. This means you'll be on the phone a lot, solving problems, asking questions and scheduling work, workers and materials. It also means buying supplies, getting permits and maybe picking up a hammer. You have to be willing to sacrifice

FIGURE 12-3 This severe case shows that structures can fail when bearing points are removed and not replaced.

BOTTOM LINE
When considering an addition to your home, be sure to calculate in all needed mechanical system upgrades and their costs.

A homemade zip wall can be made from a $3 roll of plastic sheathing and some tape. By lining a doorway with two or three layers of plastic sheeting (aka Visqueen), you can create your own separation for very little money.

GLOSSARY

Zip Wall

A ready-made partition made of two poles that extend from floor to ceiling and a sheet of plastic, sometimes with a zipper in it, that separates a work area from a living area.

GLOSSARY

Cold-air Return

An opening in the wall and duct that leads back to the furnace for air circulation. These are typically mounted high on the wall. The air that comes from the heating registers is replaced by the "cold" air that returns to the furnace through these.

a little to gain a lot. To save huge sums, you have to be willing to take some of the load upon yourself.

• **Traffic:** At times, your construction site will resemble a freeway. The busiest jobsite I ever had included a plumber, one heating contractor with two on-site workers, one sewer contractor with two on-site workers, one excavating contractor and one carpentry crew with two on-site workers — all working simultaneously. In addition, there were eight vehicles, including two backhoes. Your jobsite may not get this busy, but at times it may seem this way. If you, or your wife, stays at home with the kids, or if Grandpa lives with you and will be home all day, be prepared for company. Your workers will need access to a bathroom, electricity and some will need access to water for cleaning up. They'll also need access in and out of the work area. They'll be making noises — loud noises. Be prepared for a little disruption in your normally quiet environment.

• **Time and effort:** I touched on this in the inconvenience section, but you have to be willing to devote time and effort to your project. If you want to save big, this is absolutely necessary. If you don't want to be bothered, or are just plainly too busy to take on the extra work, hire a general contractor and be done with it. If, on the other hand, you want or need to do this project yourself, be prepared to devote yourself to it. When I know I'm going to be busy in the future, like right before I start a new project, I bank my time. By banking my time, I prepare myself for the busy period ahead. In most instances, this will last only for a few weeks at a time. Even on a large project, such as constructing a new home, I know there will be lulls in my duties where I can catch up and bank some more time for the next busy stretch.

• **Crossover exposure:** Most remodeling projects have some type of crossover, meaning the areas and ways in which your remodel will affect the rest of your home. This crossover should always be anticipated when you're considering a remodel. Let's say you're adding a room. To do this, the existing house will have to be prepared to "accept" the new room. This means that siding and roofing must be removed, and a new hole may have to be created in your existing exterior wall (you have to get to the new room somehow). Exposing your existing roof during April showers may not be wise if you're not prepared. Take the necessary precautions: have on hand the means to cover the exposed areas if nasty weather pops up.

Being mentally prepared for your remodel is half the battle. I find most people are so excited about the end result, they fail to realize what it takes to get there. I hope I haven't shattered the view of your remodeling project that you had through your rose-colored glasses. By all means, set your eyes on your goal; but be prepared to hurdle the obstacles that will present themselves along the way. Handling a project is no different from taking a trip. You may encounter some roadblocks and need to take some detours, but if you've read the map and packed the items you need to make your journey safe, you're much more apt to reach the end in one piece, on time and on budget. But, even more importantly, adequate preparation will allow you to enjoy the ride along the way.

WILL MY FURNACE HANDLE THE ADDED LOAD? HOW ABOUT MY......?

This is the most often overlooked and ignored aspect of remodeling. Most additions to our water, sewer, electric and HVAC systems are simply tacked onto the end of the existing system without regard to whether the existing setup can handle the added load. Maybe the worst violation of this is in wiring. I've heard countless times: "Oh, I'll just tap on to this outlet over here, and wire the new room(s)." While this is OK sometimes, it can be hazardous in others. If you're using licensed subcontractors for your mechanicals and the construction will be inspected by competent building inspectors, you should be OK. However, if you're doing the work yourself, live in an area where there are no building inspectors, or take my advice and want to find out for yourself, you should consult the guidelines to make sure you have adequate capacity. Pay for upgrades only when they're necessary. If you do need to upgrade, spend your money wisely.

• **Calculate the heating and cooling load:** The question here is whether your existing HVAC units can handle any added load. If you're

To save large sums of money, you must be willing to take some of the load upon yourself. This can mean scheduling services and obtaining materials and workers. In addition, it means tackling some do-it-yourself projects as well.

By banking my time, I take some of the stress out of my busy times during a project. You should bank time in whatever you're going to miss, or that'll miss you, while you're busy constructing.

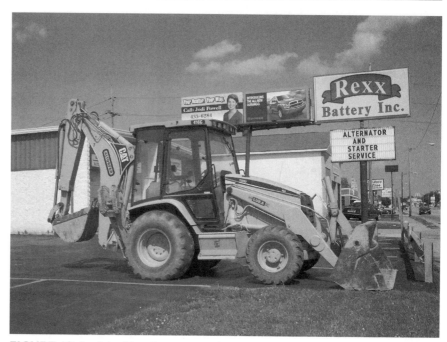

FIGURE 12-4   A backhoe is a commonly used piece of equipment.

heating and cooling any new areas with your existing system, you'll want to calculate whether you'll have adequate heating and cooling power when you need it. When calculating this for a forced warm air system, your contractor (or you) should use *Manual J*. Simple rules of thumb are inadequate for calculating load because there are so many factors that must be considered. Building design and location, floor area, air volume, insulation R-factor and type, register locations, foundation type and other factors all affect the load calculation.

 • **If you must upgrade HVAC units, don't jump into the "super-efficient" arena:** I suggest you skip the "super-efficient" systems. I do install 92-percent efficient furnaces because I get them at great prices and they save money on utility bills. However, I don't believe they do much to the bottom line when selling a home. I've never personally installed a heat pump, geothermal heating system or other "super-efficient" system because I can never figure a return on my investment; but you'll want to determine whether a "super-efficient" system may be right for you. To do this, figure out how much extra the initial cost would be, calculate interest on the difference, and see how long the savings in utilities will take to equal that amount. This is your break-even point. If you'll own the home beyond that point, you'll begin to realize a savings and should seriously consider such a system. If not, save your money.

• **If you upgrade your entire HVAC system, sell the old one:** If your system is in good working order but it's just too small to handle the added load, when you remove the old unit, sell it. Don't let it just walk away with the subcontractor or go to the dump. There is a market for good used HVAC equipment out there. People with rental property, people looking to heat a garage and even people with a very tight budget will consider buying used equipment. Sell your unit and put these dollars back into your project.

• **Consider adding a new HVAC system for the added area only, rather than replacing the entire system:** If your existing system works fine, why replace it? It may be more cost-effective and efficient to install a new unit just for the new area. For example, if you're adding two new rooms, check the figures for adding a separate system just for those two rooms and compare them to the cost of upgrading the system for the existing house and the two rooms together. You may also run into a situation where your cooling system is large enough, but your heating system is not. In this instance you'll want to add just the heating system.

• **If your HVAC system is close to handling the added load, add insulation to the existing house to lower the demand instead of upgrading your system:** You may be able to cut demand on your present system instead of having to add onto it. It's a simple matter of attacking the problem rather than just assuming that you need more power to compensate. When calculating your load, be sure to calculate what adding insulation to your existing area (and super-insulating the added area) will due to your load. If you can cut demand, you can use a smaller system — maybe the one you already have. Besides, adding insulation is much cheaper than upgrading HVAC systems — plus you get the added benefit of energy savings to boot.

• **When adding additional water lines, make sure your existing main lines will handle the extra load:** When creating extra demand on water lines, especially over long distances, you should calculate the load to

GLOSSARY

Manual J
A manual used for calculating the load on your HVAC system. It's available from: Air Conditioning Contractors of America, 2800 Shirlington Road, Suite 300, Arlington, VA 22206, or at www.acca.org.

Cathedral and vaulted ceilings add air volume that must be considered when sizing HVAC components. To get a proper fit, have your contractor provide you with a sizing using *Manual J* as the reference.

R-factor

A measure used to determine a material's resistance to heat flow. As a rule of thumb, the higher the R-factor, the higher the resistance to heat and cold transfer and the better the insulation.

FIGURE 12-5   A typical 92% efficient, considered high efficiency, forced warm air furnace.

Local codes differ from place to place. My area currently enforces the 2000 International Residential Code, 2000 International Mechanical Code, 2002 NEC and the 1998 Illinois Plumbing Code. Check to see what your local building and zoning department enforces.

ensure you'll have adequate pressure. Your local plumbing code will have charts you can use to determine whether your existing piping is adequate for the additional load. (See the 2003 International Residential Code, table 2903.7, pages 406 and 407. Be sure to check your local regulations too, in case if they're different.)

• **If you're on a septic system, make sure it will handle the added load of additional drains:** The sizing of septic systems is based on the number of bedrooms in the house. If you're adding these, check to see that the system is adequate. For a common tank and gravelless lateral system, this is determined by the linear footage of the lateral. So many feet are required per bedroom. While your overall usage may not be increasing, you'll want to ensure that the system is adequate, per the code, for subsequent owners. If you can add to the existing setup rather than replacing it, you'll save money.

• **When adding hot water lines, make sure your water heater will keep up:** If you're adding extra bathrooms, and especially if you're adding large whirlpool tubs, make sure your water heater will keep up with demand. By adding another outlet for hot water, you're creating the potential for more simultaneous demand. Your water heater will produce only a finite amount of hot water over a given time. The key is to determine how often you use hot water. If you can spread out the times you draw water from your heater, a smaller heater will suffice. I suggest trying to live with the existing heater to see whether it can keep up. If you haven't already done so, insulate the tank and water lines to increase efficiency, and spread out your usage as much as possible. If this still doesn't suffice, install a larger heater.

• **Check to see if you have space in your electrical panel for added circuits:** If you are adding any new electrical wiring, don't just blindly tap onto existing circuits and start running new circuits off of them. Do it right and find out what's acceptable and what's not. It's best to start at the panel and add new circuits as required by the code. When adding bedrooms, the new codes require arc fault breakers, so you'll need at least one

Septic system
A personal sewage treatment facility. Common systems include a septic tank and gravelless laterals. Gravelless laterals are typically round corrugated pipe or chambers. (See Figure 12-7 for a cross section of these laterals.)

BOTTOM LINE
Add new HVAC systems only when the existing system won't handle the added load. Since many systems are oversized to begin with, you may not need to upgrade.

BOTTOM LINE
When adding load to your HVAC system, you may be able to add insulation to cut demand rather than installing a bigger system. To see if this will work, have the load calculated using Manual J.

77 ILLINOIS ADMINISTRATIVE CODE   CHAPTER I §905 App. A
                                                                 SUBCHAPTER r

Section 905.Appendix A   Illustrations and Exhibits
Illustration H   Subsurface Seepage System Size Determination
Exhibit B   Gravelless System

Time (minutes) required for last 6 inches of water to fall	FOR RESIDENTIAL USE Required Absorption Area (Linear feet/bedroom) rate		FOR INSTITUTIONAL OR COMMERCIAL USE Allowable application rate (GPD/Linear Foot[3])		Recommended depth from bottom of the trench to the limiting layer
	8 inch	10 inch	8 inch	10 inch	
18 - 60	100	70	2.4	3.6	
90	105	70	2.0	3.0	3 feet
120	120	80	1.8	2.7	
150	135	90	1.6	2.4	
180	145	100	1.4	2.1	
240	160	110	1.2	1.8	
300	175	120	1.1	1.65	2 feet
360	195	130	1.0	1.5	

Note:

1.   Over 360 is unsuitable for subsurface seepage systems.

2.   Under 18 is unsuitable for subsurface seepage systems.

3.   Divide the required total gallons per day by this number to get the number of lineal feet required.

FIGURE 12-6 Sizing charts for septic systems, like this one, are available from your local health department or other enforcing agency.

77 ILLINOIS ADMINISTRATIVE CODE   CHAPTER I §905 App. A
                                                   SUBCHAPTER r

Section 905.Appendix A   Illustrations and Exhibits
Illustration J   Septic Tank Subsurface Seepage Field
Exhibit D   Section View - Gravelless and Chamber Systems

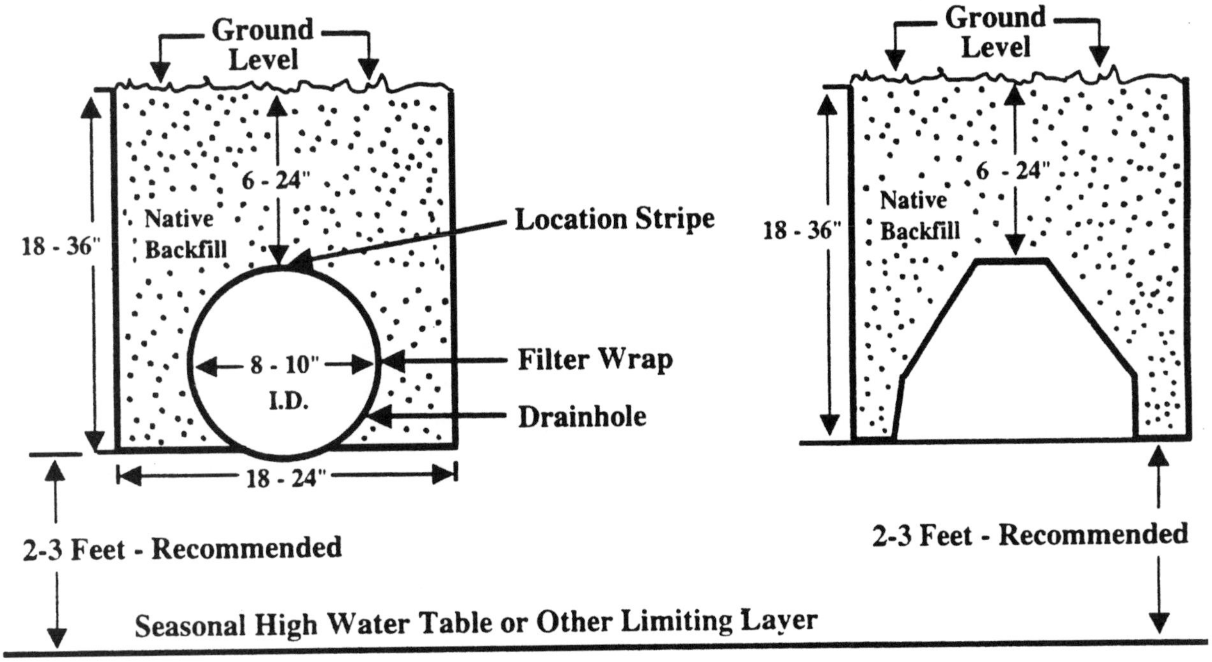

Ground Level

6 - 24"

Native Backfill

18 - 36"

Location Stripe

8 - 10"
I.D.

Filter Wrap

Drainhole

18 - 24"

2-3 Feet - Recommended

Ground Level

6 - 24"

Native Backfill

18 - 36"

2-3 Feet - Recommended

Seasonal High Water Table or Other Limiting Layer

FIGURE 12-7 A cross section of gravelless laterals made of pipe and chambers.

GLOSSARY

Arc Fault Circuit Breaker or AFCI

A fire-protection device required on bedroom electrical circuits that cuts the power to the circuit if a dangerous arc fault is detected.

space for that. Your new rooms will have to meet the existing codes, but your old ones shouldn't have to unless you want to upgrade them. I don't recommend upgrading unless you're having problems with the existing setup or have a dangerous situation. If, for example, you trip the breaker every time you run your clothes washer and microwave at the same time, you have a dangerous and improper setup. Get it fixed. Otherwise, leave what's already done alone and stick to addressing the new circuits.

• **Upgrading your existing electrical service:** If your breaker box is full, talk to your electrician about adding a subpanel or, as a last resort, upgrading your existing panel. In some instances, if you're adding enough new circuits (three in my area), you'll have to bring the rest of the house into compliance. As always, check your local codes to see what's required. Don't redo everything unless your current panel or wiring is dangerous. If you're unsure about what you're going to have to do, call an expert. You can get bids from licensed electricians, call your local code official and describe what you want to do, talk to your supplier about what's needed, search the Internet for advice on your particular situation or contact the manufacturer of your service panel to see what they suggest. You have many options; get advice, just be sure that what you finally do complies with your local electrical code. Before resorting to a total upgrade, read the next section.

• **Tapping onto existing circuits:** If you'll do some circuit tracing, in some instances you may find that you can tap onto an existing circuit without having to add a new one. Don't do this blindly; you must ensure that this is acceptable by your local code. For example, let's say you're adding a new bedroom next to an existing one. If the existing bedroom's electrical circuit is not full, you can add to that circuit to cover the new bedroom. To do this you'll need to change the circuit breaker to an arc fault; but by adding onto the existing circuit instead of adding a new circuit, you can wire the addition without extra room in your service panel.

Most of the options above are easily overlooked. You can save a lot of unnecessary headaches by getting these issues on the table up front. When systems issues come up after the budget has been decided, or after work has begun, they can add many, many dollars to the bottom line. To keep costs in line, I thoroughly investigate the scope of the entire project, carefully examining every aspect before I begin.

PROJECTS THAT PAY

When it comes to remodeling, there are two types of projects that almost always pay, and many more that don't. I'm going to discuss the two that do, but first, let's talk about the ones that don't. Generally, I don't believe

FIGURE 12-8
A water heater insulation blanket.

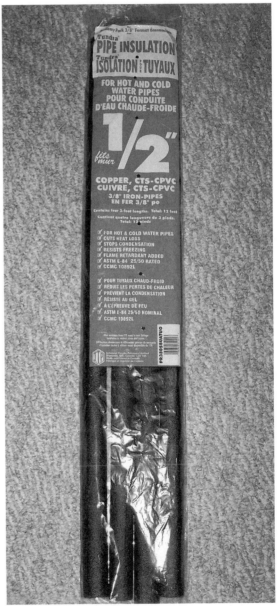

FIGURE 12-9
A length of foam pipe insulation.

FIGURE 12-10
A breaker box/service panel with two
open slots for new circuits.

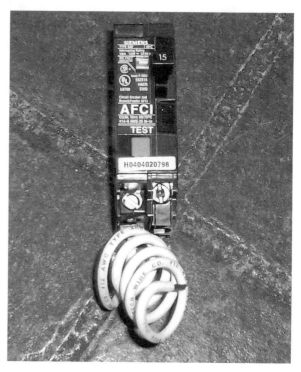

FIGURE 12-11
An arc fault circuit breaker.

in putting money into a project without the prospect of getting money out. I've seen homeowners dump tens of thousands of dollars into remodeling only to get a fraction of that money back when they sold the property. There are a few instances, however, when getting your money back should not be considered the primary goal. One of these instances is if you know you'll never move again. If you plan to stay in your house for the rest of your life, then design and remodel it to fit your needs and your needs only. If, however, you're like most of us, and you plan on moving sometime in your life, put your money where you'll be most likely to get it back.

• **Kitchens:** Kitchens sell houses. A nice, updated, clean and functional kitchen will help sell your house more quickly, and for more money. People spend more money on — and some spend more time in — the kitchen than any other room in the house. So should you. Most rooms in a house consist of four walls and a floor, but a kitchen has so much more to consider. Cabinets, countertops, sinks, faucets, appliances, pantries, lights, water filters and more affect the value of a kitchen. If you want to put your remodeling money where you're most likely to get it back — and then some — put it in the kitchen.

• **Bathrooms:** Bathrooms sell houses. A nice, updated, clean and functional bathroom will help sell your house more quickly, and for more money. Bringing a bathroom up-to-date in style and appointments will always return dollars. Nobody likes an old, dingy, musty bathroom. We spend a lot of time in this room, and our guests visit it as well, so we want it to be crisp and clean. By getting rid of that old, rotting window above the tub, or that old wall-hung sink basin, we can increase the value and comfort of our homes.

• **Other selected projects:** Remodeling other features of your home may or may not pay, depending on your particular situation. To determine what, if anything, you should do to your home to maximize its value, fill out the chart in Figure 12-14. Take a Sunday and go to the open houses of comparable houses in your area. Tour houses for sale in your home's present value range, or in your targeted value range if you're planning major remodeling project. The houses should be as similar to yours as possible. They should be in the same school district, have the same utilities, be similar in style and size and be in similar neighborhoods. Use the form to determine what, if anything, you should do to meet your targeted value. If your home is already comparable to the ones in your targeted value, remodeling won't return dollars on your investment. If, however, your home is lacking a feature that other houses in your targeted value range have (such as an updated kitchen or a finished basement), you can expect

BOTTOM LINE

In some instances, you can tap into an existing electrical circuit instead of adding (and paying for) new ones. Be sure to research the possibilities.

Seeing a return on your investment when you sell your home should be your primary objective when remodeling.

to get to get a return for the money you spend on those items.

By spending your money in the right places, you'll maximize the profit potential of your home. Let's face it: we all work hard for our money and our homes are our largest investment, so to maximize the return on this investment, we need to view it as such. Our homes serve many purposes, but none is more important than helping to secure our future. Let me give you an example of how your home is working for you right now. Let's say your home is valued at $100,000 and real estate in your area increases in value an average of 5% per year. You invested $20,000 in a down payment when you bought the home. Your $20,000 investment is growing at a rate of 5% of your home's $100,000 value. After one year, your home is worth $105,000, so you've gained $5,000 on your $20,000 investment. That's a 25% return! Now you know why so many million-

BOTTOM LINE

Kitchens and baths sell houses. You'll almost always get your money back when you invest in these two rooms.

FIGURE 12-12 An old wall-hung lavatory that is out-of-date and style.

aires invest in real estate and why smart people treat their homes as an investment. By keeping remodeling and maintenance money to a minimum, by reading and applying the information in this book, you'll get a better return when you sell.

THE PLAN AND WHY YOU NEED ONE

Remodeling is no different from anything else. It's been said countless times on countless subjects, and it's true: When you fail to plan, you plan to fail. To help you avoid failure, this chapter will help you create an intelligent plan. Such a plan will ensure that your project runs smoothly and arrives at the desired outcome, gives you the change you're looking for, and returns more money than you invested when you sell the property.

Abraham Lincoln once said, "If I had six hours to chop down a tree, I would spend the first four sharpening the axe." I believe Honest Abe was on the right track. You should spend considerable time planning — and

GLOSSARY

Targeted Value Range
The range of value you expect your home to fall in once your remodeling is done. Let's say your home is worth $100,000 now and you plan to add a master bedroom suite. Once the remodel is done, you expect your home to be worth $120,000 - $130,000. This is your targeted value range.

Feature Comparison Chart

Feature	Comp. home #1	Comp. home #2	Comp. home #3	Your Home
Siding				
Windows				
Landscaping				
Roofing				
Garage(s)				
Porches/Decks				
Kitchen				
Bathroom(s)				
Bedrooms(s)				
Basement				

FIGURE 12-14 Take this feature comparison chart with you when looking at houses that are priced similarly to your own home.

planning for — your project. By the time you're done with this chapter, you should be armed with the information you need to prepare for your remodel. When you couple that information with what you've learned from the rest of the book, you'll be able to reach the goal of completing your project for 55 percent of the national average for construction costs.

PLAN WITHIN YOUR BUDGET

Budgeting can be fun, or a nightmare, depending on your perspective. Personally, I float back and forth. On the one hand, I love designing a new project; on the other hand, I get frustrated with budgeting restraints. But when I sit down and figure out how much more I'm getting for my dollar by planning carefully and doing as much as I can myself, I'm always glad I know what I know. There's no other part-time job where I can improve my quality of life, work when and how I want, have no customers and pocket so much dough. Well, I may not be able to put the money in my pocket right away, but I know I'll get "paid" (get my money back and a whole lot more) when I sell the house. I also know that if I live in the house for two years, the money I earned will be tax free, and you can't beat that. So, if you're like me and sometimes get frustrated when you're budgeting for your project, just remember there's a pot of gold at the end of the rainbow, so to speak. To plan your budget intelligently, consider the following points.

• **Decide what you really need, then calculate the cost:** We all want beautiful homes packed with great features, but remember someone has to pay for those features: you. Rather than figuring out how much money you can afford to spend, start instead by deciding what features you genuinely need, and then cost those features out. By going this route, you'll get a home that's beautiful and functional without necessarily spending every cent you have. By keeping the remodel to what you really need, you'll help keep costs in line.

• **Multiuse rooms save money while adding features:** By giving rooms more than one task, you can cut down on the number of rooms you need. For example, you want to add on a library, guest room and office. The library and guest room will get minimal use and be needed only occasionally. Consider combining these two rooms into one — or even better,

To save money, figure out what you want in your remodeling project and then calculate the costs. Don't figure out the maximum amount you can spend and then design your project to use the full amount.

Don't add costly work by telling yourself "While I'm at it, I might as well _____." If you didn't need to do it before you planned your remodeling project, don't do it now.

all three rooms into one. By making a single room multifunctional, you'll cut square footage and save money while still fulfilling all your needs.

• **Curb the extent of the project:** If you're like most of us, your plan will grow as you develop it. It's up to you to stop this. It's so easy to think, "Well, if I'm going to do this, I might as well _____." (Fill in the blank with any number of things: Gut it down to the studs. Rip out all the electrical and start from scratch. Redo the plumbing in the whole house. Roof the whole house while we're at it.) Don't do more work than is necessary. If you didn't think it needed to be done before you began planning, don't do it now. Keep work to the minimum needed to get the results you want.

• **Work within existing parameters:** Whenever possible, work within your existing setup. Prices add up when you start moving walls, plumbing, doors and windows. By concentrating on cosmetic remodeling only, you can update fixtures, floors, doors and such without doing any structural redesigning. If you can't work within those parameters, before you decide to give in and start moving walls or fixtures, do a cost comparison between moving things and leaving them where they are; then determine if it's worth the extra money to change your structure.

Use these techniques to keep your costs down. The key is to determine what you want, then figure the most cost-effective way to get it. When you're remodeling, you have two choices if you use my techniques. First, you can save money and get more done within your budget. Second — my suggested way — you can determine what you need, and then complete your project for less and keep your saved money in your pocket or off your mortgage. Either way you win.

GREAT SOURCES FOR IDEAS AND FEEDBACK

In this section I'll highlight my favorite sources for ideas and feedback. They can help you find the perfect, affordable way to get what you want. By using these sources, my wife comes up with more ideas than I can fathom. Some are just not cost-effective enough to implement, but others are quite ingenious. She keeps a folder full of ideas, and gets it out when we begin planning a new project. Once an idea is decided upon, I rarely complete it exactly as shown in the book. I could buy ready-made

GLOSSARY

Gut
To remove everything down to the studs, including drywall and plaster. This should rarely be necessary.

GLOSSARY

Cosmetic Remodeling
Addressing surface items, the ones that show, only. Unless you have structural or mechanical problems, this type of remodeling often is all you should need.

FIGURE 12-15   A floating shelf made from a 2"x4" ledge, bullnosed shelving and crown moulding.

architectural and design features from several sources if I wanted to pay a premium. But, as I've stated, I'd much rather do the work myself for at least a 45 percent savings. For example, my wife wanted a "floating" shelf for books to line our hallway. Ready-made kits were everywhere, but they were too expensive. By buying materials at close-out prices, ripping my own brace out of 2×4s, and bullnosing the shelves myself with a router, I was able to put up 25 linear feet of shelving for $30. By using my imagination, I can almost always figure a way to get what we want, better than the ready-made alternative at the store and for half the retail price. You can too, if you'll just be a little creative. Read on for sources of inspiration and feedback when designing your project.

• **Internet:** The World Wide Web is full of free ideas for remodeling and construction. If you go to any major search engine and type in what you're looking for, you'll have thousands of sites to look at. I love this source because a picture is worth a thousand words. You can usually find a picture of what you want to do because someone has already done it.

Salespeople are a valuable resource when planning a project. Seek out their advice on products and their applications.

BOTTOM LINE
The Internet is a great free resource for ideas and information on remodeling and construction. Use it to your maximum benefit.

This visual aid is invaluable when planning. It's a great thing to actually see a completed project (or portions thereof) in a picture, to be able to check out what that flooring, window, cabinet or bathroom will look like. I equate it to a dressing room for your home. You can "try on" new looks without actually installing them, and you can do it from the comfort of your own home.

• **Sales desk:** The salespeople at these desks can be a great help to you. They have literature on the products you want to use and can offer application ideas. By describing to them what you plan to do, they can make suggestions and point out potential pitfalls. Their job is to help you determine what products you need, and then provide those products for you. Make them do their job. They can also offer some advice for installation, including the tools you'll need for the job.

• **Subcontractor:** Subcontractors can be a valuable source for information and feedback. For instance, if you're hiring electrical or plumbing subs, they not only can give you free estimates for their services, but they can inform you of code requirements and any necessary upgrades. They can also make suggestions in the planning stages to help you design your project more efficiently. When you call to set up a bid meeting, let the subcontractor know you're in the planning stages and will be open to suggestions. Have a good idea of what you want to accomplish and explain this to the subcontractor during the bid meeting. Don't be afraid to ask questions. Make a list of them before the potential sub shows up for the bid and check them off as they get answered.

• **Public library:** I love libraries. They have tons of books with immense amounts of information and it's all free! Whenever I start researching something, I'm sure to hit the library. Many good books have been written about construction and decorating, and your local library is sure to have some of them. They also have periodicals for you to peruse. Most of the books available are somewhat dated, but they still contain great information.

• **Showrooms:** Check the displays and showrooms of local suppliers and specialty stores. This allows you to see actual products up close, touch them and examine them in sample applications. It also gives you the chance to compare similar products side by side so you can discover any differences. A showroom check can often verify that the brand-

Your local library is a great source for free information and ideas. It's loaded with books and magazines for you to peruse.

GLOSSARY

Bid Meeting
A meeting between you and a potential contractor where you discuss the job you want him to provide an estimate for.

GLOSSARY

Subcontractor (or Sub)
A contractor who specializes in one field or is handling only one portion of your project. For example, you may hire a sub just for the electrical work.

FIGURE 12-16   The section of my local library with hundreds of books on construction and remodeling.

name product, once installed and stripped of its name, looks and performs no better than the not-as-well-known competitor's less-expensive product.

• **Factory representatives:** If you need in-depth information on a product and its applications, contact the factory. No one is more knowledgeable or up-to-date. Factory reps can also let you know of the latest products coming down the pike. Moreover, the factory may make and stock products that fit your particular application better than what the store stocks. For example, Menards stocks CPI Plumbing's radiant heat panel RHP-1. This is a good panel that I've installed before. However, the factory has a simpler model that sells for less, but the store doesn't stock it. When this panel fits the application at hand, I can order it through the store and save money.

Use these sources to spark your imagination and come up with the perfect features for your remodeling project. Then get the feedback you need to make sure what you want to do is not only feasible, but practical as well. Don't be afraid to get creative. If you're unsure how something will look, or work, do a test run. My wife uses a wall in our furnace room to try out various painting techniques. It looks like a patchwork quilt. But by testing her ideas on a small scale, she can visualize the actual application to see if she likes it before doing a whole wall.

MAP OUT YOUR PROJECT

Now that you've got your ideas together for your remodeling project, it's time to actually design it. This process can vary greatly from a simple bathroom makeover to a two-room addition. How deep you need to go depends on your project. Most remodeling projects aren't going to require blueprints. Most can be handled with a simple hand-drawn layout of what goes where. I'm going to give you some pointers on what to include and some suggestions for getting everything just so. I'm a big believer in the K.I.S.S. method (Keep It Simple, Stupid). Many more costly mistakes have been made by people who try to overthink and overprotect everything than by people who simply get a decent plan together and then follow through with it. Don't worry if you don't have all the answers yet; they will come as your plan develops. Now's the time to move from general ideas to more specific terms and conditions. Things tend to come together and start making more sense when you start putting them on paper. You may find that you can implement many of your original ideas, while others begin to look impractical. The key here is to get specific so you can develop a plan to get you from this conception stage to completion. Follow these steps to get a workable plan.

BOTTOM LINE

The showroom is a great place to see that the non-name-brand product, once installed, looks and performs like the name brand for as little as half the cost.

Broderbund's 3D Home Architect is a great inexpensive CAD program. It is very user-friendly and easy to learn. Your local library may even have a copy so you can try it out for free.

GLOSSARY

Scale

Proportionate in size. A scale drawing is an exact representation of what the final product will be, only a lot smaller. A common scale is $\frac{1}{4}$" = 1', meaning a quarter inch on the drawing represents a foot on the finished product. Thus if something measures 4" on the drawing, it will be 16' when finished (4 ÷ 14 = 16).

• **Scale it out, inside:** It's always a good idea to draw your project out to scale, no matter how simple it is. If you don't have a computer program (such as 3D Home Architect) or drafting equipment, this can be done for simple projects with a piece of typing paper and a ruler (see Figure 12-17). A common scale is $\frac{1}{4}$" = 1'. This drawing doesn't have to be fancy to serve its purpose. The whole goal is to ensure that your fixtures and furniture will fit into your new (or newly redefined) space and that there will be sufficient room to satisfy your needs. Be sure to include cabinets, sinks, toilets, furniture, etc. in your layout. The time to make sure everything fits is now, not later.

• **Scale it out, outside:** If you're doing any work outside the house, make a scale drawing of this too. This is very important if you're landscaping, adding on space or adding architectural features to your house.

BOTTOM LINE

Avoid costly utility problems by calling your local underground utilities locator service (such as JULIE). The number for this free service is in your local phone book.

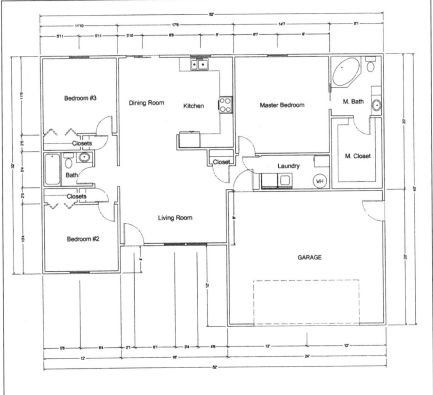

FIGURE 12-17 A ranch floor plan I designed using Broderbund's 3D Home Architect.

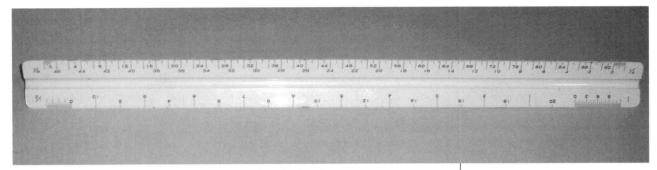

FIGURE 12-18 A scale ruler I use when I drafting by hand.

When you're drawing this out, don't forget to look up. Overhead power, phone or cable lines can get in the way. You also have to consider what's underground as well. Don't forget to call your local underground utilities locator service before doing any digging.

With your design drawing in hand, you're ready to move forward. You can begin pricing material and getting bids for the work you plan to sub-contract out. By adding all these prices together, you'll know whether your project will fall within your desired budget. If your initial figures come in over budget — which happens often — you'll have to consider what needs to be done to arrive at your goal. Before you decide to scrap your project, finish reading the book. You may learn ways to save enough money to make your project work within your budget.

YOUR ROAD MAP TO SUCCESS

I said it before and I'm going to say it again: *When you fail to plan, you plan to fail.* This section will help you take all your ideas and put them into a working plan. This plan will be your road map to success. Don't get scared if you don't have everything perfect yet, you're not supposed to. Your plan will change a little, and maybe a lot, along the way. An ancient Chinese proverb says that a journey of a thousand miles begins with one step, and remodeling is no different. By getting your ideas together, and generating a starting point, you're getting off to a good start. And, if you'll move forward a little every day, eventually you'll arrive at your destination. Follow these steps to generate your map.

• **Brainstorm:** Get out a pad of paper and start writing down what you know you need to do. Don't worry about order or how trivial you think something is. Don't tell yourself, "Oh I won't forget that!" and then not write it down. Write down *everything*. Don't forget little items such as moving furniture, sealing off work areas, obtaining permits, getting bids, measuring, contacting the utilities locator service, providing power for workers and so forth. I always try to start at the beginning and work my

GLOSSARY

Underground Utilities Locator Service
The service provided by local utilities that locates under-ground utility lines before you do any digging. In my area the service is called JULIE, and you're required by law to call at least two days, but no more than fourteen days, prior to any digging.

way through the whole process, but I write down whatever I think of as soon as I think of it. It also helps to look around at a finished room to remind you of things that need to be done. A checklist like the well-used one in Figure 12-19 will not only help you estimate costs, but also help you to remember things that need to be handled.

• **Step by step:** Now that you've brainstormed and written everything down, rearrange the list into chronological order. For example, your mechanical work should follow this order: HVAC, plumbing, then electrical. You'll save headaches, subcontractor conflicts and possibly money by scheduling correctly.

Now you have a step-by-step outline for your project. Use this to estimate cost. By estimating each item on your list, you'll have a very good idea of what your bottom line will be. Once you get this in line with your budget, you should be just about ready to start. For the additional information you'll need for assessing the value of materials and furnishings, I refer you to chapters three and thirteen. Whether you're building new or remodeling, your thought process should be the same: always ask, "Will spending extra money increase the bottom-line value of the house?"

1	2	3	4	5	6	7
Name and Address	Kind of Work	Amount of Contract	Retention (incl Current)	Net of Previous Payments	Net Amount This Payment	Balance to Become Due (incl. Ret.)
Pinkston	Footings, Foundation	5,000 $18,995.00	4.7	2500		
Sims	Lumber	$28,600.00	27	20K		
	Drywall	$6,100.00	5.8	5.5K	materials + Fixtures	
Closs Electric	Electric	$5,640.00	5.3	2K		
Design Air	HVAC	$5,980.00	5.7	5K	5K plumber 3K Fixtures	3.8
Burdick	Plumbing	$9,800.00	9.3	8K — 5K		
Interior Comfort	Insulation	$1,657.00	1.5	1.7		
C&A Custom Kitchens	Cabinets - Allowance Material and Labor	$4,950.00	1.9	2K	Kit. only	
Flooring Depot	Flooring - Allowance Material and Labor	$3,200.00	3	3K		
Allowance	Lights	$800.00	.7	—		
	Painting	$2,200.00	2	.8K		
Allowance	Appliances	$1,700.00	1.6	—		
North East Construction	Labor	$12,010.00	11			
By Owner	Permit	1,000 $0.00	.9	1K		
Illinois Power/By Owner	Gas/Electric Hookup	1,000 $0.00	.9	1K		
North East Construction	Layout/Administrative	$500.00	.45	—		
Landscaping/By Owner	Allowance Labor and Material	800. $0.00	.7	.8K		
Fireplace	Allowance Labor and Material	$1,375.00	1.3	?		
North East Construction	Profit & Overhead-5%	$5,650.00	5.3			
Contingency-%5		$5,380.00	5.2			
Burdick	Spetic System	2500 $4,300.00	7.3	2.5K		
TOTAL		$118,837.00	96.55	55.8		

104,842

2K crete
.5K Gutt
.3K OH. Doors   NO BACK Fill
60K   NO Insurance

FIGURE 12-19 A well-used general price breakdown sheet helps me figure costs accurately.

BUILDING MATERIAL CHECKLISTS FOR HOUSES

Wall, Stoop and Post Footings
- [ ] ReRods - OSP x number of rods
- [ ] Drain pipe and fittings - OSP + fittings
- [ ] Crushed stone
- [ ] Concrete - Length x width x depth (in feet) = cubic feet divided by 27 = cubic yards

Basement and Stoop Walls
- [ ] Basement windows
- [ ] Area walls

CONCRETE BLOCK
- [ ] Concrete blocks
- [ ] Glass blocks
- [ ] Mortar cement
- [ ] Mortar sand
- [ ] Block reinforcing
- [ ] Portland cement (parg.)
- [ ] Mortar sand
- [ ] Foundation coating
- [ ] Anchor bolts
- [ ] Styrofoam
- [ ] Foundation vents

POURED CONCRETE
- [ ] Form material
- [ ] Form tiles
- [ ] Form oil
- [ ] ReRods
- [ ] Concrete
- [ ] Foundation coating
- [ ] Anchor bolts
- [ ] Styrofoam
- [ ] Foundation vents

PERMANENT WOOD FOUNDATION
- [ ] Pea rock
- [ ] Footing plate
- [ ] Bottom plate
- [ ] Screed board
- [ ] Studs
- [ ] Top plate
- [ ] Tie plate
- [ ] Plywood sheathing
- [ ] Caulking
- [ ] Adhesive
- [ ] Wood strip protector
- [ ] 6M poly
- [ ] Blocking
- [ ] Joist hangers
- [ ] Framing anchors
- [ ] Insulation
- [ ] Interior finish
- [ ] Nails

Basement Floor
- [ ] Expansion joint
- [ ] Pit run fill
- [ ] Poly
- [ ] Reinforcing mesh
- [ ] Concrete
- [ ] Plinth blocks
- [ ] Concrete blocks (curb)

Concrete Stoop
- [ ] ReRods
- [ ] Reinforcing mesh
- [ ] Fill
- [ ] Concrete

Masonry (Brick or Stone Veneer)
- [ ] Brick
- [ ] Stone
- [ ] Mortar cement
- [ ] Mortar sand
- [ ] Lintels
- [ ] Brick tiles

FIGURE 12-20   A multi-paged, very detailed, checklist I use when I figure material lists.

LOAD 1

Basement Framing
- [ ] Posts - Count from basement plan
- [ ] Girders - See "How To Find"
- [ ] Bottom plates (treated)
- [ ] Upper plates
- [ ] Studs - Use "long way" method

Basement Stairs
- [ ] Stair horse (Stringer) 12" length for 7' - 2" ceiling height; 14' for 8'
- [ ] Treads - One less than riser quantity
- [ ] Risers* - See note on floor or basement plan
- [ ] Handrail* - Same length as stair horse
- [ ] Handrail brackets* - Two up to 6' ; Three up to 12'
- [ ] Landing materials

* Items not delivered until millwork load

Floor Framing
- [ ] Sill sealer - Use O.S.P.
- [ ] Sill plate - Use O.S.P.
- [ ] Floor joists
- [ ] (Headers)
- [ ] (Trimmers)
- [ ] Box/Band joist - Across "end" of joists
- [ ] Bridging
- [ ] Joist hangers
- [ ] Subfloor - Floor area or floor area minus opening + 5% waste
- [ ] Adhesive - See manufacturer's literature for coverage
- [ ] Nails
- [ ] Termite shield

"LONG WAY" FOR STUDS
- [ ] Multiply length x spacing factor (Table 4).
- [ ] Add one starter for each new wall.
- [ ] Add three per O.S. corner.
- [ ] Add three per opening (doorways, windows, etc.)
- [ ] Add two per intersection.

LOAD 2

Wall Framing
- [ ] Sole and top plates - LFT walls x 3 (+ 1/3)
- [ ] Studs - LFT x 1.1 (16" o/c)
- [ ] Headers - Add 1" to RO, round up
- [ ] Pocket door frames - Count
- [ ] Wall sheathing
- [ ] Corner bracing - If required, two per corner
- [ ] Nails

If Attached Garage
64a. Garage plates
65a. Garage studs

LOAD 3

Roof Framing

TRUSS CONSTRUCTION

☐ Trusses - Spacing factor minus 1
(for each side)
☐ Gable end assemblies
☐ Ladder rake assemblies
☐ Truss bracing - See manufacturer's literature
☐ Ladder rake materials
☐ Fly rafters

CONVENTIONAL CONSTRUCTION

☐ Ceiling joist - Spacing factor + 1
☐ Built-up ceiling girder - Figure 4-4
☐ Joist hangers
☐ Strong back - Figure 4-4
☐ Gable end studs
☐ Common rafters
☐ Hip rafters
☐ Valley rafters
☐ Bracing
☐ Collar ties - Figure 4-4
☐ Garage ties
☐ Ridge board

☐ Nailer (parallel partitions) - Use vertical ISP
☐ Roof sheathing - Roof area + 5%
☐ "H" clips
☐ Nails

LOAD 4

☐ Sub facia - Length of eaves
☐ Facia - Length of eaves + 2' per length
☐ Rake - Same length as rafter (goes up gable end)
☐ Aluminum, vinyl or steel system accessories
☐ Roof edge - Add up eave and rake
☐ Gutter apron
☐ Lookouts - Width of overhang x number of rafters using
☐ Lookout nailer - LFT along house
☐ Soffit - Both eaves and rake square feet
☐ Cove
☐ Soffit louvers - Count or figure (see section 2)
☐ Gable end louvers - Count or figure (see section 2)
☐ Roof vents - Count or figure (see section 2)
☐ Starter roll - If used, along eaves (33'/roll)
☐ 15# felt - Divide roof area by 400 (round up)
☐ Staples
☐ Lap cement
☐ Shingles + ridge and hip cap
☐ Valley tin/Flashing
☐ Tin shingles
☐ Plastic cement
☐ Nails

☐ Siding
☐ Starter
☐ Undersill trim
☐ OS Corner
☐ S Corner
☐ J Channel
☐ Miscellaneous

LOAD 5

Windows & Exterior
- [ ] Windows (drip cap, exterior jambs, extras)
- [ ] Combination storm windows
- [ ] Exterior door frames
- [ ] Exterior pre-hung units
- [ ] Patio/sliding doors
- [ ] Siding - 8' OS wall area + gable end minus 30 square foot openings + factor table 10
- [ ] Siding corners and dividers (same amount of each)
- [ ] Caulking - one carton
- [ ] Siding nailer for vertical siding
- [ ] Tyvek/15# felt
- [ ] Wood lath/siding starter
- [ ] Aluminum, steel, vinyl siding and accessories
- [ ] Flashing
- [ ] Garage door frame
- [ ] Garage door stop
- [ ] Garage door o.s. casing
- [ ] Nails

- [ ] J Channel
- [ ] F Channel
- [ ] Soffit-Plain
- [ ] Soffit-Vented
- [ ] Facia
- [ ] Miscellaneous

LOAD 6

Insulation
- [ ] Wall insulation - 8' OS wall area
- [ ] Ceiling insulation - floor area
- [ ] Floor insulation
- [ ] Rim joist insulation - Usually enough with walls
- [ ] Proper vents/air chutes
- [ ] Poly film/vapor barrier
- [ ] Staples
- [ ] Foam cans/canisters

STRUCTURAL VERSUS COSMETIC REMODELING

GLOSSARY

Cosmetic Remodeling

Light remodeling that includes only visible items such as paint, fixtures, trim, doors and floor coverings.

GLOSSARY

Structural Remodeling

Intensive remodeling that involves removal or addition of structural components, including framing, drywall, plaster, plumbing or electrical systems.

Unless you have had a flood, have structural problems, mechanical problems or just can't get what you want otherwise, I don't recommend structural remodeling. I use the old adage, "If it ain't broke, don't fix it." I even go further and try to repair what's broke while disturbing other items as little as possible. I've seen too many novices get into trouble by jumping in and ripping out walls, plaster, drywall, cabinets, wiring and plumbing, only to find themselves in over their head — both financially as well as figuratively. Before you decide to gut the area for your remodeling project, read the following points to see if they'll work for you. They may save you time, work and money.

- **Cracked walls and ceilings:** If your walls or ceilings are cracked, here are three possibilities you should consider before gutting the room: 1) *Patch the cracks only*. Remove the loose material, tape and patch the cracks. 2) *Skim coat the entire damaged area to smooth it out*. Remove the loose material, tape the cracks, and put a thin layer of patching compound over the entire area. 3) *Cover the wall with $1/4"$ drywall and finish normally*. Any of these methods would be easier and less expensive than demolition.

- **Refinish your old wood floors:** Many homes have nice wood floors that have been covered up by carpet. If you're in this situation and want to update your floor coverings, consider removing the old carpet and refinishing the floors. Some people pay a premium for wood floors. It's a shame that so many of the older wood floors have been covered. By salvaging yours, you can save a bundle over new flooring.

FIGURE 13-1   A beautiful wood floor that was once covered with carpet. This floor was refinished by the owner.

• **Cabinet refacing:** By refacing your cabinets instead of ordering completely new ones, you can save time and money. There are many companies that offer this service, although it is a task that can be handled by many homeowners for much less than the cost of paying to have it done. The process isn't nearly as difficult as building new cabinets from scratch. You can purchase or order ready-made cabinet doors and drawer fronts from most large home centers and building supply stores, which will make the job much easier. New facings can be made from wooden laminate or $\frac{1}{4}$" plywood. With a little research about the process, you can get the kitchen look you've always dreamed of without paying for a custom kitchen.

• **A glove for your tub:** Instead of ripping out and replacing your old worn-out tub, have it lined with a new one. Companies such as Illinois Re-Bath can install a bathtub liner in less than a day, and they'll install it for a fraction of the cost of replacing your existing

BOTTOM LINE

If you have wood flooring under your old carpet, remove the carpet and refinish the wood. If you do this yourself, instead of buying carpet and paying for installation, you'll get a beautiful floor and save a bunch of money.

Cabinet Refacing
Giving your cabinets a "face lift" by replacing the doors, rails and drawer fronts of your existing cabinets.

tub with a new unit. By sleeving your old unit with a new liner, you get a new tub without having the expense and trouble of getting rid of the old one. This is the same concept as cabinet refacing. By using the existing structure and simply covering it with a pretty new surface, you can save a ton of time and materials — and saving time and materials will always save you money.

- **Convert a tub to a shower for less:** Suppose you want or need to convert an existing tub to a shower, but there's a window right above the tub. You could remove the window, frame in the opening, struggle to make the filled-in hole match the interior and exterior surfaces of your home, then open up the wall to install the new plumbing for your shower — or you could do it my way. I suggest you leave the

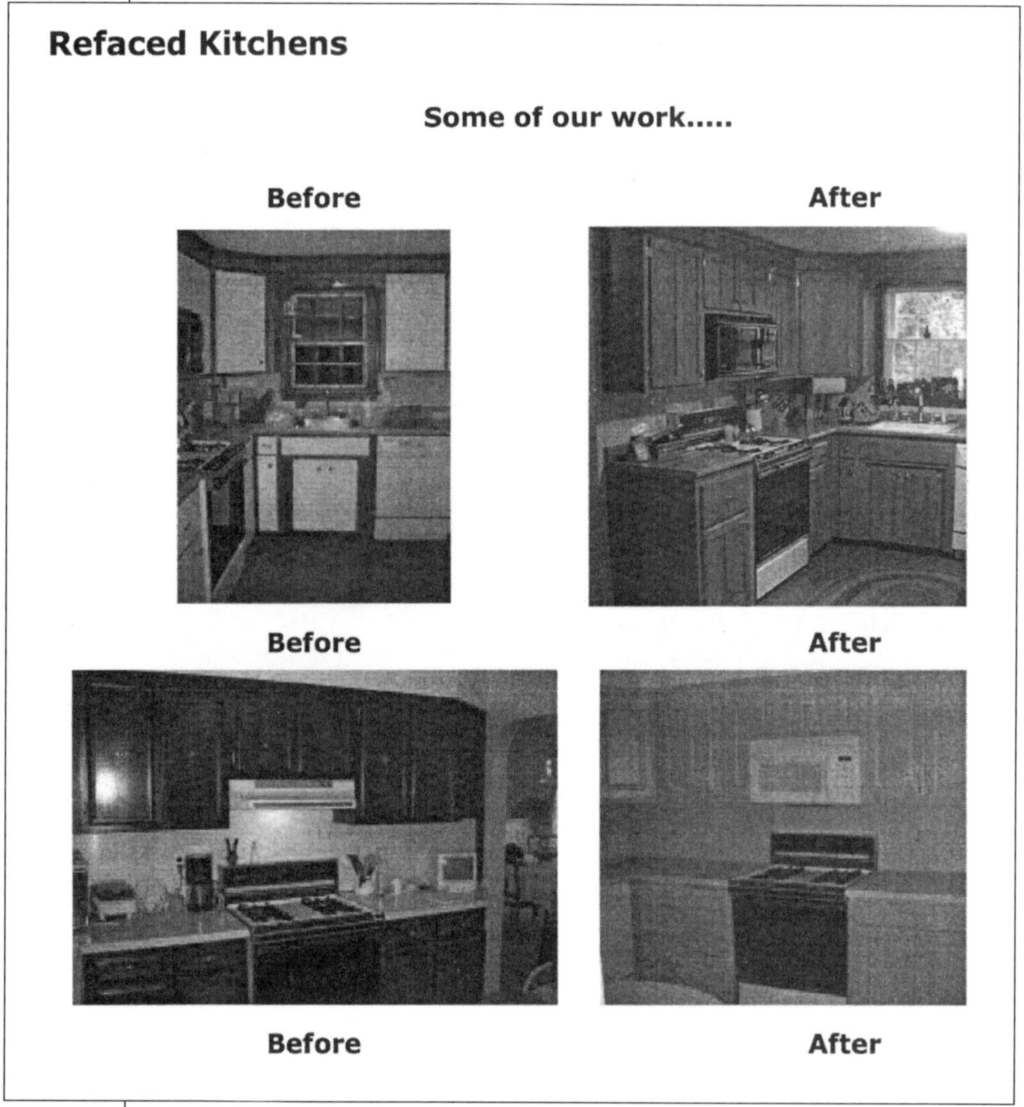

FIGURE 13-2 Before and after pictures of a cabinet refacing job. Courtesy of Concept One Remodeling, www.concept1Remodeling.com, 866-720-5200.

Relax, Re-Bath Has You Covered!

Quality That Spans Three Decades

State-of-the-art manufacturing and over 750 bathtub molds make Re-Bath number one.

"Put A New Bathtub Over Your Old One"™

Professional installation of your new Bathtub will be completed in a matter of hours.

Wall Surround Installation Is Quick and Clean

Your lustrous Wall Surround System is professionally installed in less than one day.

FIGURE 13-3 A brochure that shows how a new tub sleeve can be fit over your existing tub. Courtesy of Re-Bath Inc., www.re-bath.com.

FIGURE 13-4 An installed tub diverter and circular shower curtain rod.

window alone, install a diverter spout on the tub with a surface-mount pipe, and hang a circular shower curtain rod. By eliminating the structural work of removing the window and installing plumbing lines behind the wall, you'll save a ton of time and materials, and therefore, money. (See Figure 13-4 to see a diverter and circular curtain rod installed in a home.)

- **Floor over floor:** If your vinyl floors have seen better days, consider installing a new layer over the old one using embossing floor leveler. By smoothing and leveling the old surface, you can lay new vinyl right over the old flooring instead of having to remove it.
- **Don't get talked into it now:** Stick to your plans. Don't get talked into doing it now while you're building because it's easier. You know how you live and what you need, and you designed your addition around this and the code. There are times when thinking ahead can save you some trouble down the line, but in general I don't build for

"I might's". For example, "I might buy that welder someday, and I'll need a circuit for it", or "Eventually, I might want to put a ceiling fan there", or "I might as well do it now while the wall is open". In my experience, most of these "I might's" just don't happen. Circuits can and do get added to existing houses everyday. It may not be as easy as adding a circuit to a new one while it's being built, but it isn't impossible either. Save your money now, and if an "I might" arises, that you want bad enough, you can still get it when the time comes.

- **If you must add to your HVAC system, skip the "super" heating and cooling units:** Geothermal, heat pumps and high efficiency furnaces are all great things, but skip them if the return isn't there. When you can see on paper, calculated for your specific example, where you'll get your money back, please use these devices. However, in my experience, I can't get the numbers to work in my favor. The biggest reason for this is I don't plan on building a "final" house anytime soon. I haven't settled in a house for more than four years and I always plan to move every 2-4 years, at least for the near future. When I build a home my family will stay in for the long haul, I'll seriously consider such a heating system. But for now, I know that my dollars in won't equal dollars out. However, if you can show where you'll save money over the long haul, definitely use the more energy efficient systems.

Follow the previous guidelines to keep your addition to code. Decide for yourself when/if the time to go over and beyond what's required arises. Never forget that you should only go over for two reasons; 1) a practical use specific to you or your family, or 2) when a dollar in will result in more than a dollar out. When in doubt get another opinion, take it with a grain of salt, and then decide what's best for you.

COMMON TRAPS TO AVOID

There are several very common traps that have cost remodelers countless dollars. They're very easy to get snared in. They seductively pull you in with their siren song or they're so sneaky that you don't even know you've been caught. But the key to avoiding the snare is the same as it is with any trap. You must know where it is and have an alternate route to get around it. Sounds simple enough, and it is, but it's also one of those things that's so easy to forget. To arm yourself against these money wasters, read this

GLOSSARY

Geothermal heating
A very efficient water-based heating system that circulates water through the earth or a pond to transfer heat and cold.

Figure your return on investment before spending extra money unnecessarily.

chapter very carefully. Commit the words to memory and review Figure 4-4 in chapter four often. Copy it, or tear it out, and keep it with you. If you read it before making decisions, it'll save you from the money pits that are out there.

- **I'm spending thirty grand on this remodel, what's an extra thousand?** If these words ever escape your mouth, one of us has failed. I've heard it time and time again from homeowners and contractors. When money ceases to be important to you, it will flee from you. This happens when you look at bids; "Honey, Uncle Joe's plumber is only a thousand dollars higher than this other company and Uncle Joe really likes his guy." It happens when you're shopping for materials; "Jim's Lumber Yard was only a thousand dollars higher on their lumber package, and they're so much more personal than the super store." It happens all the time and people are spending thousands upon thousands of dollars unnecessarily. I'm not saying I haven't ever went with a higher bid, because I have. But when I do, you can bet there's a darn good reason and that it doesn't happen often.

- **You can't remodel your house without _____!** Now fill in the blank. If the item you filled in isn't required by the code, you don't have to have it. You may think you do, and that's alright, but when you're installing it because everyone else says you have to, you're wrong. I've heard all kinds of statements to this effect; "When you're spending the money to remodel your house, you might as well go ahead and add the three car garage. You can hardly sell a house without one anymore." and "When I redid my kitchen, I just went ahead and ordered the custom cabinets. You just have to have a John Doe kitchen to sell a home in this market." and "If I was ever going to remodel my home, I'd install a skylight in every room, they're all the rage these days." Now, if you really want, or need, a particular item, and it's in your budget, by all means put it in. Just don't let keeping up with the Jones's separate you from your hard earned cash. Remember, your goal is to remodel for 55 cents on the dollar, so hold tight to your money.

- **If I'm going to install the siding on the house, I have to have a new saw!** This one's tough, especially for us guys. We love the chance to get a new tool, and the cooler the tool, the harder it is to resist. If we wire an addition, we need new wire strippers, if we install a new furnace, we need a new tap and die set for the pipe and if we plumb the new bathroom, we have to have that right angle drill. There are countless tools and gadgets out there to make working on a house easier. Some of them are absolutely necessary and absolutely expen-

BOTTOM LINE

For every $1,000 borrowed, you'll repay $2,394 on a 7% loan amortized over thirty years.

sive. Try everything possible to avoid the trap of buying every tool you'll need. Tools can be borrowed, rented or leased. So, if you can't pay for the tool on this job, meaning it'll cost you more to rent it than to buy it, consider an alternative. Just don't consider the cost, remember you have to store it after you're done with it. If you buy all the tools you need to complete your remodel, not only will you go broke, but you'll have to park your car outside because the garage will be full of your tools.

- **I saved $500 on the demolition and clean up, so I can spend an extra $500 on windows.** Wrong! Your entire budget will work because the ups hopefully match the downs. For every item you bring in under budget, there'll be one that comes in over budget. It's a constant battle to keep your costs down. You'll win some battles, lose others, and hopefully in the end you come out where you wanted to be. For example, on the last house I built, I had spec'd the concrete at around $2 a square foot. I can usually get it done for this and even had a guy on the line at this price; plus I had a back up if he failed. Everything's fine and dandy until it comes time to pour. I call guy #1 two weeks before I'm going to be ready for him (I always try and give my subs as much notice as possible) and he crawfishes on me. OK, on to guy #2 who just hurt his back and will be down for at least six weeks. So I end up paying over $3 a foot for it. For the happy ending, I hadn't spent saved dollars from other portions of the project and the whole thing came in on budget. If I had blown the saved money when I first had it, I would've blown the *whole* budget.

- **Skip the last minute changes:** You'll lie awake at night wandering if you should move the kitchen wall over 6". You can't sleep. How can you live with the kitchen if you don't move that wall? Don't laugh. This happens all the time. It usually starts with the statement "I've been thinking". Let me tell you to do your thinking when you're planning your project. Don't start rearranging walls once you've started. This takes materials, labor and time. All of which cost money. You're going to make a couple of mistakes, some of which may include moving that wall at the last minute, but don't drive yourself crazy with them. Most people would change something about their house if they could, and that's why people remodel. And I know that any project I design just gets my house closer to the dream of the perfect house. But don't beat yourself up over getting it perfect. Once you're done, you'll love the results and you'll be a lot happier if you don't lie awake at night wandering whether you're doing everything perfect.

FIGURE 13-5 A right angle drill commonly used by plumbers and electricians.

BOTTOM LINE

The bottom line is usually more like the bottom hilly road; full of ups and downs. This price goes up while this other one comes down. The idea is to maintain the average so your project comes in on budget.

- **It's only $50 more for the better one:** Everyone will try and get you to spend your money on the "better" one. Or the better grade or the thicker this or the faster that, don't let them talk you into it. Stick to what you've spec'd the item out at. It's real easy to think it's OK to spend a few dollars on the "better" one. Don't do it. There's always a "better" grade, it doesn't mean you have to have it or that the lower grade is not any good. Think about it this way; A Chevy is a fine car, but a Cadillac is better, but a Lamborghini is better than the Cadillac, and so on. The point is that a Chevy is still a fine car even though there is a "better" one, and most entry level materials are the same. The big factor is usually warranty. Many times the less expensive line has the same warranty as the "better" one, and sometimes the cost difference outweighs any longer warranty you may get with the upgrade.

If the entry level product has a lifetime warrantee, why upgrade? Good examples are vinyl siding and faucets.

To keep your dollars, stay close to them. Don't let someone get to you with terms like tightwad or miser, you should wear those badges with pride. Let them have a little laugh at your expense, you'll be the one laughing all the way to the bank when your house payment is half of theirs. Then, when you're packing your bags for that week long trip in Cancun, and they ask you "How in the world can you afford a trip like that?" You can reply with a sly smile, "Oh, I don't know, maybe I'm just a little miserly."

BOTTOM LINE

Some warranties simply aren't worth it. For example, you can buy a toilet for $44 that comes with a 1 year warrantee. You can buy a different toilet for $99 that comes with a 5 year warrantee. The replacement parts to rebuild a toilet, if it fails, cost about $8. So the "cheap" toilet would have to fail almost twice a year, every year, for the four year difference in warranties, before you lose money.

END OF CHAPTER CHECKLIST

1. Don't upsize framing from what the code book or the span charts tell you to use.

2. Use the rated sheathing.

3. Don't add extras once you start.

4. Skip the super systems and the upgrades.

5. Every $ you spend can cost you $2.40 over the life of your loan, so save every $2.40 you can.

6. Don't listen to the family, neighbors, subs or anyone else when they try to get you to spend extra money.

7. Don't buy that new tool unless you can't do the job without it. Then see if you can borrow it or rent it for less.

8. If you've saved on part A, don't blow your savings on part B. You may need it for part C.

9. Don't buy the upgrade without very good reason.

10. Hold tight to your money, or it will flee from you!

FIGURE 13-6   Pull out or copy Figure 13-6 and keep it with you when you go shopping or make decisions on what to put where. Read the advice, and keep it at the top of your mind when deciding where to invest your money. Remember, a lifetime warranty is as long as you'll get or ever need.

RECOMMENDED WEBSITES, PERIODICALS AND OTHER RESOURCES

I try to have all of my automotive mechanical work done by friends who have the proper skills. Not only does this save me money, but I trust my friends. I know very little about automobiles and have no desire to learn more. If I were to have my work done by someone I don't know, I would be taking a large risk because I'd have no way of knowing whether they're being honest with me or taking me to the cleaners. When you're hiring a contractor to do construction work for you, if you know nothing about construction, you're in the same boat as I am with vehicles. It's a good idea to at least know the basics. If you have no experience you'll have to obtain your information from other sources. These are my favorites; they offer basic, in-depth information about construction.

CONSTRUCTION INFORMATION IN YOUR LOCAL LIBRARY

I love using the library in my community. It has lots and lots of books with a wealth of information and it's all *free*! When compared to the Decatur Public Library, however, my local library is pretty small. By using a reciprocal card, I can access the larger library even though I don't live within the required boundaries for membership. I also have a reciprocal card at the Illinois State Library in Springfield, Illinois. When you need access to more materials, contact your local library to find out how to use the resources of other libraries. If you don't know where your local library is or wish to find a larger one in your area, use this link:

www.publiclibraries.com
> This Web site has links to libraries by state. It also has links to:
> University and college libraries
> Presidential libraries
> Library of Congress
> National Library of Medicine
> National Archives and Records Office
> National libraries in many foreign countries.

The Journal of Light Construction

This is a great magazine filled with excellent articles about construction materials and practices. The information is presented in useful and applicable ways. It is a great way to stay up-to-date on new materials and new application standards. The only drawback I see for homeowners is that nonprofessionals are charged a higher subscription rate. At the time of this writing, an annual subscription for a professional was $39.95; the rate for a nonprofessional was $59.95. For subscription information, or to learn more about this magazine, write to:

The Journal of Light Construction
186 Allen Brook Lane
Williston, VT 05495
Web site: **www.jlconline.com**

This Old House

While I like the television show that airs on PBS, I'm talking more specifically about the Web site: **www.thisoldhouse.com.**

The site has a "Homeowner Knowhow" link that is full of useful tips for you to ingest. There are articles on everything from glazing a window to hanging a flower box. By researching your proposed projects, you can gain the information you need to make informed decisions.

INTERNET SEARCH ENGINES

By using search engines such as Yahoo or Google you can find information on just about anything. The amount of information that can be had for free on the Internet never ceases to amaze me. What used to mean hours of poring over printed material can now be done in seconds by your computer. Simply type in a few key words, and you're off and running.

INSPIRATIONAL RESOURCES

As discussed in chapter eleven, a positive mindset is critical in allowing you to reach your goals, both in construction and in life. I hope these resources help you as much as they've helped me.

Early To Rise (ETR)

This is a daily newsletter I get by e-mail. Its main goal is to provide information on health and wealth, pertaining to both your professional and your personal life. It takes a few minutes each morning to read, but I believe it is well worth it. The people who produce ETR also produce other daily newsletters that you can subscribe to. For more information, contact

www.earlytorise.com/SuccessPartnership.htm
    If you have trouble with the site, write:
        Order Processing Center
        Attn: Customer Service
        P.O. Box 925
        Frederick, MD 21705

MyDailyInsights.com

I get a daily "insight" and a weekly "eMeditation" from here. The daily insight is an inspiring quote and takes about twenty seconds to open and read. Whenever I get a quote that really strikes me, from here or another source, I print it out and put it up on my office wall. (At present, I have eight posted. I would probably have more, but I'm running out of room.) The e-meditation is several pages of information on the successful mind-set that comes once a week. Some of these are really great and I'll read every word; with others I'll just scan the highlights. For more information go to:

www.AsAManThinketh.net
    If you have trouble with the link, write:
        MyDailyInsights.com LLC
        P.O. Box 2087
        St. Augustine, FL 32085

I highly recommend reading the free downloadable version of James Allen's classic book, *As A Man Thinketh*. For me, it was one of the best 30 minutes I've spent doing something for myself.

Success.com

I get a daily quote and a daily "powerword" from **www.success.com**. It takes about twenty seconds to open and read. Several of the quotes I've received from here are on my walls. For more information click on the newsletters link. If you have trouble with the connection, write:

Success.com
P.O. Box 5015
North Muskegon, MI 49445

MORE SAMPLE FLOOR PLANS

n this appendix you'll find ten sample floor plans, each with a brief description and some thoughts about the plan in general. By reviewing the plans, you'll start to get a feel for what's possible in a new home or an addition, and see some typical design features. Evaluate the way you use your existing home, and then try to envision how your lifestyle would fit in to a new one.

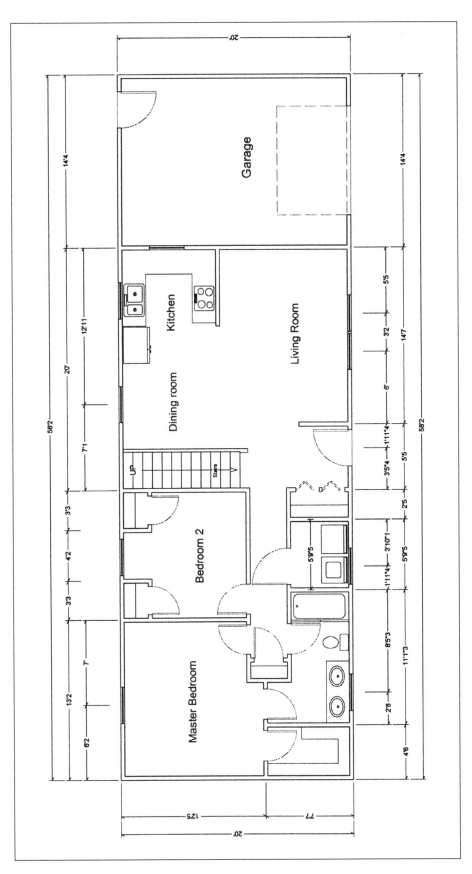

FIGURE APPENDIX B-1
Floor plan for the 880-square-foot ranch home.

FIGURE APPENDIX B-2   The false gable over my garage.

880-SQUARE-FOOT RANCH

This is a minute little plan reminiscent of the designs of the late 1960s and 1970s. If you're looking for a very inexpensive house to build, or are looking for a plan for a second home or vacation cabin, this plan just might fit your needs. It has two bedrooms and one bathroom. The laundry room is located directly across from the bedrooms for easy access. Even with its minuscule footprint, this plan still offers a walk-in closet, linen closet and foyer. The dual closets in the smaller bedroom could be modified to include a study center for your teenager or a window seat with toy storage underneath for a younger child. A staircase is included in case you'd like to add a basement or attic storage or living area. The exterior of this house could be left plain, or it could be dressed up with the addition of a front porch and/or false gable over the garage. For a rustic look, install cedar siding and leave the rafter tails exposed.

1,800-SQUARE-FOOT RANCH

This plan is a derivative of my home. It's a very livable plan that features three bedrooms, two baths, a den or office, a fireplace, an attached garage, a covered front porch, a large kitchen and a laundry room. The angled hallway adds flair to the main entrance and foyer. The master suite features his-and-hers closets, a whirlpool tub, dual sinks and a stand up

---

GLOSSARY

False Gable

A gable feature that has no structural purpose. It is installed merely for aesthetic reasons.

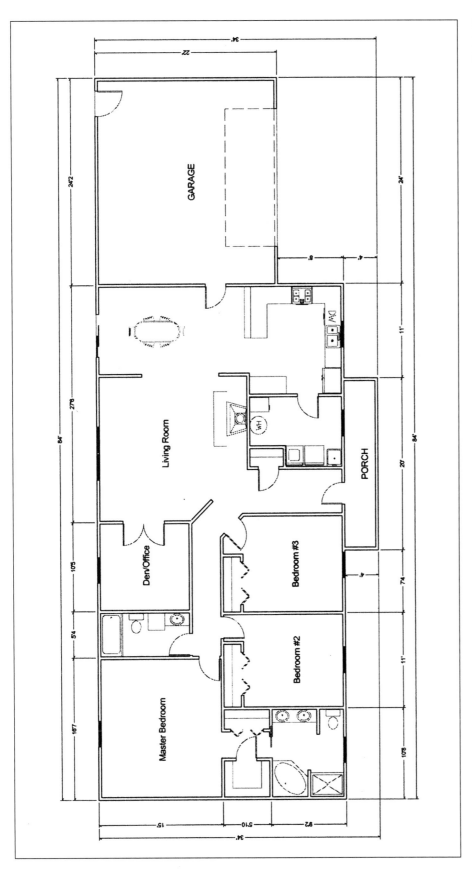

FIGURE APPENDIX B-3
Floor plan for the 1,800-square-foot ranch home.

FIGURE APPENDIX B-4 The half circle with sunburst over my front door.

shower. I dressed up the exterior by adding a half circle with sunburst over the front door. The sunburst is a nice addition to the gable over the front porch. The double doors in the den can be opened to enlarge the main living area for entertaining guests. This plan would be a great first project for beginners because it is a basic box and simple to build.

1,488-SQUARE-FOOT TWO-STORY WITH OPTIONAL BASEMENT

This plan, while still being a basic box, can be dressed up to look pretty elaborate on the exterior if you wish. With a hip roof on the porch, a gable over bedroom no. 2 and a forward-facing gable over the garage, this home could shine. The layout is not typical due to the fact that it was designed to sit on a pond and I wanted all the views to be out the front and right sides. It packs a lot of living in a small area with four bedrooms, two and a half baths and room for expansion with an optional bonus room over the garage. The 19' ceilings and catwalk (missing in print) in the living room and foyer make for a dramatic entrance area. Finishing the optional basement would increase your total finished square footage to 2,400 square feet. This plan provides a lot of features on a footprint that could easily fit on most building lots — even small ones.

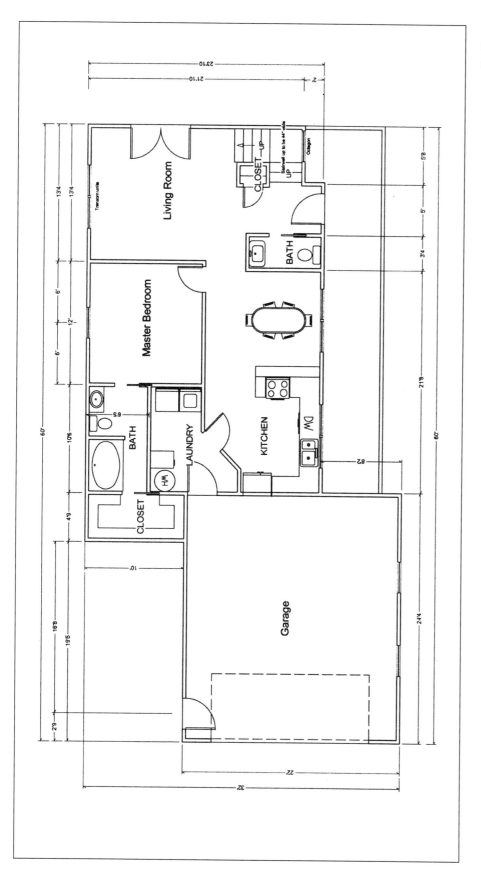

FIGURE APPENDIX B-5
First-floor plan of the 1,488-square-foot two-story home.

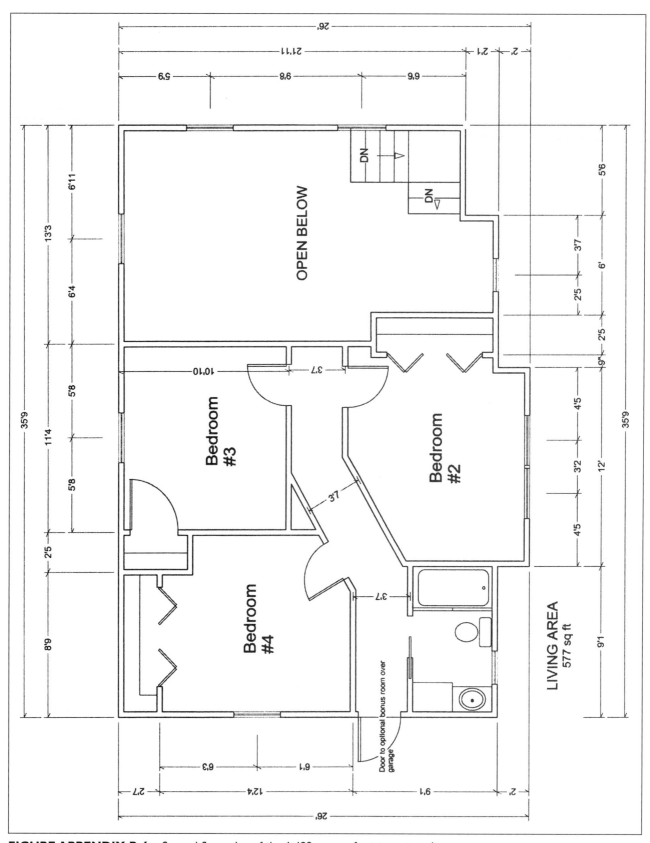

FIGURE APPENDIX B-6   Second-floor plan of the 1,488-square-foot two-story home.

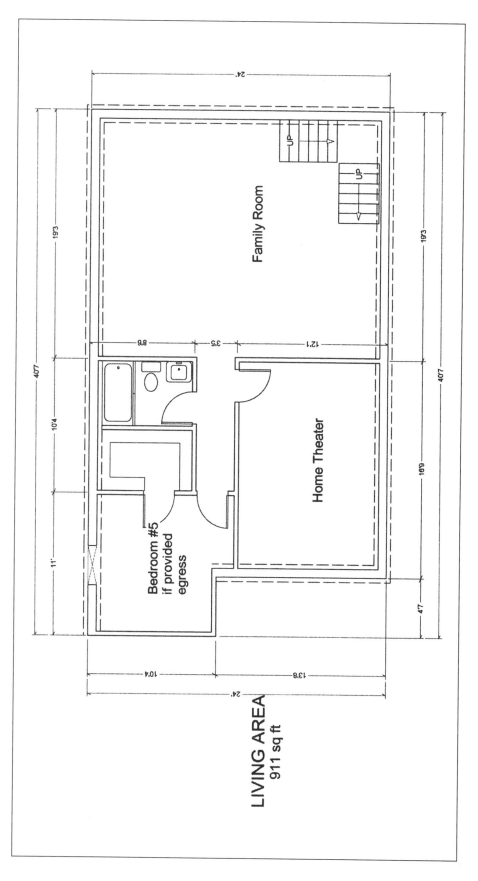

FIGURE APPENDIX B-7
Optional basement plan of the 1,488-square-foot two-story home.

GLOSSARY

Gingerbread
Ornamental moulding installed to decorate a structure. This moulding is usually seen at the peaks of gables and on porches.

1,900-SQUARE-FOOT TWO-STORY WITH OPTIONAL BASEMENT

This plan could be built with Victorian features such as gingerbread moulding, or could be built more simply by removing the veranda and the sitting area from the master bedroom. It has a dramatic two-story foyer and an open flow between the living areas. Bedroom no. 4 could be used as an office or den if so desired. It features four bedrooms, three and a half baths, front and rear porches and a huge master suite. The extra bathroom downstairs makes this room perfect for a teenager. The optional basement is designed as a pure leisure area. It features a large family room, a home theater, a library and a small craft room so you don't have to assemble the children's projects on the kitchen table. This is a lot of house for most of us and is full of extra features. Don't forget that the extra features won't come free, but by using this book you can get them at deep discounts.

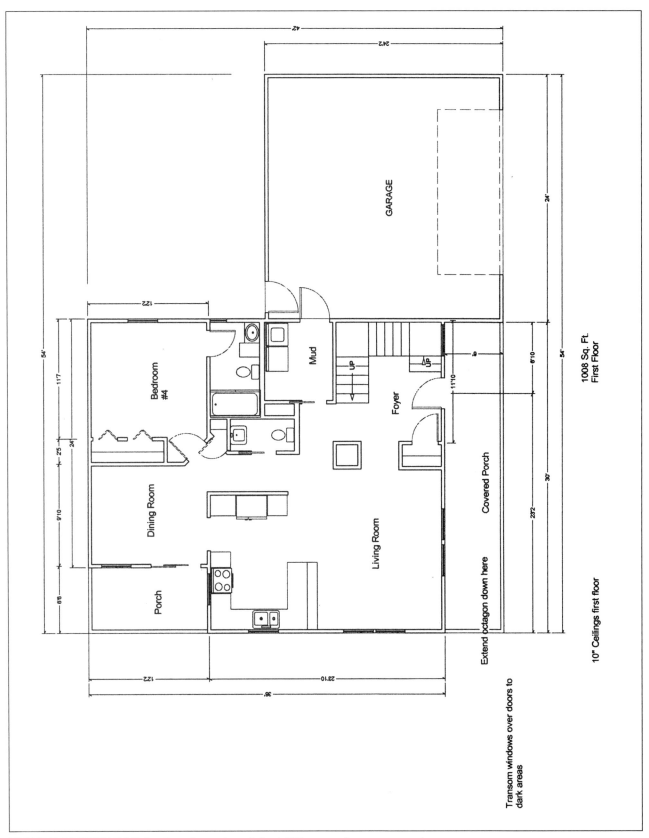

FIGURE APPENDIX B-8 First-floor plan of the 1,900-square-foot two-story home.

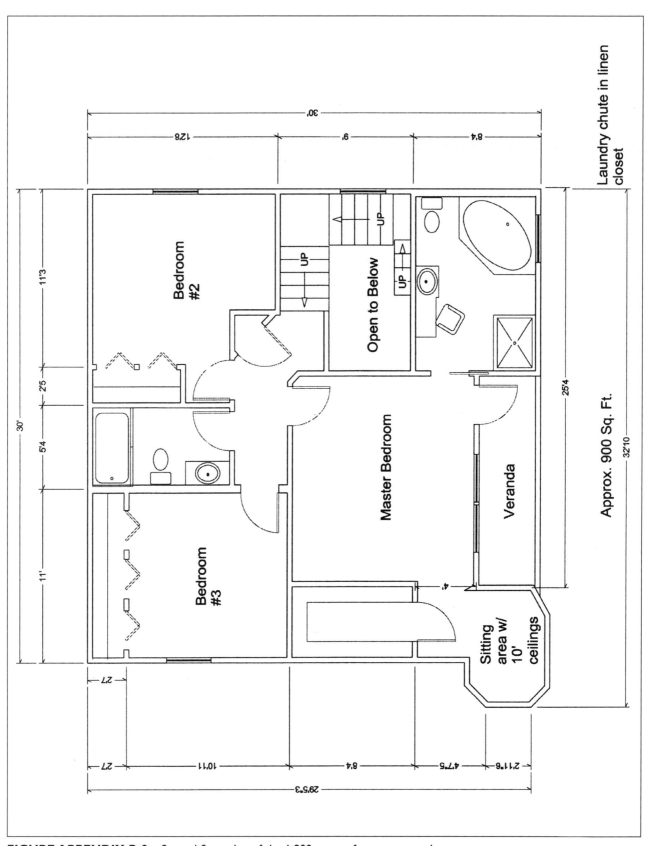

FIGURE APPENDIX B-9   Second-floor plan of the 1,900-square-foot two-story home.

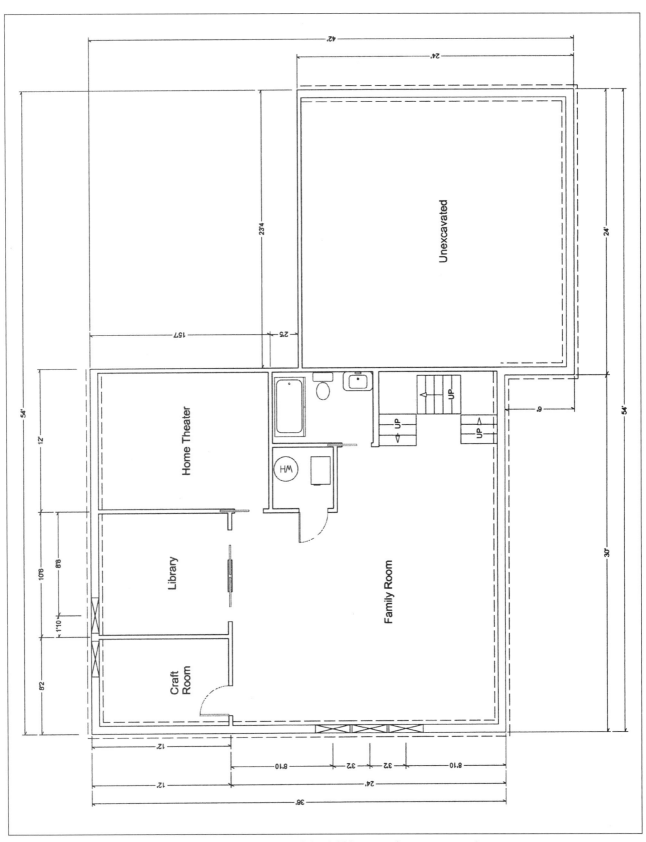

FIGURE APPENDIX B-10 Optional basement plan of the 1,900-square-foot two -story home.

1,144-SQUARE-FOOT CAPE COD WITH OPTIONAL BASEMENT

This very small home packs a lot in tight spaces. Everything that's included in larger homes is here, but on a smaller scale. If you're on a budget but still need three bedrooms, two or more baths and room for future growth with the optional basement, this may be the plan for you. The exterior of the home can be left as is (very plain) or could be dressed up with a covered porch and dormers. The optional basement can add an additional 768 square feet of finished area for you to utilize. This plan delivers big features in a small, affordable package.

FIGURE APPENDIX B-11
First-floor plan of the 1,144-square-foot Cape Cod home.

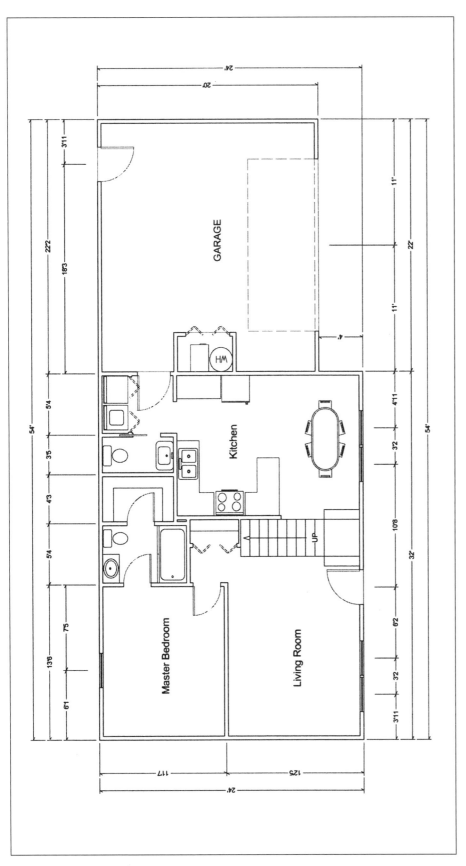

FIGURE APPENDIX B-12
Second-floor plan of the 1,144-square-foot Cape Cod home.

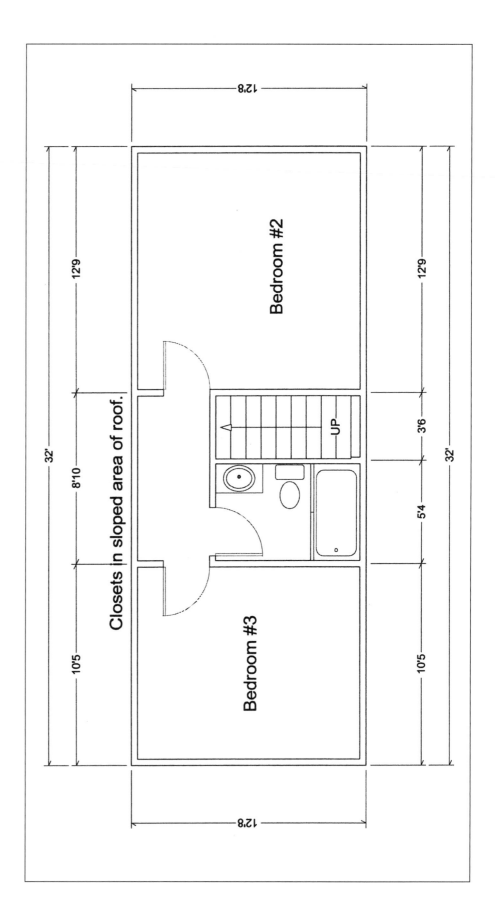

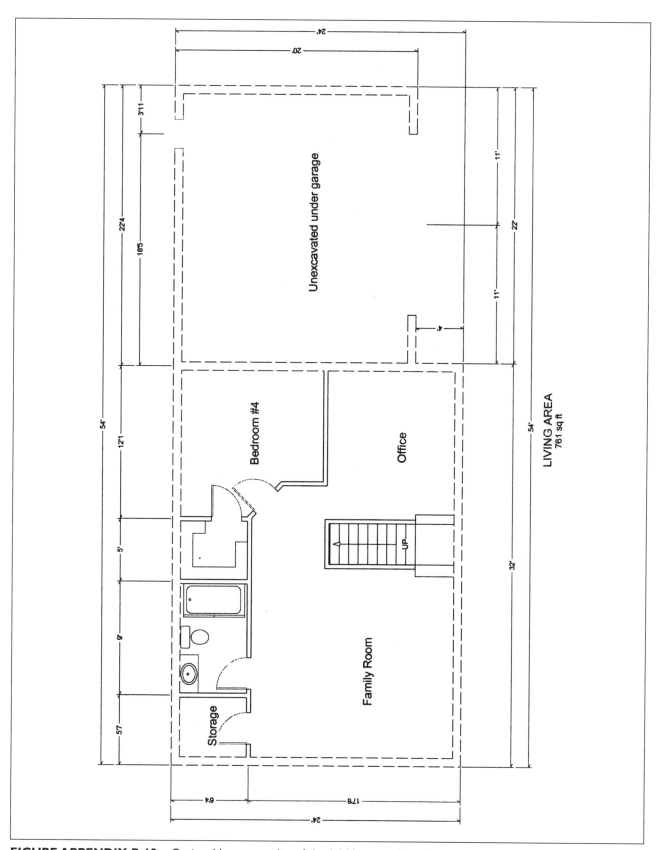

FIGURE APPENDIX B-13 Optional basement plan of the 1,144-square-foot Cape Cod home.

1,934-SQUARE-FOOT CAPE COD WITH OPTIONAL BASEMENT

This plan has it all. From the huge master bath to the kitchen center island to the sunroom to the home theater, it encompasses almost everything I could ever need in a home. It has four bedrooms, two and a half baths, a large covered porch, a mud room, a kids' play area, a two-story foyer and more. The optional basement adds a library, a guest room, a home theater, a family room and even some extra storage. The single distinctive feature of the octagonal sunroom sets this house out from the crowd. The other special features just add to its uniqueness. The only alteration I'd consider is enlarging the garage to accomodate three cars. This house has a wonderful charm that's all its own.

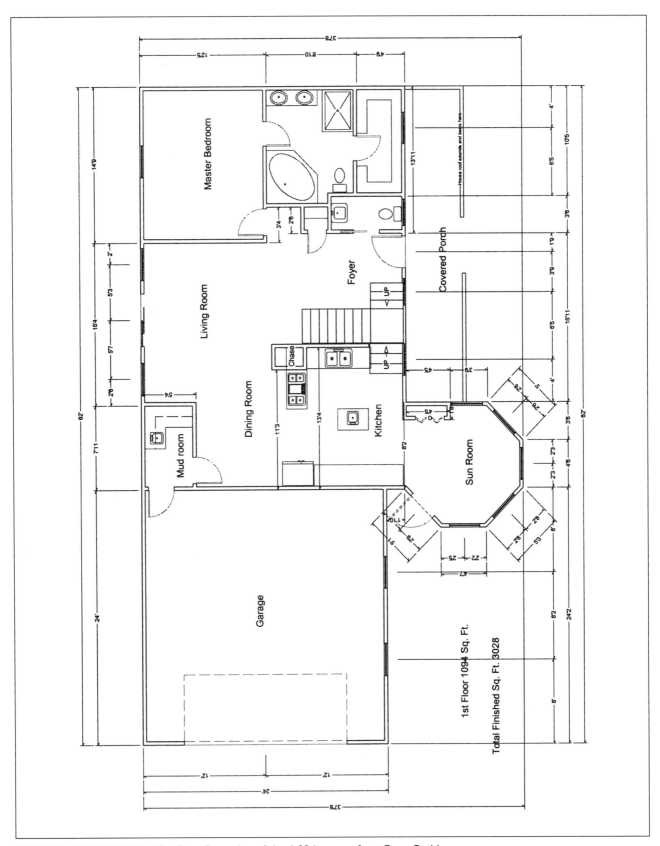

FIGURE APPENDIX B-14   First-floor plan of the 1,934-square-foot Cape Cod home.

FIGURE APPENDIX B-15
Second-floor plan of the 1,934-square-foot Cape Cod home.

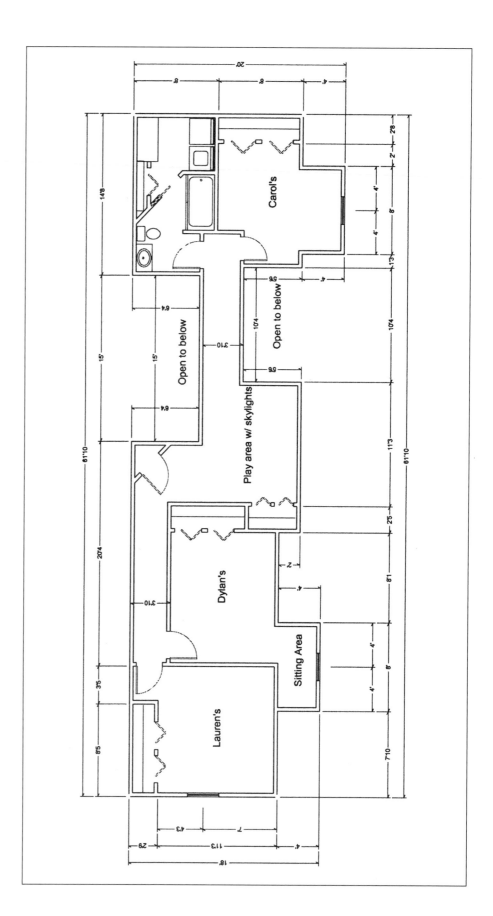

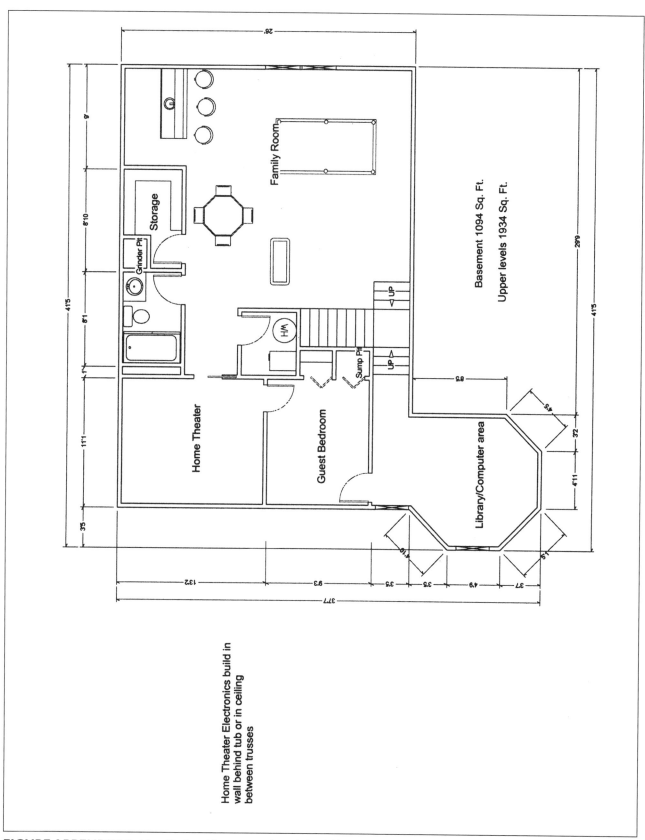

FIGURE APPENDIX B-16   Optional basement plan of the 1,934-square-foot Cape Cod home.

1,503-SQUARE-FOOT SALTBOX WITH OPTIONAL BASEMENT

This plan squeezes all its features into a tiny footprint. It would be excellent for a lot with a small buildable area. The small footprint is possible because all the bedrooms are upstairs and over the garage. The small optional basement allows for some separation of living areas by adding a family room and two small rooms that could be used for several purposes. This plan features four bedrooms, two and a half baths, his-and-hers closets in the master bedroom, and a vaulted foyer ceiling. The dormers keep the exterior from being plain; the house also could be accented with a covered porch if desired. This basic box is inexpensive to build, yet it's practical and has lots of curb appeal.

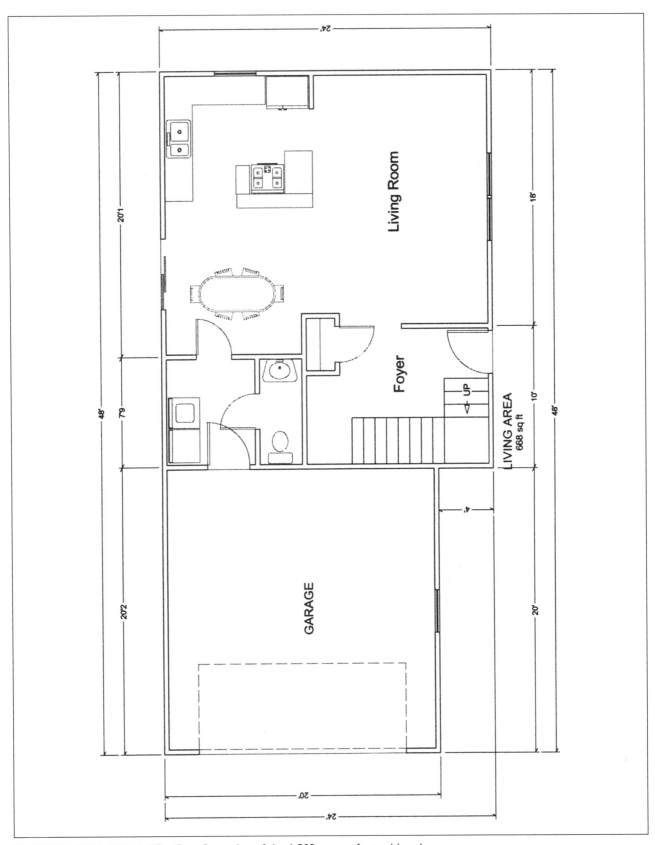

FIGURE APPENDIX B-17 First-floor plan of the 1,503-square-foot saltbox home.

FIGURE APPENDIX B-18
Second-floor plan of the 1,503-square-foot saltbox home.

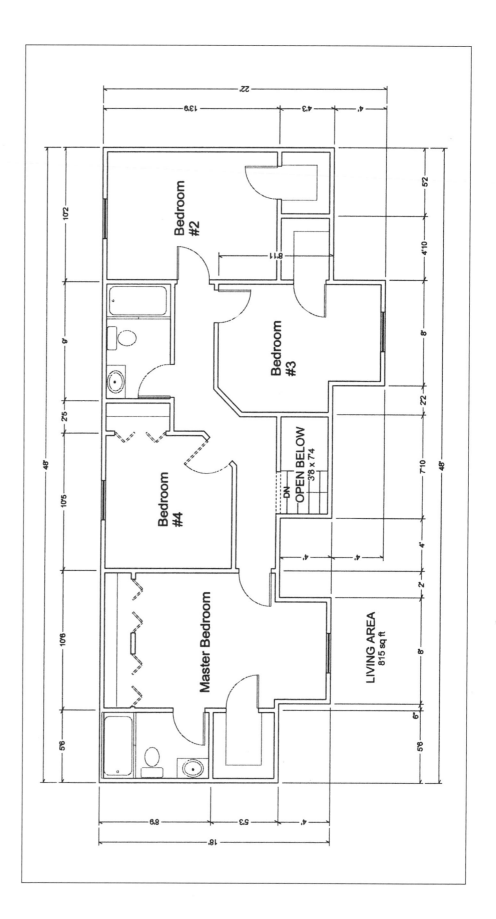

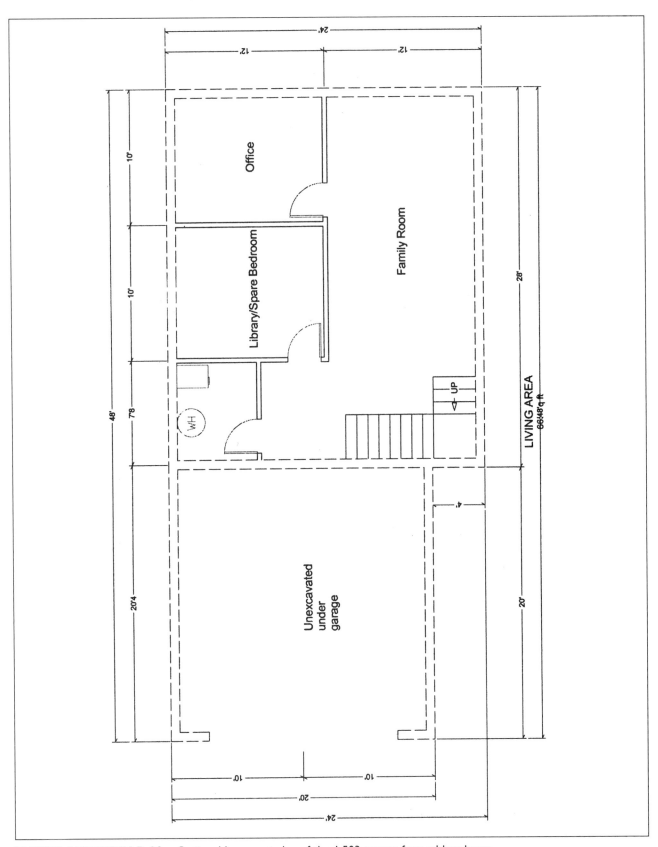

FIGURE APPENDIX B-19 Optional basement plan of the 1,503-square-foot saltbox home.

1,582-SQUARE-FOOT SALTBOX WITH OPTIONAL BASEMENT

The thing I love best about this plan is the sunroom. There are so many things you can do in this one room to make it a cozy place to spend your time. Imagine sitting at the table and reading the morning paper. You sip your steaming coffee while you watch the rabbits play in the morning dew just outside the windows.

I envision 10-foot sidewalls with transom windows over the already oversized double-hung windows below. By placing the transoms 12 inches higher than the double-hung, a continuous shelf could be installed on three sides of the room and filled with plants. Then by vaulting the ceiling and leaving the rafters and beams exposed, the volume of the room would belie its small size of 12'x 14'. It could be further accented by "sinking" the room approximately 8 inches below the adjoining kitchen area.

This plan also features three bedrooms, two and a half baths, vaulted ceilings in the foyer, a living room and kitchen and a bonus room over the garage if desired. With the optional basement, even more finished square footage can be added. This plan would be very practical to build, yet could be dressed up with some additional features to be an impressive home. To make the home more dramatic, consider a full-length covered porch and dormers.

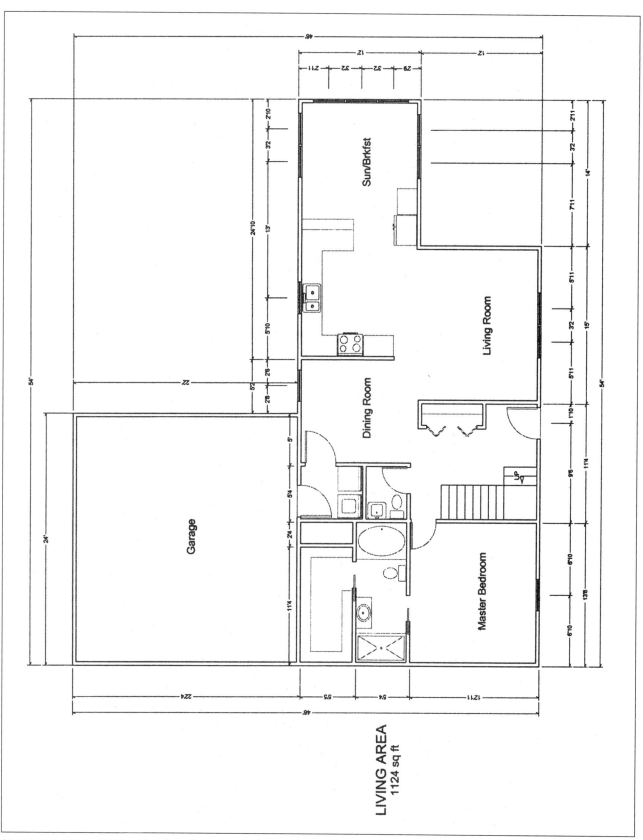

FIGURE APPENDIX B-20 First-floor plan of the 1,582-square-foot saltbox home.

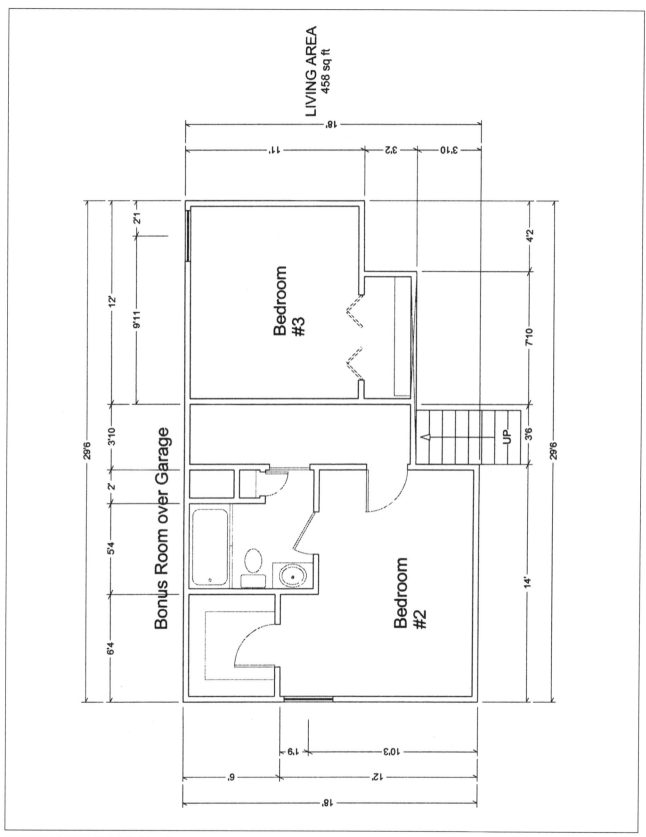

FIGURE APPENDIX B-21   Second-floor plan of the 1,582-square-foot saltbox home.

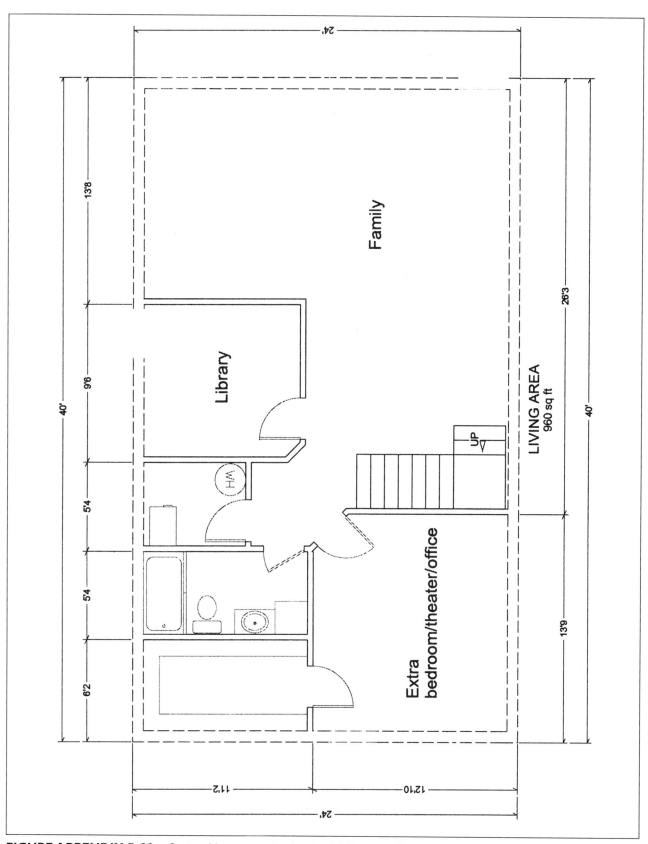

FIGURE APPENDIX B-22 Optional basement plan for the 1,582-square-foot saltbox home.

1,816 SQUARE-FOOT MULTILEVEL HOME

Multilevel homes are attractive because you can get more square footage for fewer dollars than with other types of plans. If you need as much square footage as you can squeeze out of your budget, one of the next two plans may be for you. This plan features four bedrooms, two and a half baths, open living areas and floor separation between the bedrooms. This plan offers a lot of living on a small footprint, making it a good choice for a tight lot. One improvement to consider might be expanding the bathroom on the lower floor to a full bath.

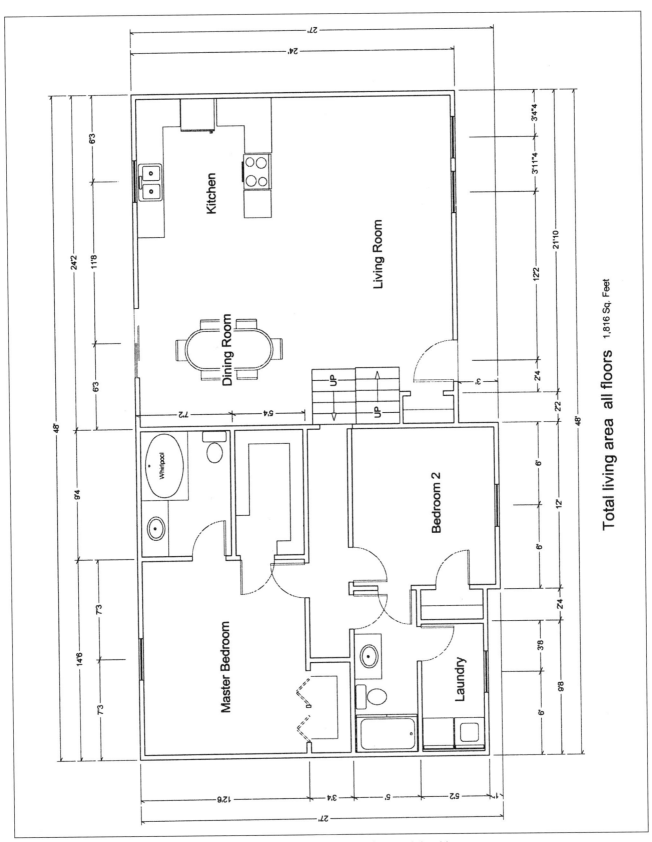

FIGURE APPENDIX B-23 Upper-floors plan for the 1,816-square-foot multilevel home.

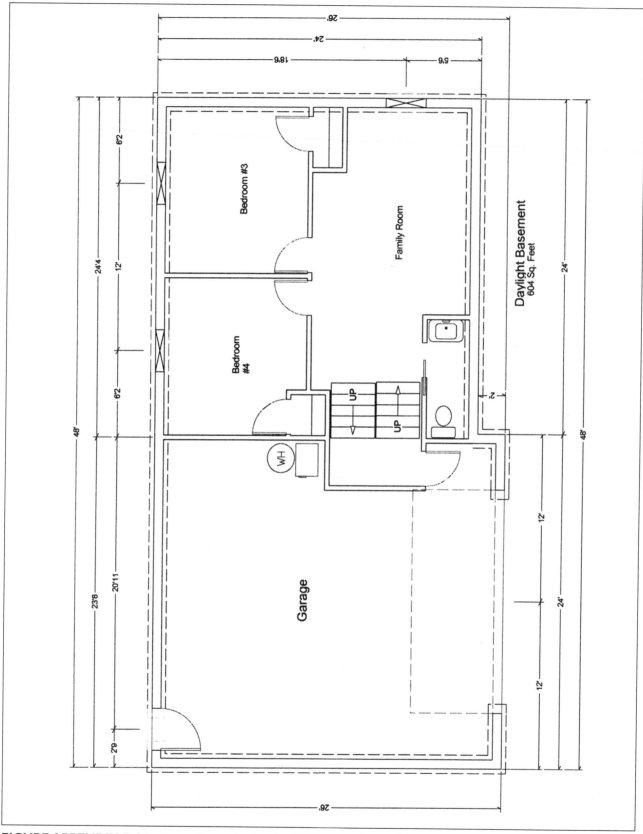

FIGURE APPENDIX B-24 Lower-floors plan for the 1,816-square-foot multilevel home.

1,540-SQUARE-FOOT MULTILEVEL HOME

This plan is a smaller version of the previous plan with one less bathroom, no laundry room and no family room. If your budget is really tight, but you need four bedrooms, this may be a plan to consider. Additions could include the extra bath and laundry room. With a footprint of only 24'x42' this house would fit almost anywhere. Nearly everything has been simplified on this plan in an effort to make it as affordable as possible.

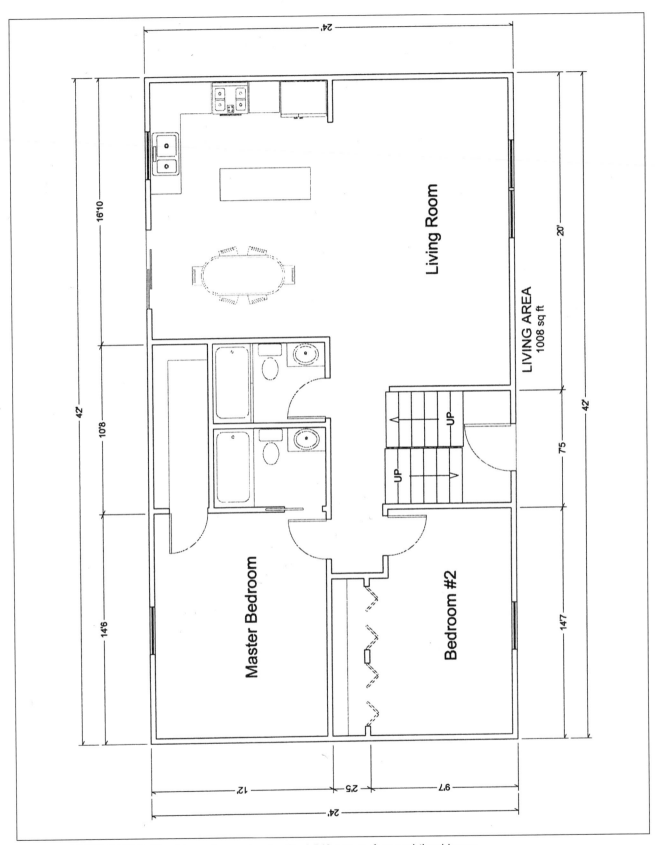

FIGURE APPENDIX B-25 Upper-floors plan for the 1,540-square-foot multilevel home.

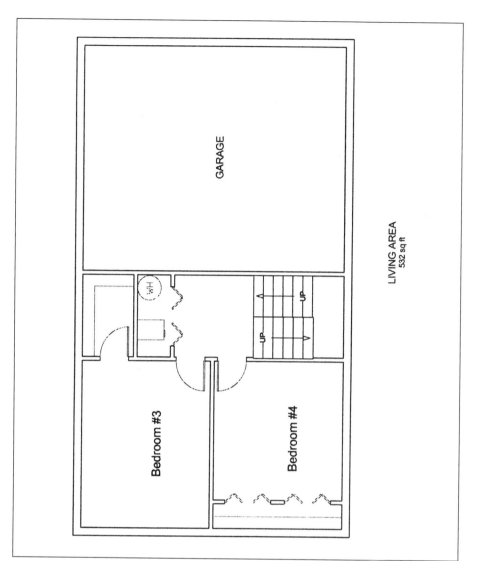

FIGURE APPENDIX B-26
Lower-floors plan for their 1,540-square-foot multilevel home.

CONVERSION CHARTS AND FORMULAS

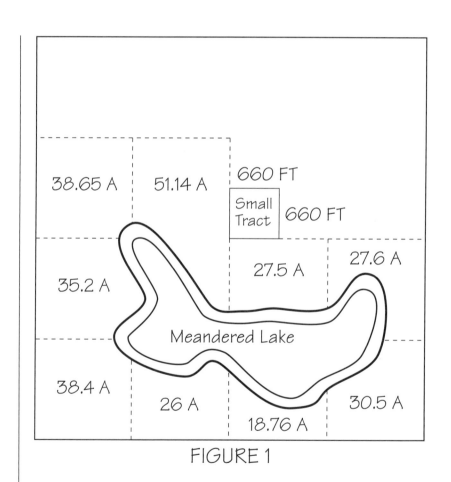

FIGURE 1

IMPORTANT FACTS ABOUT LAND DESCRIPTIONS

LAND MEASUREMENTS, TOWNSHIPS, SECTIONS, MEANDERED WATER, GOVERNMENT LOTS, ETC.

WHAT IS A LAND DESCRIPTION?

A land description is a description of a tract of land in legally acceptable terms, so as to show exactly where it is located and how many acres it contains.

TABLE OF LAND MEASUREMENTS

LINEAR MEASURE				SQUARE MEASURE			
1 inch	.0833 foot	16½ feet	1 rod	144 sq. in.	1 sq. ft.	43560 sq. ft.	1 acre
7.92 inches	1 link	5½ yards	1 rod	9 sq. ft.	1 sq. yd.	640 acres	1 sq. mile
12 inches	1 foot	4 rods	100 links	30¼ sq. yd.	1 sq. rod	1 sq. mile	1 section
1 vara	33 inches	66 feet	1 chain	16 sq. rods	1 sq. chain	36 sq. miles	1 township
2¾ feet	1 vara	80 chains	1 mile	1 sq. rod	272½ sq. ft.	6 miles sq.	1 township
3 feet	1 yard	320 rods	1 mile	1 sq. chain	4356 sq. ft.	208 ft. 8 in. sq.	1 acre
25 links	16½ feet	8000 links	1 mile	10 sq. chains	1 acre	80 rods sq.	40 acres
25 links	1 rod	5280 feet	1 mile	160 sq. rods	1 acre	160 rods sq.	160 acres
100 links	1 chain	1760 yards	1 mile	4840 sq. yd.	1 acre		

In non-rectangular land descriptions, distance is usually described in terms of either feet or rods (this is especially true in surveying today), and square measure in terms of acres. Such descriptions are called Metes and Bounds descriptions and will be explained in detail later. In rectangular land descriptions, square measure is again in terms of acres, and the location of the land in such as N½ (north one-half), SE¼ (southeast one-fourth or quarter), etc. as shown in Figures 2, 3, 4 and 5 on the next page.

MEANDERED WATER AND GOVERNMENT LOTS

A meandered lake or stream is water, next to which the adjoining landowner pays taxes on the land only. Such land is divided into divisions of land called government lots. The location, acreage and lot number of each such tract of land, was determined, surveyed and platted by the original government surveyors.

The original survey of your county (complete maps of each township, meandered lakes, government lots, etc.) is in your courthouse, and this original survey is the basis for all land descriptions in your county (see Figure 1). IMPORTANT: The government lot number given to a piece of land is the legal description of that tract of land.

HOW CAN YOU TELL WHETHER WATER IS MEANDERED OR PRIVATELY OWNED?

On township maps, if you find government lots adjoining a body of water or stream, those waters are meandered. If there are no government lots surrounding water, that water is privately owned, the owner is paying taxes of the land under the water, and the owner controls the hunting, fishing, trapping rights, etc., on that water, within the regulations of the state and federal laws, except where such water is deemed navigable, other rulings may sometimes pertain.

As a generality (but not always), meandered water is public water which the public may use for recreational purposes, fishing, hunting, trapping, etc., provided that there is legal access to the water, or in other words, if the public can get to such waters without trespassing. There still is much litigation concerning the same to be decided by the courts.

SAMPLE SECTIONS SHOWING RECTANGULAR LAND DESCRIPTIONS, ACREAGES AND DISTANCES

THE BEST WAY TO READ LAND DESCRIPTIONS IS FROM THE REAR OR BACKWARDS

Always read descriptions of land first from either the north or the south. In Figures 2, 3, 4 and 5, notice that they all start with N (north), S (south), such as NW, SE, etc. They are never WN (west north), ES (east south), etc. IMPORTANT: It is comparatively simple for anyone to understand a description, that is, determine where a tract of land is located, from even a long description. The secret is to read or analyze the description from the rear or backwards.

EXAMPLE: Under Figure 4, the first description reads E½, SE¼, SW¼, SW¼. The last part of the description reads SW¼, which means that the tract of land we are looking for is somewhere in that quarter (as shown in Figure 2). Next back we find SW¼, which means the tract we are after is somewhere in the SW¼ SW¼ (as shown in Figure 3). Next back, we find the SE¼, which means that the tract is in the SE¼ SW¼ SW¼ (as shown in Figure 5). Next back and our last part to look up, is the E½ of the above, which is the location of the tract described by the whole description (as shown in Figure 4).

TO INTERPRET A LAND DESCRIPTION — LOCATE THE AREA ON YOUR TOWNSHIP PLAT, THEN ANALYZE THE DESCRIPTION AND FOLLOW IT ON THE PLAT MAP.

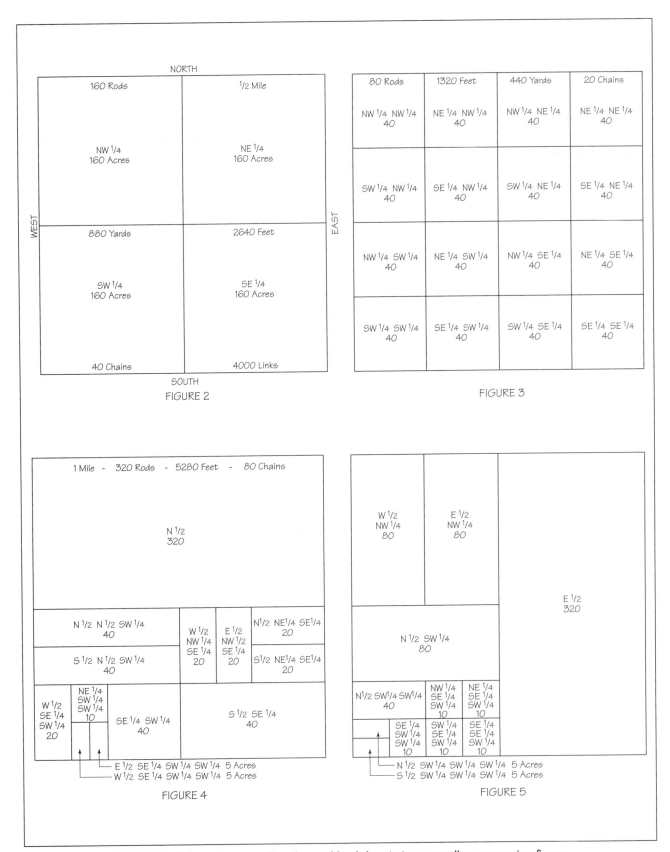

FIGURE APPENDIX C-1 Information regarding plats and legal descriptions as well as conversion figures.

DESIGNING A HOME THEATER

L.W. Sepmeyer developed three formulas for configuring the room's dimensions when designing a home theater. They are known as Sepmeyer's Three Golden Room Ratios:

1. Ceiling height C, Room width 1.14C and Room length 1.39C.
2. Ceiling height C, Room width 1.28C and Room length 1.54 C.
3. Ceiling height C, Room width 1.60C and Room length 2.33C.

So, for example, if your room is 8' tall and we use Formula 2, we would calculate the length and width as follows:

Width = 8' (C) × 1.28 = 10.24'
Length = 8' (C) × 1.54 = 12.32'

The suggested room size would then be 10.24' wide by 12.32' long.
Source: **www.hometheatervillage.com**

OTHER USEFUL FORMULAS

The area of a square equals its length times its width.
The area of a triangle equals half the length of its base times its height.
The area of a circle equals pr^2.
A square yard equals 9 square feet, or an area 3' wide × 3' long.
A cubic yard equals 27 cubic feet, or an area 3' wide × 3' long × 3' high.

To determine the long angle of a right triangle, such as a rafter length, use the Pythagorean theorem, which says that $A^2 + B^2 = C^2$. A is the base of the triangle, B is the height of the triangle and C is the long side of the triangle.

CALCULATING ROOF AREA

To calculate an existing roof's area without climbing a ladder, count the number of shingle tabs along the eaves and the rakes. Each tab along the eaves is one foot long and each tab up the rake is approximately five inches long. Multiply the number of tabs up the rake by five. Take that figure and divide it by 12. Then multiply that figure by the number of tabs along the eaves. The result is the area of the roof in square feet. For triangular sections of roof, do the same and divide the final answer by two.

TERMS, SAFETY TIPS AND MISCELLANEOUS FORMS

When you're planning an overseas trip, it's always a good idea to know the native language. When you're considering a construction project, it's no different: you have to know the lingo or you'll be lost. Study the diagrams and terms in this section so that when your contractor, a retailer, or your uncle talks about jambs, sills and eaves, you will at least know the basics.

MAJOR FRICTION AND IMPACT POINTS

WINDOWS

• Paint deteriorated from moisture/weather
• Sash rubbing jamb, stop and parting bead
• Sash banging against well and parting bead
• Impact against edge of stool

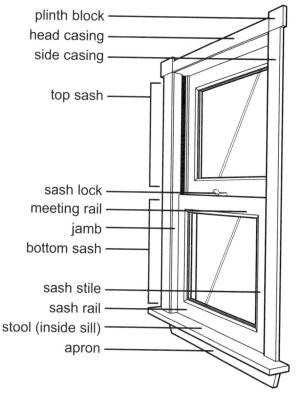

plinth block
head casing
side casing
top sash
sash lock
meeting rail
jamb
bottom sash
sash stile
sash rail
stool (inside sill)
apron

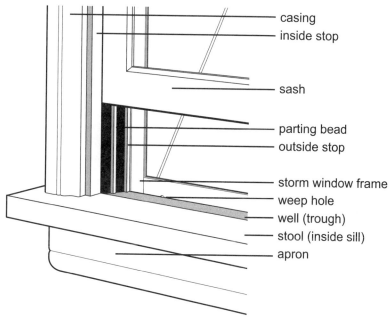

casing
inside stop
sash
parting bead
outside stop
storm window frame
weep hole
well (trough)
stool (inside sill)
apron

FIGURE Appendix D-1   Window and door components, courtesy of EPA, Model Worker Tool Box Guide.

DOORS

- Paint weakened by impact and friction at jamb, stop and door edge
- Exterior door paint weakened by moisture and weather
- Paint weakened by crushing on hinge side

transom
transom light
head jamb
rail
stile
hinge jamb
latch jamb
panel
stop
latch
casing
hinge
threshold
door

STAIR/FLOOR

- Floor boards
- Stair treads
- Paint exposed through walking, moving objects and impact against risers, treads and newel post

rail
baluster
newel post
tread
riser
stringer

FIGURE Appendix D-2   Stair and porch components, courtesy of EPA, Model Worker Tool Box Guide.

MOISTURE

Moisture is a major cause of paint failure. Moisture usually attacks the painted surface from behind the paint.

EXTERIOR SURFACES

- Sun, heat, cold, rain cause paint failure, flaking and peeling
- Some exterior paint is designed to chalk
- Clogged or separated gutters and downspouts damage paint
- Standing water on porch floors, window wells and sills damage paint
- Moisture from inside the house migrating to behind exterior paint damages paint

INTERIOR SURFACES

- Steam/moisture from cooking and washing
- Roof and roof flashing leaks
- Plumbing leaks
- Rain water entering walls
- Condensation in ceilings and walls
- Water splashed in kitchen and bath
- Dampness from crawl spaces

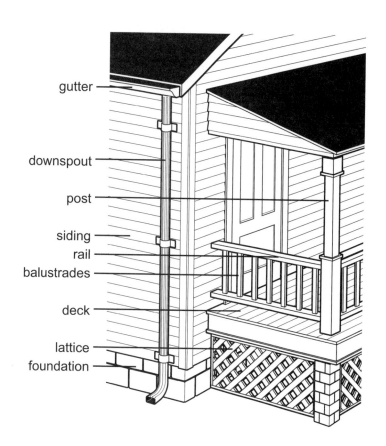

gutter

downspout

post

siding

rail

balustrades

deck

lattice

foundation

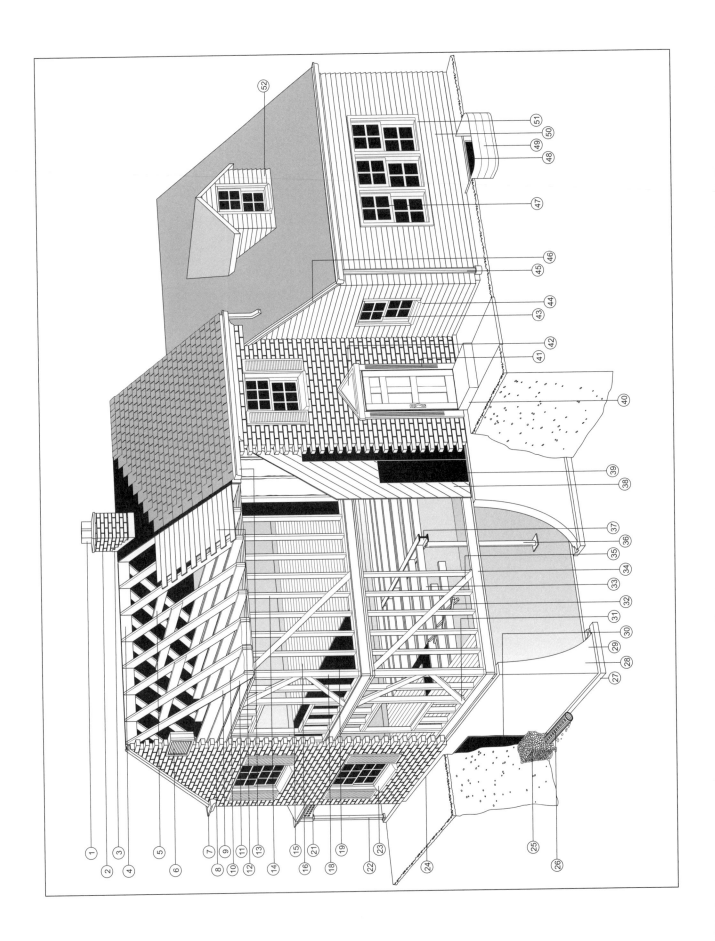

FIGURE Appendix D-3
Exterior and interior components of your house. Courtesy Illinois Administrative Code.

1. Chimney flues or pots
2. Chimney
3. Flashing
4. Ridgeboard
5. Collar beam
6. Vent; louver
7. Cornice return
8. Brick veneer
9. End rafter
10. Insulation
11. Top double plate
12. Roof decking
13. Gutter
14. Stud
15. Flooring paper
16. Finish flooring
17. Shutter
18. Corner post
19. Subfloor
20. Lintel; header
21. Porch frieze board
22. Porch post
23. Brick sill
24. Grade line
25. Cinder or gravel fill
26. Drain tile
27. Footing
28. Keyway
29. Foundation wall
30. Waterproofing
31. Knee brace
32. Bridging
33. Floor joists
34. Sill plate
35. Corner brace
36. Steel column
37. Beam; girder
38. Wall sheathing
39. Building paper
40. Stoop
41. Trim pilaster
42. Pediment door trim
43. Double-hung window
44. Windowsill
45. Downspout
46. Rake mold
47. Mullion
48. Basement window
49. Areaway well
50. Bevel siding
51. Wood window trim
52. Dormer

HEALTH AND SAFETY

Your health and safety can never be taken for granted. This appendix also includes some basic guidelines that should be followed on every jobsite.

When you start your project you'll need to fill out an application for a building permit. I've included a sample application from the City of Decatur, Illinois, as an example. All municipalities are different, but most should require similar information.

This appendix also includes an itemized estimate sheet that will help you calculate the overall cost for your project.

HEALTH AND SAFETY

1. BLOOD SCREENING

- When you work with lead, your employer must provide medical screening at no cost to you.
- Whenever you work with lead you must have blood tests. They are the Blood Lead Level test and the ZPP blood test. Both of these tests can be taken from the same sample.
- If you work with lead for 30 or more days in a year, above the action level, you must have these blood tests every two months and then every six months.
- You should get a blood test when you leave your job.
- The Blood Lead Level test will tell you how much lead is in your blood.
- You can also receive medical exams and consultations whenever you feel any of the symptoms of lead poisoning, have difficulty breathing or are concerned about having healthy children.
- You have a right to your medical records.
- If your blood level is over 25ug/dl, NIOSH recommends a worker be removed from the worksite and be provided a job away from lead exposure. Medical research shows reproductive hazards at 30ug/dl. (The OSHA interim law requires removal at 50ug/dl with the requirement of being provided a job of equal pay for as long as the job lasts or 18 months.)

FIGURE Appendix D-5A   Construction safety guidelines, courtesy of EPA, Model Worker Tool Box Guide.

2. HEAT

PROTECT AGAINST HEAT STROKE

Danger signs to look for:

- Hot, dry skin
- Headache/dizziness
- Sick to stomach
- Fainting
- Sweating stops, suit drys

Actions to take:

- Call for ambulance
- Remove individual from work area
- Remove respirator/suit
- Cool body with water

PROTECT AGAINST HEAT STRESS

Danger signs to look for:

- Cool, sweaty, pale skin
- Headache, dizziness, sick to stomach

Actions to take:

- Remove individual from work area
- Remove respirator/suit
- Cool body with water
- If fainting, call ambulance
- Do not give water to a person who has fainted.

PREVENTING THE PROBLEMS:

- Drink lots of water
- Drink orange juice and eat bananas
- Take breaks
- Get used to heat gradually
- Cut down on alcohol

3. CARBON MONOXIDE

Carbon monoxide is a potentially deadly gas that comes from engines such as air compressors, generators or un-vented combustion heaters. You cannot see, taste or smell this gas. Never use an engine in a closed space!

Signs to look for:

- Dizziness, faintness, sleepy feeling
- Headache
- Stomach ache, vomiting

Actions to take:

- Remove worker from the work area and remove respirator
- If worker becomes unconscious, use CPR

FIGURE Appendix D-5B   More construction safety guidelines, courtesy of EPA, Model Worker Tool Box Guide.

4. ELECTRIC SHOCKS

Electric shocks can stop your heart!
Electricity is particularly dangerous in the
presence of water. Always remember to:

HAVE SOMEONE ON SITE WHO KNOWS CPR

- Keep worksite dry
- Use double-insulated tools on grounded cords
- Remove damaged tools from worksite or cut off plug
- Keep power tools sharp
- Never carry tools by cord or unplug them by pulling cord
- Never use metal ladders near electricity
- When demolishing walls, always turn off central power and test for confirmation
- If another worker is shocked, move them with a wooden object and then turn off electricity. Use CPR if necessary.
- When you are working with electricity near water, a ground fault interrupter is required. Workers should wear rubber gloves and boots in these conditions.

5. FIRES AND EXPLOSION

A lead abatement site is in danger of fires starting and spreading.

These materials burn very fast:
- Poly sheets and duct tape
- Disposable suits
- Some encapsulants
- Floor finishes and solvents

Keep the following offsite:
- Cigarettes
- Internal combustion machines
- Damaged electrical tools and cutting or welding tools

Have an ABC extinguisher onsite and have a fire exit plan.
No smoking on worksites — ever. NO EXCEPTIONS.

FIGURE Appendix D-5C   More construction safety guidelines, courtesy of EPA, Model Worker Tool Box Guide.

6. LADDERS

Before using ladders check for:
- Broken steps
- Broken hinges
- Broken or absent non-slip base
- Wobbly frame
- No rubber feet
- Slippery rungs

The top of the ladder should be tied off to structure or braced inside of structure. After you tie off the top, hook a safety belt above you. When working on window, use stand-off so you do not have to lean to the side or reach behind the ladder.

7. EYES

ALWAYS wear goggles when you are:
- Scraping
- Cutting
- Using strippers
- Using power tools
- Doing demolition
- Working overhead
- Hammering hardened nails

All worksites should have an eye wash station in the cleanup area.
If irritants get into eyes, wash for 15 minutes and call the doctor.

8. CUTS AND BLEEDING

Whenever someone has a cut that is bleeding heavily, cover the wound with a clean cloth. Press on the cloth to give direct pressure on the wound. Elevate the limb. If the wound does not stop bleeding within a few minutes, call 911 for emergency help. As necessary, press pressure points as learned in first aid class.

FIGURE Appendix D-5D   More construction safely guidelines, courtesy of EPA, Model Worker Tool Box Guide.

9. BURNS

If you or one of your co-workers is burned, get the person away from the hot object. Run clean, cold water over the burned skin for at least 15 minutes. If the burn is red or is small and has only a few blisters, clean and cover it with a sterile non-stick gauze pad. The dressing should be changed twice daily and checked for signs of infection. Never heat a needle and puncture a blister. Never use butter, oil or petroleum jelly for burns.

Call 911 for emergency help if:
• The injured person is going into shock
• The burned skin covers more than 20% of the body
• The burns have blisters and are on the hands, feet, face or genitals
• The burned skin is charred or black

You can treat the injured person for shock until emergency personnel arrive. Run cold water over the burned areas. Do not put any covering over the burn.

10. NOISE

If you are working around very noisy machinery, it is essential to use earplugs or muffs. Power tools using compressed air create high levels of noise. Protect your hearing. Hearing loss is for life.

11. BACK INJURIES

• Do not lift an object heavier than is comfortable
• Bend your legs, keep your back straight and lift close to your body
• Don't lift and twist or turn at the same time
• Always get help to lift heavy objects

RIGHT TO KNOW

OSHA says you have to be trained about the dangers of your work. Your employer must provide you with training for the chemicals you work with. This is part of the Hazard Communication (or "Right to Know") law (29 CFR 1926.59). Your employer has to have a list of the hazardous chemicals that workers could potentially be exposed to. They must have fact sheets about all the chemicals you work with. These fact sheets are called Material Safety Data Sheets or MSDS's. MSDS's tell you about how the chemicals can harm your health. They also tell you how to protect yourself from the chemicals. You must be trained to use the data sheets. The MSDS's for each hazardous material must be at the worksite.

FIGURE Appendix D-5E   More construction safety guidelines, courtesy of EPA, Model Worker Tool Box Guide.

CITY OF DECATUR, ILLINOIS
APPLICATION FOR BUILDING PERMIT

PROJECT ADDRESS_____ ZIP CODE_____

LEGAL DESCRIPTION: LOT_____ BLK_____ SUBDIV._____

ZONING_____ CENSUS TRACT_____ TOWNSHIP_____

100 YR. FLOOD PLAN (Y/N)_____ CORNER LOT (Y/N)_____

VARIANCE NUMBER (IF REQUIRED)_____

OWNER NAME_____   TYPE OF PERMIT(S)

ADDRESS_____   BUILDING   _____

CITY_____STATE_____ZIP_____   ELECTRICAL   _____

OWNER PHONE_____   MECHANICAL   _____

CONTACT PERSON_____   PLUMBING   _____

ADDRESS_____   FOUNDATION   _____

CITY_____STATE_____ZIP_____   FIRE SUPPR   _____

TELEPHONE_____   TENT (TEMP)   _____

                                                          SWP   _____

                                                          FAC   _____

PROJECT EVALUATION $_____

DESCRIPTION OF WORK

****

CONTRACTORS:

GENERAL_____ PH_____ LIC#_____

ELECTRICAL_____ PH_____ LIC#_____

PLUMBING_____ PH_____ LIC#_____

MECHANICAL_____ PH_____ LIC#_____

SPRINKLER_____ PH_____ LIC#_____

SIGNED SUBCONTRACTOR OR HOMEOWNERS DECLARATION MUST ACCOMPANY THIS APPLICATION

****

A SITE PLAN IS REQUIRED FOR ALL NEW CONSTRUCTION AND ADDITIONS TO EXISTING CONSTRUCTION OF THE PRINCIPAL AND/OR

ACCESSORY STRUCTURES USE THE BACK OF THIS FORM OR ATTACH A SITE PLAN. COMPLETE THE FOLLOWING SQUARE.

FOOT INFORMATION

MAIN FLOOR: LIVING AREA_____ SQ.FT.   GARAGE_____SQ.FT.

                     PORCH_____ SQ.FT.   DECK_____SQ.FT.

SECOND FLOOR: LIVING AREA_____ SQ.FT.

BASEMENT: FINISHED AREA_____ UNFINISHED AREA_____

TOTAL FINISHED AREA _____ TOTAL UNFINISHED AREA_____

BUILDING MAX WIDTH/DEPTH _____ x _____

SET BACKS: FRONT_____ REAR_____ SIDES_____

****

ALL CONSTRUCTION DEBRIS MUST BE REMOVED FROM THE SITE AND LEGALLY DISPOSED. BURNING IS NOT ALLOWED.

APPLICANT SIGNATURE_____ DATE_____

FIGURE Appendix D-6   The front page of an application for a building permit, courtesy of the City of Decatur, Illinois.

INDICATE WHERE POWER ENTERS LOT AND ATTACHES TO HOUSE

ABOVE GROUND_____ BELOW GROUND_____

REAR PROPERTY LINE

SIDE
LINE

FRONT PROPERTY LINE

LOT DIMENSIONS   L_____   W_____   SQ.FT._____

SET BACKS   FRONT_____   REAR_____   SIDES_____

OTHER STRUCTURES   I_____   2_____   3_____   4_____

CORNER LOT?   _____

FIGURE Appendix D-7   The back page of an application for a building permit, courtesy of the City of Decatur, Illinois.

ESTIMATE SUMMARY

BUILDING	ADDRESS	NO.
OWNER	ADDRESS	DATE
ARCHITECT	ADDRESS	ESTIMATOR

NO.	DESCRIPTION AND SPECIFICATION	TOTAL ESTIMATED COST	TOTAL ACTUAL COST
1	Survey		
2	Stake-out		
3	Excavating		
4	Rough Grading		
5	Sewer or Septic System		
6	Foundation		
7	Masonry		
8	Lumber		
9	Millwork		
10	Plumbing		
11	Plumbing Fixtures		
12	Heating		
13	Air Conditioning		
14	Sheet Metal		
15	Roofing		
16	Wiring		
17	Fixtures		
18	Plastering		
19	Drywall		
20	Cabinets		
21	Built-ins		
22	Appliances		
23	Hardware - Rough		
24	Hardware - Finish		
25	Ceramic Tile - Marble		
26	Windows		
27	Glazing		
28	Mirrors		
29	Painting		
30	Floor Coverings		
31	Carpeting		
32	Concrete		
33	Wrought-iron		
34	Stairs		
35	Garage Doors		
36	Steel		
37	Labor		
38	Overhead - Labor		
39	Overhead – Gen. (Permits, Fees, Insurance)		
40			
41			
42			
43	Subtotal		
44	Profit		
45	TOTAL		

FIGURE Appendix D-8   Estimate summary sheet.

ABOUT LEAD-BASED PAINT

Everyone should know the basics about lead-based paint (LBP). Although its use has been against the law since 1978, almost all of us will encounter LBP at some time. Whether it's your home, your neighbors' home, your child's babysitter's home, Grandma's house or that quaint bed and breakfast you like so much, you will inevitably find yourself in a structure built before 1978, and 75 percent of them contain some LBP. Does this mean you should avoid these older buildings? Not necessarily. But, if you have young children or grandchildren, I highly suggest you get some education on the subject. Reading this appendix is a good start. For further information, contact the nearest office of the Department of Housing and Urban Development or visit their website at **www.hud.gov**.

FIGURE APPENDIX E-1   Caution: Lead Paint Handle With Care, courtesy of the U.S. Department of Housing and Urban Development.

HUD wants every home to be a healthy home.

LEARN THE FACTS ABOUT WORKING WITH LEAD PAINT

- Any home built before 1978 could have lead paint. Homes built before 1960 have the most lead paint.

- Lead paint in good condition usually is not a problem.

- Dangerous lead dust can be released from peeling or damaged paint or by sanding or scraping paint in older homes.

- When working on or remodeling a home with lead paint there are important safety tips you need to follow.

KNOW THAT LEAD PAINT CAN POISON CHILDREN

- Lead is toxic. It can harm a child's brain and cause learning and behavior problems. It can even harm unborn babies.

- Most children are poisoned by lead dust that gets on their hands and then in their mouths.

- Almost one million children under age six in the U.S. suffer from lead poisoning.

FIGURE APPENDIX E-2   Courtesy of the U.S. Department of Housing and Urban Development.

Handle lead paint with care when you paint or repair.

Here are five things you can do:

1. Keep lead dust away from people.
2. Use the right tools.
3. Work safely and clean up lead dust.
4. Don't bring lead dust home with you.
5. Learn the laws about lead and obey them.

Follow HUD's simple checklist for working safely.

1. Keep lead dust away from people.

- Keep children and pregnant women away from the work area.
- Seal off the work area by covering floors, vents, doors and windows with heavy plastic.
- If possible, remove furniture from the room. Cover any remaining furniture with heavy plastic.

2. Use the right tools.

- Use vacuum cleaners and power tools with HEPA filters.
- If you use a power sander or grinder, be sure it has a HEPA filter as well as a hood to trap dust.
- Never power wash or sand blast painted surfaces.
- Never use tools that create dust, chips, high heat or fumes.
- Never use open flame torches or heat guns at temperatures above 1100°F.
- Never use paint strippers that contain methylene chloride.

FIGURE APPENDIX E-3   Courtesy of the U.S. Department of Housing and Urban Development.

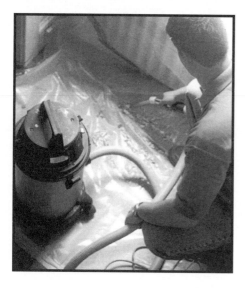

3. Work safely and clean up lead dust.

- ◦◦Fix water damage that can make paint peel.
- ◦◦Wet down the paint before you sand or scrape to control lead dust.
- ◦◦Use heavy plastic bags to remove dust and other trash.
- ◦◦After the job, wash floors and other surfaces with soap and water and rinse with fresh water. Remember lead dust can be too small to see.
- ◦◦Inform customers about the importance of maintaining the paint in their home.
- ◦◦Give customers the option to test for lead dust after the job is done. Call 1-888-LEADLIST for a list of lead service providers.

4. Don't bring lead dust home with you.

- ◦◦Clean your shoes before you leave the work area.
- ◦◦Change from work clothes before going home.
- ◦◦Don't wash your work clothes with the family laundry.
- ◦◦Take a shower and wash your hair at the end of each workday.

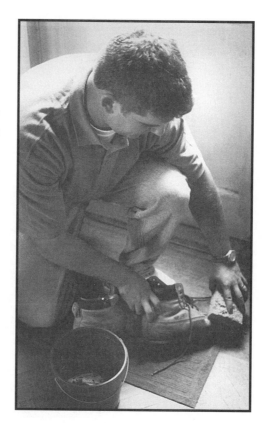

FIGURE APPENDIX E-4   Courtesy of the U.S. Department of Housing and Urban Development.

5. Learn the laws about lead and obey them.

○ ○○Federal law requires contractors to provide a brochure, *Protect Your Family From Lead in Your Home*, to owners and occupants before starting jobs that involve lead paint. Call 1-800-424-LEAD for free copies.

○ ○○Learn what state and local laws apply to you.

HUD wants every child to have a lead-safe home!

For more information about making homes lead-safe or to order a free copy of *Lead Paint Safety: A Field Guide for Painting, Home Maintenance, and Renovation Work*, call 1-800-424-LEAD.

For a free brochure on other home safety issues call HUD's Healthy Homes hotline at 1-800-HUDS-FHA or visit HUD's Web site at www.hud.gov. HUD is on your side.

FIGURE APPENDIX E-5
Courtesy of the U.S. Department of Housing and Urban Development.

SOURCES OF LEAD PAINT DUST

BREAKING SURFACES

- Lead paint is usually below several layers of non-lead paint
- If left unexposed/undamaged, it produces little if any dust
- Some practices produce so much lead dust that they should always be avoided: (insert art)
- Removal of cabinets, window trim, etc. produces dust when paint joints are broken
- Removal also may release large amounts of dust and chips that have accumulated behind objects or molding being removed
- Demolition creates large quantities of dust
- Stripping creates toxic paste which releases toxic dust when dried
- Heat guns are permitted but not encouraged

DO NOT DRY SCRAPE

DO NOT DRY SAND
Power sanding is
most dangerous

DO NOT DRY BURN

FIGURE APPENDIX E-6   Lead in dust created by work can be harmful. Avoid these dangerous practices. Chart courtesy of the EPA, Model Worker Tool Box Guide.

RENOVATION

How to safely remove old paint

LEAD-BASED PAINT DANGER

Most Illinois homes built before 1978 were painted with lead-based paint. Renovating or refinishing lead paint surfaces creates dust, fumes and debris that can cause lead poisoning.

Lead poisoning is a condition caused most often by eating lead paint chips or inhaling or eating leaded dust. Lead poisoning is one of the most common and most serious child health problems. It is estimated that two out of every 10 children in Illinois have blood lead levels that are too high. City, suburban and rural children are all at risk.

Children ages 6 months through 6 years are at greatest risk for lead poisoning in part because young children put everything into their mouths. Lead is especially harmful to infants and toddlers because their bodies absorb lead more easily than adult bodies do. Lead poisoning can slow a child's development and cause learning and behavior problems. Even small amounts of lead can seriously harm a young child, causing damage to the brain, kidneys and stomach. Lead also can harm pregnant women and their unborn children.

If you plan to renovate your home, have your home inspected for lead paint.

FIGURE APPENDIX E-7 Renovation: How to safely remove old paint, courtesy of the U.S. Department of Housing and Urban Development.

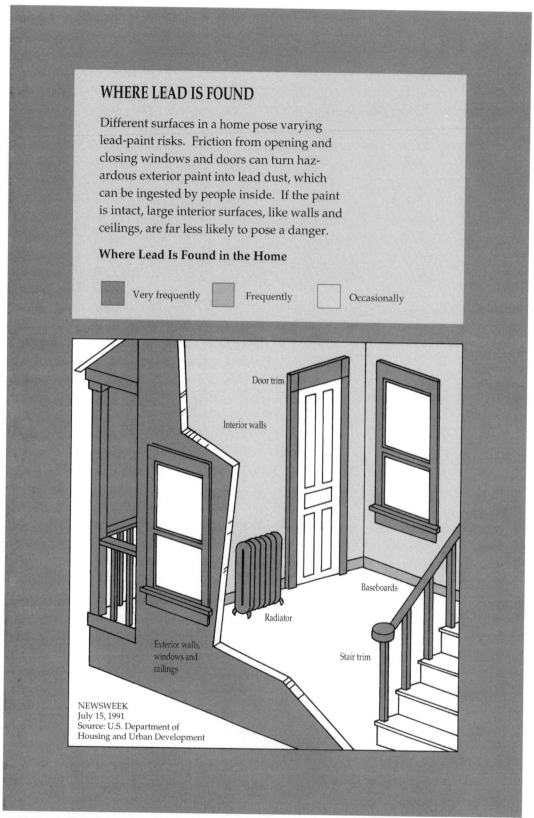

WHERE LEAD IS FOUND

Different surfaces in a home pose varying lead-paint risks. Friction from opening and closing windows and doors can turn hazardous exterior paint into lead dust, which can be ingested by people inside. If the paint is intact, large interior surfaces, like walls and ceilings, are far less likely to pose a danger.

Where Lead Is Found in the Home

Very frequently   Frequently   Occasionally

Door trim

Interior walls

Baseboards

Radiator

Stair trim

Exterior walls, windows and railings

NEWSWEEK
July 15, 1991
Source: U.S. Department of
Housing and Urban Development

FIGURE APPENDIX E-8   Where lead is found, courtesy of the U.S. Department of Housing and Urban Development.

The only way to find out if your home contains lead paint is to have an inspection. Contact your local health department for information on lead inspections.

BE ALERT TO THE DANGERS OF REMOVING OLD PAINT

To protect your family from lead during renovation —

- Do not remain at home during the renovation. It is especially important that young children and pregnant women not remain in areas where work is underway. When work is complete, do not reenter the area until it has been thoroughly cleaned.

- Only properly protected workers should enter the work area.

- Renovators working in residential dwellings and day care facilities must provide the owner and occupant with an educational pamphlet. Additionally, the owner and occupant must sign a statement that the renovator distributed the pamphlet. If you hire contractors, make sure they understand the notification requirements and are familiar with the causes of lead

poisoning and how to prevent lead exposure.

- If you must do the work yourself, use proper precautions to remove old paint and painted surfaces safely. Contact the Illinois Department of Public Health's Childhood Lead Poisoning Prevention Program at 217-782-3517 or 217-782-0403 or 800-545-2200 or TTY 800-547-0466 for information on safe methods of renovation or re-modeling.

RENOVATION SAFETY TIPS

- The safest time to renovate or remodel is when the house is unoccupied.

- Protect all food appliances, cooking and eating utensils, furniture, bedding, toys and clothing from lead dust. Remove these items from the work area or cover or bag them in plastic and seal tightly.

- Do not eat or smoke in the work area to avoid getting dust from your hands or clothing in your mouth. Wash your hands thoroughly.

- Place a damp floor mat outside the work area to collect dust from the bottom of shoes.

- Even removing wallpaper or loose plaster can create lead dust. To clean up, use a clean damp cloth or mop dampened with a cleaning product. Do not vacuum dust

FIGURE APPENDIX E-9 Courtesy of the U.S. Department of Housing and Urban Development.

and debris as vacuuming may push lead dust into the air, spreading it to other parts of the house.

- Wash work clothes and clean-up rags separately from other laundry.

WHAT ABOUT RENOVATING MY HOME'S EXTERIOR?

- When removing exterior paint, seal windows and vents so dust cannot get inside the house.

- Wipe shoes on damp floor mat. Remove shoes before entering the house.

- Do not walk around clean areas of the house in work clothes.

- To remove paint chips and dust from around the outside of the house, hose off porches, sidewalks, driveways and the sides of buildings. Scrub with a stiff brush or broom and soapy water; then rinse as clean as possible. Pick up and dispose of paint chips.

SCREENING FOR LEAD POISONING

Have family members, particularly children 6 months through 6 years of age, tested for lead poisoning by a physician or other health care provider when renovation of an older home is complete.

A child may have lead poisoning yet not have any symptoms. Or a child may have symptoms like those of a cold or the flu. The only way to detect lead poisoning early is to bring your child to your local clinic, public health clinic or physician to have a simple blood test.

For additional information on how to safely remove old paint and clean up lead debris, paint chips and dust, or for information on lead poisoning, call the Illinois Department of Public Health's Childhood Lead Poisoning Prevention Program at 217-782-0403 or 800-545-2200 or TTY 800-547-0466.

FIGURE APPENDIX E-10 Courtesy of the U.S. Department of Housing and Urban Development.

INDEX

A

Adding on, 164
Advertising, yard signs, 87
Advice, free, 89-90
Aesthetics and quality, 61-63
AFCI. See Arc fault circuit breaker
American Plywood Association, 72
Arc fault circuit breaker (AFCI)
    for bedrooms, 173
    costs, 139
    defined, 117, 176
    illustrated, 118, 178
Architect, review of plans, 57
Architectural shake shingle, 133
Argon gas, 134, 164
AsAManThinketh.net, 208
Asphalt shingle, 133
Attitude, 148, 152. See also Mindset

B

Back injuries, safety guidelines, 258
Backfill, 61, 128, 129
Backhoe, 170
Ballpark price, 96
Banking time, 170
Bargain hunting, 152
Barrel vault ceiling, 150

Barter
    bottom line, 10
    defined, 93
    reducing labor costs, 92, 93
    work swap group, 94
Basements
    cape cod floor plan, 42, 222-229
    multilevel floor plan, 49
    saltbox, 230-237
    two-story floor plan, 214, 217-218, 221
    walk-out, 23
Bathroom. See also Tub-and-shower
    remodeling, 179, 180, 197-199, 200
    vent fans, 139
    wall-hung lavatory, 180
Bearing point
    defined, 167
    remodeling, 167
    span length, 70, 72
Bids
    customer-supplied materials, 86-87
    meeting, 186
    negotiations, 87
    by the piece, 86-87
Blocks
    foundation walls, 106, 108, 109, 128, 130
    inside corner, 62, 63, 113

outside corner, 62, 63, 113
plinth, 62, 63, 113
rosette, 62, 63, 113
Blood screening, 254
Bobcat, 98, 99
Borrowing tools, 98, 203
Box cabinet, 141-142
Brad nailer, 112, 113
Brainstorm, 189-190
Brand names vs. generics, 64-65, 124-125
Breaker box (subpanel), 179
Bridging, 131
Broderbund's 3D Home Architect, 56, 127, 188
Buddies as labor resource, 92
Budget
    bargain hunting, 152
    cabinets, 141-142
    carpet, 142-143
    closet trim, 144
    design features, 23-24, 26
    drywall, 139
    electrical, 139, 143, 145
    estimate summary sheet, 260
    excavation, 128
    exterior doors, 134-135
    fireplaces, 144, 145
    floor beam, 130
    floor coverings, 142-143
    footings, 128
    foundation, 128, 130
    heating and cooling system, 137, 138
    insulation, 139
    interior doors and trim, 139-140
    lot price, 20
    overhead garage doors, 145
    paint, 139
    plans or designs, 127-128
    plumbing, 138, 144
    remodeling, 182-183, 191
    roof, 132-133
    room size determination, 28
    room use checklist, 27
    siding, 135, 136
    soffit and fascia, 136, 138
    stairs, 131, 144-145
    temporary power, 128, 129
    walls, 132
    windows, 134
Buildable area, 23, 24, 25
Builders, free advice, 89-90
Building codes. See also Inspectors
    adding circuits, 173
    additional costs cautions, 75
    building permit, 259-260
    design code, 128
    energy efficiency, 74
    last-minute changes, 77, 203-204

needs and code requirements, 75
    plan changes, 74
    review of plans, 56-57
    sheathing, 72-74
    spans, 69-72
    spending your savings, 76-77, 203
    tool trap, 75-76, 203
    upselling, 77, 204-205
Building inspectors, on-site consultations, 90
Building permit, 258-259
Bullnose, 183, 184
Burns and fire, safety guidelines, 258
Bystanders as labor resource, 93

C

Cabinets
    box, 141-142
    budget, 141-142
    custom, 52-53, 141-142
    overhead lighting, 29
    refacing, 197, 198
    scratch and dent, 59
Cable TV
    do it yourself installation, 108
    free installation, 103-104, 108
Cantilever, 33
Cape Cod home
    cross section, 39
    features, 38, 39, 43
    floor plans, 40-42, 222-229
    pros and cons, 43
Carbon monoxide, health and safety guidelines,
    255
Carpet
    Berber, 152, 155
    budget, 142-143
    do it yourself installation, 105, 106, 107
    Internet purchasing, 120
    pad attached, 105, 106
    seaming, 106
Cathedral ceiling, 150, 171
Ceiling price, 165
Ceilings
    barrel vault, 150
    cathedral, 150, 171
    cracked ceilings, 196
    type-x drywall, 138
    vaulted, 171
Chain stores, materials purchasing, 120-122
Changes in plans
    contractors, 88
    at end of project, 160
    last-minute, 74, 77, 203-204
Checklists
    materials, 78, 192-195
    quality elements, 67
    remodeling, 205

room use checklist, 24, 26, 27

Church members as labor resource, 93-94

Cleanup. See Debris cleanup

Clearance items, 29

Closeout materials, 29, 64, 120, 123

Closet trim, 144

Codes. See Building codes

Cold-air return, 168

Comparable house, 18, 179-180

Construction loan, 110

Construction material waste, example declaration, 15

Construction plans, 55-57

Consult, 83

Contractors. See also General contractors; Subcontractors

    material discounts, 124

    material markups, 124, 125

    part-time, 95, 96

Convenience shopping, 125

Conversion chart, 244

Conversion figures, 246

Corner blocks, 62, 63, 113

Corners, cost-effective design, 50

Cosmetic remodeling, 183, 197

Cost per square foot, 7

Cost-effective design, 50, 52-53

Counter top, 141

Covenants and restrictions

    defined, 10

    duration, 16

    example declaration, 13-17

    purpose, 10

    severability, 16

    violations, 16

Crawfish, 77, 203

Crawl space, 128, 130

Credit cards for prepurchased materials, 119-120

Crossover exposure, 168-169, 170

Curb appeal, 31, 33

Custom features

    cabinets, 52-53, 141-142

    cost-effective design, 52-53

Cuts and bleeding, safety guidelines, 257

D

Damp-proofing, 130

Dead load, 70

Debris cleanup

    bid negotiations, 101

    in contractor bids, 88

    do it yourself, 110

    pickup truck, 100, 103

    production time loss, 100, 101, 102

    prompt removal at job site, 94

    trash removal costs, 100-101

Decks, 54

Declaration example, 13-17

Deficiency, withholding payment, 100

Deflection, 73

Delivery statement, 88, 90

Department of Housing and Urban Development (HUD), 262

Design

    budget considerations, 23-24, 26, 27-28, 127-128

    buildable area, 23, 24, 25

    cape cod home, 38-43

    code, 128

    construction plans, 55-57

    cost-effective, 50, 52-53

    features, 26, 29-30

    for the lot, 22-23

    multilevel home, 47-50

    ranch home, 31-34

    saltbox, 43-47

    two-story home, 35-38

Discipline, 91

DIY. See Do it yourself

Do it yourself (DIY)

    carpet, 105, 106, 107

    cleaning, 110

    electrical, 117-118

    foundation, 106, 108, 109

    gutter professional installation, 115, 136

    insulation professional installation, 114

    laminate flooring, 105-106, 107

    landscaping, 110, 111

    painting, 109

    phone and cable, 108

    plumbing, 116-117

    roofing professional installation, 114-115

    shoveling, 110

    siding, 114-115, 116

    trim, 110, 113

Doors

    components, 250

    exterior, 134-135

    garage, 145

    interior, 139-141

    jamb, 123, 139

    keyed alike, 135

Drafting, 187-189

Drills, right-angle, 76, 98, 204

Driveways, example declaration, 15

Drywall

    budget, 139

    market fluctuations, 123

    type-X (firecode), 138

E

Ear protection, 2, 105

Early To Rise (ETR) newsletter, 208

Easement, 12, 14

Eave, 135
Egress, 35
Electric miter saw, 112, 113
Electrical
  arc fault circuit breaker. See Arc fault circuit breaker
  budget, 139, 143, 145
  do it yourself installation, 117-118
  fixtures, 29, 143, 166
  GFCI (ground fault circuit interrupter), 117, 118, 139
  locator service, 188-189
  nail-it box, 117, 118, 139
  remodeling, 165, 167, 173, 176, 179
  Romex, 138, 139
  rough-in budget, 139
  service entrance, 117, 118, 139
  service panel. See Service panel
  shocks, health and safety guidelines, 254
  subcontractor, 80
  subpanel (breaker box), 178, 179
  switched outlet, 29
  temporary power, 128, 129
Elements checklist, 67
Elevation, 56
E-mail newsletters, 149
Energy efficiency, HVAC, 74, 172
Engineer, review of plans, 57
Engineered Wood Association, 72
Equipment. See also Tools
  backhoe, 170
  Bobcat, 98, 99
  borrowing, 98, 203
  free use, 98
Equity, 7, 17
Erosion control, example declaration, 14-15
Estimate summary sheet, 260
ETR (Early To Rise) newsletter, 208
Example declaration, 13-17
Excavation, 128
Existing features, 10, 12
Explosion, safety guidelines, 256
Exterior
  components, 251-252
  cost-effective dimensions, 50, 52
  doors, 134-135
Eye protection, 2, 105, 257

F

Factory representatives for product information, 187. See also Manufacturers
False gable, 212
Family involvement in lot purchase, 20
Fascia cover, 135
Fear and doubt, 153
Features
  Cape Cod home, 38, 39, 43

comparison chart, 181
custom, 52-53, 141-142
designing, 26, 29-30
existing, 10, 12
lots, 22, 23
multilevel home, 47, 50
ranch home, 31
saltbox, 43
two-story home, 35
Fiberglass shingle, 133
Fill sand, 110, 128, 130
Finishing. See Wrapping up
Fire and burns, safety guidelines, 256
Firecode drywall, 138
Fireplaces, 144, 145
Fixtures
  electrical, 29, 143, 166
  purchases, 124
Floating shelf, 183-184
Flood plain insurance, 17
Floor
  beams, 130
  budget, 130-131, 142-143
  floor over floor, 199
  laminate, 105-106, 107, 142-143
  refinishing of wood, 196-197
  span length, 70, 72
  subfloor, 106
Floor plans
  basic plan, 55
  Cape Cod home, 40-42, 222-229
  layout, 56
  multilevel home, 48-49, 238-243
  ranch home, 32, 188, 211-213, 214
  saltbox, 45-46, 230-237
  two-story home, 36-37, 214-221
Footings, 128
Footprint, 34
Formulas, 247
Foundation
  block, 106, 108, 109, 128, 130
  budget, 128, 130
  crawl space, 128, 130
  footings, 128
Frieze runner, 135, 136
Functionality, 61
Furnace. See Heating and cooling system
Furnace room, 187

G

Gable roof, 51
Garage
  options, 54-55
  overhead doors, 145
  storage, 55
General contractors. See also Contractors; Sub-contractors

bids, 86-87
comparison chart, 82
consultants, 83
contractor referrals, 84-85
finding, 84-86
hiring subcontractors, 81
payouts, 86
roles, 79, 80
saving money, 87-89
when to hire, 82-83
Generics vs. brand names, 64-65, 124-125
Geothermal heating, 74, 201
GFCI (ground fault circuit interrupter), 117, 118, 139
Gingerbread, 218
Glass. See also Windows
low-E glass, 134, 164
polished edges, 2
tempering, 2
Grade, defined, 22
Grapevine, to find location
covenants and restrictions, 10
existing features, 10, 12
flood plain insurance, 17
historical districts, 10
school districts, 9-10
style of homes, 10
subdividing possibilities, 12
surrounding areas, 10
taxes, 10, 11
unwanted lots, 17
utility hookups, 12, 17
utility lines, 12
Ground fault circuit interrupter (GFCI), 117, 118, 139
Guarantees, 122. See also Warranty
Gut, 183
Gutters, 115, 136

H

Hazard Communication law, 257
H-clip, 133
Headers
defined, 59
double 2x12, 61
plywood, 59
wood structural panel box, 60
Health. See Safety
Heat, health and safety guidelines, 255
Heating and cooling system
for added area only, 171
added insulation, 171, 173
budget, 137, 138
cold-air return, 168
energy efficiency, 74, 172
furnace room, 187
geothermal heating, 74, 201

passive solar, 55
radiant heat system, 90, 91
remodeling, 169-171, 172, 201
return on investment, 74, 170, 201
selling old unit, 171
warranty, 138
Hip roof, 52
Historical districts, 10, 165
Home Depot, 121
Home theater, 247
House of Fara, 113
Housewrap, 132
Housing and Urban Development (HUD), 261
HUD (Department of Housing and Urban Development), 262
HVAC (heating, ventilating and air conditioning). See Heating and cooling system

I

Illinois Department of Public Health, 268
Inconvenience of remodeling, 167
Inside corner blocks, 62, 63, 113
Inspections, before payout for project, 100
Inspectors
disciplines, 91
electrical, 118
on-site consultations, 90
plumbing, 117, 118
Inspirational resources, 208-209
Insulation
blown cellulose, 115, 139
budget, 139
foam pipe, 177
housewrap, 132
lowering HVAC demand, 171, 173
professional installation, 114
R-factor, 172
sheathing, 132
water heater, 177
windows, 134
Insurance
builder's risk, 20
flood plain, 17
high deductibles, 20
liability, 20
outriders, 20-21
part-time workers, 97
pay in full, 21
worker's compensation, 97
Interest on loans, 21, 120
Interior
components, 252-253
doors and trim, 139-141
Internet
e-mail, 149
free advice, 90

materials purchasing, 91, 120, 121
remodeling information, 184, 185
search engines, 207

J

Jamb, 123, 139
JLG, 99
Jobsites
    for finding contractors, 84, 85
    frequency of visits, 88
Joints, cantilevered, 33
Joists, 130
The Journal of Light Construction, 132, 207

K

K.I.S.S. (Keep It Simple Stupid), 187
Kitchens, 141, 179

L

Labor costs
    cable installations, 103-104
    cutting costs, 92
    discount rates, 95-97
    equipment and tools, 98-99
    helping a licensed person, 96, 97
    laid-off workers, 97
    learners as resource, 93
    licensed workers, 96, 97
    making-a-living contractor, 97
    part-time contractors, 95, 96
    resources, 92-94
    retired workers, 95-96
    rules of thumb, 100-104
Ladders, safety guidelines, 257
Laid-off workers, 97
Laminate flooring, 105-106, 107, 142-143
Land, 245, 246. See also Lots
Landscaping
    do it yourself, 110, 111
    nursery, 109, 110
    options, 55
    waste, example declaration, 14-15
    web site, 111
Laundry box, 144
Laundry chute, 29, 30
Laws and regulations. See also Covenants and re-
        strictions
    Hazard Communication law, 257
    Right to Know law, 257
    Layman, 126
    Laziness, 158, 159
LBP. See Lead-based paint
Lead, blood screening, 254
Lead-based paint (LBP), 262-272
Learners as labor resource, 93
Legwork, 151
Library resources

listing, 206-207
    remodeling, 185, 186
    web site, 207
Licensed workers, 96, 97
Life adjustments for remodeling, 165, 167-169
Lighting, 29, 143, 166
Lincoln, Abraham, 181
Lineal foot, 86, 87
Livability, 61
Live load, 70
Loads, live or dead, 70
Loans
    construction, 110
    interest accumulation, 21, 120
Location
    grapevine as resource, 9-17
    importance of, 18
    investment insurance, 20-21
    price negotiations, 19-20
    resale value, 17-19
Locks
    keyed alike, 135
    passage, 141
    privacy, 141
Lots
    distinctive features, 22
    example declaration, 16
    first in a subdivision, 19-20
    fronted, 19
    house design and, 22-23
    land, 245, 246
    last in a subdivision, 19
    natural features, 22, 23
    obstructions, 23
    restrictive features, 22
    setbacks, 23
    timing of offers, 20
    unwanted, 17
    vistas, 23
Low price guarantees, 122
Low-E glass, 134, 164
Lowe's, 121, 122
Lumber price comparison, 121

M

Making-a-living contractor, 97
Man lift, 99
Manufacturers
    free advice, 90, 187
    knowledgeable, 121, 122
Market fluctuations, 123-124
Markup, 125
Masterson, Michael, 124
Material Safety Data Sheets (MSDS), 257
Materials
    chain stores, 120-122
    checklist, 78, 192-195

closeouts, 29, 64, 120, 123
contractor's discounts, 124
convenience shopping, 125
customer-supplied, 86-87
delivery charges, 124, 125
fixtures, 124
market fluctuations, 123-124
markup, 125
money-back guarantees, 122
online shopping, 91, 120, 121
prepurchase, 119-120
rebates, 122
returning unused materials, 125-126
salvage, 29, 123
scrap, 126
shop on Sunday, 119
Meandered water and government lots, 245
Mechanicals, 104, 166
Menard's, 121, 122, 124, 187
Mental preparation
bargain hunting, 152
be a rock, 152
e-mail/newsletter, 149
fear and doubt, 153
goal, 149
legwork, 151
mindset to save money, 153
move forward, 151
question everyone, 152
research, 150
tracking another's project, 83, 150
warming up, 150-151
Microlam, 72
Mindset
mental preparation, 83, 149-153
saving money, 153
speed bumps, 154, 156-158
wrapping up, 159-161
Miter, 63, 112, 113
Money-back guarantees, 122
Money-saving techniques, 7
Mortgage-free plan, 146-147
MSDS (Material Safety Data Sheets), 257
Mullion, 134
Multilevel home
features, 47, 50
floor plans, 48-49, 238-243
pros and cons, 50
Multiuse rooms, 182
MyDailyInsights.com, 208

N
Nail-it box, 117, 118, 139
Natural features of lots, 22
Neighbors
as labor resource, 93
vandalism or theft prevention, 94

New products and contractor bids, 87
Newsletters, 149
Noise safety guidelines, 258
Nuisances, example declaration, 15-16
Nursery, 109, 110

O
Obstructions on the lot, 23
On center, 70
Online. See Internet
Options
decks and patios, 54
garages, 54-55
landscaping, 55
passive solar, 55
porch, 54
Order of work, 101-104, 159-160, 190
Orient strand board. See OSB
OSB (orient strand board)
price fluctuations, 123
roof sheathing, 133
scraps, 126
span ratings, 73
for walls, 132
OSHA, 257
Outside corner blocks, 62, 63, 113
Overhead, defined, 96
Overhead cabinet lighting, 29

P
Painting, 109, 139. See also Lead-based paint
Paperwork, 160-161
Part-time contractors, 95, 96
Passage lock, 141
Passive solar, 55
Pasteur, Louis, 149
Patios, 54
Payouts, 86, 100
Performance, 59
PEX pipe, 117, 138
Pickup truck
hauling fill sand, 110
for trash hauling, 100, 103
Plat, defined, 12
Plinth blocks, 62, 63, 113
Plumbing
budget, 138, 144
do it yourself installation, 116-117
locator service, 188-189
PEX and PVC pipe, 117, 138
remodeling, 167, 171, 173
sweat a joint, 117
Pop-up, 143, 144
Porch, 54, 250
Possible Return Chart, 19
Power vent water heater, 137
Prepurchasing materials, 119-120

Price
    ballpark, 96
    budget, 20
    ceiling, 165
    first or last lots, 19-20
    guarantees, 122
    lumber comparisons, 121
    market fluctuations, 123
    negotiations, 19-20
    per piece, 86-87
    timing, 20
Privacy lock, 141
Problems. See Speed bumps
Pulling wire, 97
PVC pipe
    furnace flue, 137
    illustrated, 117
    water and waste lines, 138
    water heater flue, 137

Q

Quality
    aesthetics, 61-63
    alternatives, 66, 68
    brand names vs. generics, 64-65, 124-125
    elements checklist, 67
    functionality, 61
    livability, 61
    perform, 59
    resale value, 59
    structural integrity, 59
    upgrade costs, 63, 64, 65
    visibility, 59
    windows, 63
    worth, 65-66
Question everyone, 152

R

Radiant heat system, 90, 91
Rake, 135
Ranch home
    features, 31
    floor plans, 32, 188, 211-213, 214
    pros and cons, 34
Real estate listing, 11
Rebates, 122
Re-Bath, 197, 199
Relatives as labor resource, 93
Remodeling
    adding on, 164
    bathrooms, 179, 180, 197-199, 200
    budgeting, 182-183, 191
    cabinet refacing, 197, 198
    checklist, 205
    considerations, 163-165
    cosmetic, 183, 197
    cost-effective projects, 176, 179-180, 181

cracked walls and ceilings, 196
    electrical, 165, 167, 173, 176, 179
    floors, 196-197, 199
    historic district regulations, 165
    HVAC, 169-171, 172, 201
    information sources, 183-187
    kitchens, 179
    life adjustments, 165, 167-169
    map out the project, 187-189
    material checklist, 192-195
    multiuse rooms, 182
    planning, 181, 189-190
    plumbing, 167, 171, 173
    reasons for, 162
    return on investment, 163-164
    septic system, 173, 174, 175
    structural, 164-165, 197
    traps, 202-205
    water lines, 171
Resale value
    considerations, 17-19
    defined, 17
    Possible Return Chart, 19
    quality and, 59
    remodeling, 163, 164
    windows, 63
Research, 150
Resources
    inspirational, 208-209
    library, 185, 186, 206-207
    search engines, 207
Restrictions. See Covenants and restrictions
Restrictive features of lots, 22
Retailers
    free advice, 89
    nursery, 109, 110
    for remodeling information, 185
Retired workers, 95-96
Return on investment, remodeling, 163-164
Returning unused materials, 125-126
R-factor, 172
Ridge vent, 134
Right to Know law, 258
Right-angle drill, 76, 98, 204
Rights of way, example declaration, 14
Rock solid attitude, 152
Roller coasters, 154. See also Speed bumps
Roll-off, 100, 102
RomexË, 138, 139
Roof
    budget, 132-133
    calculating area, 247
    cost-effective design, 50
    example declaration, 16
    gable, 51
    hip, 52
    pitch, 50, 52

professional installation, 114-115
ridge vent, 134
sheathing, 72-74, 133
shingles, 133
Room size determination, 26, 28
Room use checklist, 24, 26, 27
Room-in-attic truss, 43
Rosette blocks, 62, 63, 113
Rough in, 108, 139
Rough opening, 59, 61

S

Safety
back injuries, 258
blood screening, 254
burns, 258
carbon monoxide, 255
cuts and bleeding, 257
ear and eye protection, 2, 105
electric shocks, 256
eyes, 257
fires and explosions, 256
glass, 2
heat, 255
ladders, 257
noise, 2, 105, 258
notice, 2
Right to Know law, 258
work order, 103
Salespeople
free information, 89
for remodeling information, 185
Saltbox
features, 43, 47
floor plans, 45-46, 230-237
pros and cons, 44
Salvage shops, 29, 123
Scale, 187-189
Schedules, 156
School district locations, 9-10
Scratch and dent
cabinets, 59
materials, 123
value, 64
Seaming, 106
Seamless gutter, 115, 136
Search engines, 207
Septic system
defined, 173
laterals, 175
remodeling, 173
sizing chart, 174
Service entrance, 117, 118, 139
Service panel
adding circuits, 173, 176
brand names vs. generics, 64-65
budget, 139

defined, 66
illustrated, 178
Setbacks, 23, 166
Severability of covenants and restrictions, 16
Sewer system. See Plumbing; Septic system
Shake shingle, 133
Sheathing
floor, 130-131
insulated, 132
market fluctuations, 123
rating, 72-74
roof, 72-74, 133
subfloor, 106
Shell, 80, 81
Shingles, 133
Shoveling, 110
Showrooms for remodeling information, 185, 187
Sidewalks, example declaration, 16
Siding
budget, 135, 136
do it yourself installation, 114-115, 116
warranty, 136
Six-year mortgage-free plan, 146-147
Skid steer, 98, 99
Social gatherings, for finding contractors, 84
Sock tile, 130
Soffit and fascia, 136, 138
Software
3D Home Architect, 56, 127, 188
CAD, 56, 127, 188
Spans
building codes, 69-72
floor beams, 130
floor joist chart, 71
length, 70, 72
sheathing, 72-74
span chart, 70, 72
Spec house, 123, 124
Specified (spec'd), 59
Speed bumps. See also Traps
believe you can do it, 157-158
communication, 157
don't hurry, 156
don't panic, 154
finish each task, 157
keep your cool, 158
laziness, 158, 159
love your dollars, 156
think it through, 156, 157
Spending your savings, 76-77, 203
Split jamb, 139
Split jobs, 89
Square, 87
Square foot, 86, 87
Stairs
budget, 131, 144-145

components, 250
lead-based paint, 273
materials, 131
railings, 144-145
Stakes, 128
Stick-frame, defined, 39
Structural integrity
quality and compromise, 59
remodeling, 164-165, 167
Structural remodeling, 197
Studs
prices compared, 121
wall, 132
Style of homes, 10
Subcontractors. See also Contractors; General
contractors
bids, 86-87
contractor referrals, 84-85
defined, 186
electrical, 80
finding, 84-86
hired by general contractors, 81
payouts, 86
for remodeling information, 185
review of plans, 57
roles, 79-80
saving money, 87-89
specialists, 80
supplying materials, 86-87, 124
Subdividing, 10, 12
Subfloor, 106
Subpanel (breaker box), 178, 179
Success.com, 209
Sunburst, 214
Sunday materials shopping, 119
Surface bonding, 106, 108, 109
Surrounding areas, 10
Sweat a joint, 117
Switched outlet, 29

T
Targeted value range, 181
Taxes
considerations before purchase, 10
real estate listing, 11
timing of offers, 20
Telephone installation, 108
Television cable, 103-104, 108
Theater design, 247
Theft prevention by neighbors, 94
Think it through, 156, 157
This Old House, 207
3D Home Architect, 56, 127, 188
Time and effort of remodeling, 168
Toilets
budget, 138
upgrades, 63, 64, 65

warranties, 78, 205
Tools. See also Equipment
borrowing, 98, 203
brad nailer, 112, 113
electric miter saw, 112, 113
Internet purchasing, 120
for painting, 109
renting or leasing, 76, 203
right-angle drill, 76, 98, 204
unnecessary, 75-76, 203
Tracking a job, 83, 150
Trades, 108
Traffic during remodeling, 168
Training, 151
Transition strips
alternatives, 66, 68
carpet installation, 107
ready-made vs. custom, 142
Transom, 234
Traps. See also Speed bumps
last-minute changes, 77, 203-204
needs vs. wants, 75, 202
small additional costs, 75, 202
spending your savings, 76-77, 203
Trash
example declaration, 15-16
removal, 100-101. See also Debris cleanup
Trim
budget, 139-141
do-it-yourself, 110, 113
finger-jointed, 141
miters, 110, 112-113
Trusses
cantilevered, 33
room-in-attic, 43
Tub-and-shower
budget, 138
costs, 67
quality, 65-66
shower conversion, 198, 200
tub sleeve, 197, 199
Two-story home
features, 35
floor plans, 36-37, 214-221
pros and cons, 38
Type-X drywall, 138

U
Underground utilities locator service, 188-189
Underlayment, 142, 143
Upgrades
cellulose insulation, 115
flooring, 130-131
heating and cooling system, 74
toilets, 63, 64, 65
Upselling, 77, 204-205
Use restrictions, 13-14

Utility. See also Electrical; Plumbing
    hookups, 12, 17
    lines, 12
    locator service, 188-189

V

Vandalism prevention by neighbors, 94
Vaulted ceiling, 171
Violations of covenants and restrictions, 16
Visibility, 59
Vistas, 23

W

Walk-out basement, 23
Walls
    budget, 132
    cracked walls, 196
    zip wall, 168
Warming up, 150-151
Warranty
    guarantees, 122
    heating and cooling system, 138
    lifetime, 78
    siding, 136
    supplying own fixtures, 124
    toilets, 78, 205
    upgrades, 77, 205
Wasted space, 52
Water. See Plumbing
Water heater
    budget, 138
    insulation, 177
    power vent, 137
    remodeling, 173
Web sites
    AsAManThinketh, 208
    Early To Rise (ETR) newsletter, 208
    House of Fara, 113
    HUD, 261
    Illinois Department of Public Health, 268
    The Journal of Light Construction, 207
    landscaping, 111
    library, 207
    MyDailyInsights, 208
    Success.com, 209
    This Old House, 207
Windows
    budget, 134
    closeout prices, 122
    components, 249
    low-E glass, 134, 164
    quality, 63
    resale value, 63
Wiring. See Electrical
Word of mouth referrals, 84
Work order, 101-104, 159-160, 190
Work swap group, 94

Worker's compensation, 97
World Wide Web, 184. See also Internet
Worth, 65-66
Wrapping up
    changes, 160
    finish the job, 159
    paperwork, 160-161
    work order, 159-160

Y

Yellow pages to find contractors, 85

Z

Zip wall, 168
Zoning setback, 23, 166

notes

notes

notes

notes

MORE GREAT TITLES FROM F+W PUBLICATIONS!

Plan and design a new bathroom or makeover your existing one with help from this complete guide to updating and adding value to one of the most important rooms in your home. Incorporate one of ten stylish decorating plans and any of the nineteen easy-to-do-follow projects or pick and choose elements of each to show your own creative design flair.

ISBN 1-55870-696-8, paperback, 144 pages, #70647

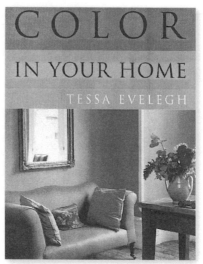

Rid your home of boring white walls! Add the zing of color to your home with this ultimate guide for novice home decorators. *Color In Your Home* provides clear, visual instructions to help you choose the hues that work best for the moods you want to create.

ISBN 1-58180-322-2, paperback, 128 pages, #32286

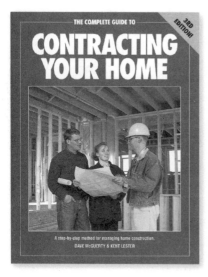

With more than 183,000 copies sold, this book is the classic manual you'll want to guide you through the often difficult, confusing world of building your own home. From beginning construction to financing and working with inspectors, *The Complete Guide to Contracting Your Home* takes the headaches and worries out of your home construction plans.

ISBN 1-55870-465-5, paperback, 320 pages, #70378

Don't settle for less than the home of your dreams! *Build Your Dream Home For Less* is filled with wise advice, tips and lessons for saving you money on every aspect of your home-building project without compromising on quality. This is a reference every prospective homebuilder should have.

ISBN 1-55870-383-7, paperback, 192 pages, #70286

These and other great books are available at your local bookstore or online supplier.